Dreadful

Dreadful

The Short Life and Gay Times of
JOHN HORNE BURNS

David Margolick

WITHDRAWN

OTHER PRESS
NEW YORK

Frontispiece: John Horne Burns, Harvard graduation photo, 1937

Production Editor: Yvonne E. Cárdenas
Text Designer: Jennifer Daddio/Bookmark Design & Media, Inc.
This book was set in 11.8 pt Horley Old Style
by Alpha Design & Composition of Pittsfield, NH.

1 3 5 7 9 10 8 6 4 2

Library of Congress Cataloging-in-Publication Data

Margolick, David.
Dreadful : the short life and gay times of John Horne Burns / by David Margolick.
pages cm
ISBN 978-1-59051-571-6 (hardcover) — ISBN 978-1-59051-572-3 (ebook)
1. Burns, John Horne, 1916–1953.   2. Authors, American—20th century—Biography.
3. Gay authors—United States—Biography.   I. Title.
PS3503.U6385Z75 2013
813'.54—dc23
[B]
2013002151

To Mark Bassett

Acknowledgments

This has been the most magical kind of book—a volunteer, like a seed that survives the winter (or, in this case, forty-odd winters) and then sprouts and grows, seemingly on its own. Even volunteers can need nurturing to bear fruit, though, and I want to thank all those who fed and nourished this seedling.

First, there are the many former Loomis and Chaffee students and teachers, and members of the Loomis Chaffee community, who either provided me with their recollections of John Horne Burns or helped me find others with them. They include Jody Adams, Elihu Berman, Donald Cantor, John Stuart Cox, Sebastian DiMauro, W. Barrett Dower, Joel Graham, Jane Hazelton, Lucretia Hickok, John Howard, Albie Hurwit, Donald Kaplan, Tom Lehrer, Taylor Mead, James Munves, John Nichols, Lyman Page, Robert Louis Purinton, Richard Rifkind,

Robert Rifkind, Judy Stevenson, and Guy Wiggins. Several others to whom I spoke—David Brewer, David Haller, Glover Howe, Henry Krotzer, Russell Rhodes, and Michael Sudarsky—have since died, and I cherish my conversations with them. Loomis Chaffee's highly capable and dedicated archivist, Karen Parson, was indispensable. So, too, was Seth Beebe, and I also want to thank Loomis Chaffee's former head of school, Sheila Culbert. At Phillips Academy in Andover, Paige Roberts ferreted out some wonderfully useful material from the school's impressive archive, and Amy Morris was a source of encouragement and inspiration throughout.

Several people who seem forever to be helping me assisted with this book as well: David Smith of the New York Public Library; Charles Niles and Sean Noel at the Howard Gotlieb Archival Research Center at Boston University, and Jeff Roth, master of the *New York Times*'s incomparable morgue. Also helpful were Heather Cole at the Houghton Library at Harvard; Anthony Nussmeier at the University of Indiana; Andrew Garsky and William Workman at the Harry Ransom Center of the University of Texas; Bill Hooper of the Time-Life archives; and the capable staffs at the Firestone Library at Princeton, the Rare Books & Manuscripts Library at Columbia, and the Biblioteca Nazionale in Florence.

Retracing Burns's path in Italy was made infinitely more rewarding, and edifying, by Francesco Durante, Gaia Pianigiani, Selene Salvi, Alessandra Serrano, Jeff Matthews, Larry Ray, Nino Delogu, Paolo Delogu, Gianfranco Vallini, Andrea Fiano, and Antonio Lombardi. Others helping me along the way include Victoria Barstow, Rhonda Chahine, Gerald Clarke, Brian Glanville, Sarah Gross, Bruce Hotchkiss, Andrew Huebner, Fred Kaplan, Betty Katkov, Eugenia Klein, Jack Larson, Ken Maley, Celia McGee, John Mitzel, Michael Morris, Donald Nuner, Reinhard Pauly, Jerry Rosco, Susan Searles, Jesse Sheidlower,

Risa Sodi, Susan Spanier, Jay Trask, and Berny Wolff. I'm also grateful to the folks at Bauman Rare Books for sharing an important Burns letter. Many, many people helped me pursue the innumerable dead ends that a project like this entails. I thank them for the peace of mind they gave me, for convincing me—whether justly or not—that I left few stones, or even pebbles, unturned.

Many people read, and improved, my manuscript: Michael Henry Adams, Daniel Blue, Christopher Bram, David Bray, Elizabeth Cohen, Phillip Isenberg, Charles Kaiser, Robert Loomis, John Loughery, Gertrude Margolick, Joseph Margolick, Michael James Moore, James Rugen, Michael Shnayerson, and Tim Zagat. Harvard Knowles, who endured plenty of my prose as an English teacher at Loomis, nonetheless agreed to read the manuscript, too; whether he believes it marked an improvement from my student work he (very graciously) didn't say.

I bless the day I met Judith Gurewich of Other Press. She embraced this book enthusiastically without reading a word of it, and at a time when it mattered greatly to me. I'm grateful to her and all of her colleagues—including Paul Kozlowski, Sulay Hernandez, Yvonne E. Cárdenas, Jessica Greer, Tynan Kogane, Iisha Stevens, Libby Riefler, Lauren Shekari, and Bill Foo—for creating such a lovely home for my work. Thanks, too, to my copyeditor, Walter Havighurst, who was punctilious in multiple languages.

I'd like, finally, to single out three people for special thanks.

I know it was not easy for him to revisit the life, and death, and afterlife, of his difficult older brother, but Thomas D. Burns, Esq., did so unflinchingly. He was also encouraging, gracious, good-humored, and patient with me. Working with him was one of the high points of this experience. I want also to thank two of his sisters, Constance Silverman and Anne Laskey, for their cooperation and goodwill.

Thirty years ago, Mark Bassett wrote his doctoral dissertation on Burns, an act of great courage in a homophobic time.

Conditions thwarted him from circulating that thesis, let alone turning it into a book. But he held on to the material he had gathered and, in an act of extraordinary generosity, shared it all with me. Without that—without *him*—this book would have never come to be, which is why I have dedicated it to him.

Finally, I'm thinking of the Loomis boy who, sometime in the fall of 1966, pulled me aside and bared to me the great secret of John Horne Burns and his scandalous book. It was he who really launched me on this project, though he could never have imagined how long it would take me to do it, nor that I'd let so many eyewitnesses to the Burns story—people like Mr. Grubbs, Mr. Howard, Mr. Stookins, Mr. (Charles) Pratt, Mr. Norris, and Mr. Fowles, all of them then still very much alive—slip through my fingers. I would thank this boy more personally—if only I could remember who he was.

Dreadful

1

The old library at the Loomis School, off the grand entrance to Founders Hall, was a cramped and uninviting place, with giant tables, cork floors, and books shoehorned into caged stacks in a back room. Students would go in there as much to kill time and rile up the famously stern and schoolmarmish librarian, Winifred Adams, as to study or read.

Libraries are generally best known for the items they contain rather than those they don't. But when I reached Loomis, a prep school in Windsor, Connecticut, in the fall of 1966, what soon came to intrigue me most about its library was a book that wasn't there. Only a few weeks after I arrived, another student told me—in the hushed tones of someone disclosing an ancient but still embarrassing secret—that many years earlier there'd appeared a scabrous novel about Loomis called *Lucifer with a Book*, written by a man named John Horne Burns. It was, he revealed, filled with thinly veiled caricatures of its teachers and administrators, many of whom were still there, the people we saw walking around every day. But, he went on, the one place where you would never find the book was the Loomis library: Mrs. Adams had seen to that. Around the school, the book was in permanent exile: not to be taught or read or in any way acknowledged. Nearly twenty years after its messy debut, it remained totally taboo.

In my time, boarding schools like Loomis were still very insular places. Really, things had changed little since Burns's days there on either side of World War II, and it felt that way. Immured in the plaster and brick and marble and wood and wainscoting were the ghosts of dead students and their teachers. You sensed their presence when you passed the old photographs of athletic teams on the gymnasium walls, where the doddering instructors you knew appeared as youthful and robust young men, and the boys, by contrast, looked precociously mature, wearing baggy uniforms, parting their hair in the middle. Climbing the marble steps in Founders en route to class, past the painted names of Loomis's fallen from World War II, Korea, and now Vietnam, you stepped into the grooves that generations of wing tips, penny loafers, and bucks had left in the stone. You sensed their hands as you leafed through the dusty and neglected copies of *Victory* and *Look Homeward, Angel* in the classroom bookcases, or in the ancient graffiti in the dignified cupola that looked out over the Quadrangle. When, in the grand, spacious dining hall, beneath the painting of King Arthur and one of his knights and the carved words of Tennyson's *Idylls of the King*, you cheered on some team's latest victory—"*Tah! Rah-rah! Football!*"—you heard the echoes of the same chants reverberating through the hall from decades earlier. You smelled the dead boys, too, in the musty air of sweat and jockstraps entombed in the locker rooms and in the slightly less pungent stench of spoiled food and dirty feet in the old dormitories, where the bell for lights-out echoed along the corridors at ten o'clock each night.

Somewhere in that same netherworld resided the ghost of John Horne Burns. From the first time I heard it that day, his very name conveyed to me something vaguely remote, sinister, tragic, *truncated*. Maybe its formal, archaic ring, maybe the realization that one had never encountered it anywhere else, suggested that this Burns had come to a sudden, premature, and maybe even an unnatural end. I got the distinct sense of a young life snuffed out, and as a young man then myself, I found it sad and unnerving. Because our teachers knew we liked reading about ourselves, prep school novels like *A Separate Peace* and *The Catcher in the Rye* were staples in our English classes. But no teacher dared assign or even discuss *Lucifer*, though it would surely have engaged us, and, unbeknownst to us, some of them had managed, after considerable effort, to procure their own copies of the contraband in secondhand bookstores, many containing inside their front covers handwritten lists detailing who was supposedly who. The book clearly skewered the school's first headmaster, after whom a dormitory and the main road leading to the campus were named, and his wife, whose sculptures and bas-reliefs were scattered throughout. It turned out the book may also have played a small role in another ancient and still-whispered-about campus tragedy: the suicide of the man for whom the school theater was named. A third character in it, pockmarked and unctuous, was said to have been modeled after our current headmaster. Nor had Loomis students been immune from Burns's barbs. With but few exceptions—the Jewish student council president; the school's only Negro; an artsy scholarship boy on whom the book's (male) hero has an overpowering crush (and on whom the boy has a crush back); some flamboyantly effeminate types given to fey soirees and gang bangs—*Lucifer*'s students were almost uniformly spoiled blockheads. If they had been, then what were we?

For a time, among more literary and historically minded students or irreverent types who just savored a good scandal, tracking down and reading *Lucifer* was an illicit rite of passage, like sneaking cigarettes behind the Power House or buying condoms for the school prom. Anyone intrepid and curious enough could find it in the nearby Windsor Public Library, to which Winnie Adams's tentacles did not extend. Others found it very easily once they got to college, for Burns had grown famous outside Loomis and his books were readily available. "This is about Loomis!" an anonymous student wrote breathlessly in the copy still in Yale's Sterling Library, at a time when the Ivy League was still so stocked with preppies that such information would have mattered. But by the time I reached Loomis, almost no one—besides my informer, and then me—would have much cared. Burns was not just dead but forgotten, even in the place with which, along with a city in Southern Italy, he was once most closely associated.

Long after I'd left Loomis, I remained haunted by John Horne Burns. But it took me more than ten years to track down and read *Lucifer with a Book*. As time passed I gathered some material on him, but another thirty years went by before I tried to learn who Burns was, and how he had come to write the book, and what else he wrote before and after it, and what had become of him. I learned he was best known for what was once considered one of the finest novels of World War II, *The Gallery*, a book blessed by such chroniclers of the previous Great War as Ernest Hemingway and John Dos Passos and powerful contemporary critics like Edmund Wilson and John Aldridge. As important as it was, the book was more significant for what it heralded: seemingly out of nowhere a major new literary star had suddenly appeared, and once his immaturities had burned off, who knew what even greater works he might one day produce? *The Gallery* was good enough both to inspire and to intimidate notable novelists to come, like William Styron and Joseph Heller, who had war books of their own still in them, waiting to be born. "There was nothing I could add to war literature that was not in *From Here to Eternity* and had not been produced before by Norman Mailer and a very excellent novel—and it's been forgotten now—by John Horne Burns," Heller, reflecting on the long and difficult gestation of *Catch-22*, once recalled.

I learned how, by presenting an unflinching and unsanitized account of the conduct of American soldiers in occupied Naples in 1944 and 1945, documenting their contempt for the locals and their own despicable behavior—the black-marketing, the sexual predations, the rampant venereal disease—Burns provided an important, contemporaneous counterweight to the more senti-mental accounts of the time as well as a corrective to the revision-ist talk decades later of a "greatest generation." In its hardheaded portrayal of American parochialism and insularity, *The Gallery* anticipated books like *The Ugly American* and reportage from Vietnam, Iraq, and Afghanistan. Burns elaborated upon these themes in hundreds of remarkable wartime letters to his family and friends, most of which have languished unread for decades. Never had he come close to combat himself—officially, his war was largely spent reading the letters of homesick Italian prison-ers of war, safely behind the lines in Casablanca, Algiers, and Naples—but wherever he had been he had witnessed something else: as he put it to a friend, "the effects of war after the wedge has gone through and left nothing but splinters and pain."

The playwright David Mamet has called *The Gallery* "the best book to have come out of the war." To the war historian and essay-ist Paul Fussell, it was "an extraordinary contribution to American literature. There is nothing like it." It was also, he went on to say, "undeniably an oddity produced by an undeniably odd author mo-tivated by rare moral convictions." Rare, and in some ways, eva-nescent and fragile: the story of how Burns struggled to shed his youthful cynicism, then to find and retain the compassion that war had nurtured in him is in some ways the greatest drama of the man himself. It had the makings of his second great novel, the one he never got to write and quite possibly never could have.

I learned *The Gallery* was perhaps America's first great gay novel, in large part because it was among the first to depict homosexuals at considerable length and generously—as alternately lonely, proud, unpleasant, sensitive, and a range of other things: in other words, as *normal*, rather than as the suicidal freaks and criminals featured in the gay novels coming before it. And how the book's most remarkable chapter—describing a gay bar frequented by Allied soldiers in the heart of Naples—was what many, including Burns's great rival, Gore Vidal (who found Burns's manifest talent positively painful), agreed is one of the most brilliant pieces of gay writing in English of the twentieth century. It is also a startlingly courageous plea for tolerance long before the term "gay rights" even existed, though so explosive was his plea that most straight reviewers—which meant virtually all reviewers—simply ignored it, including those who praised the book.

I learned, further, how through his unpublished letters to one of his gay students at Loomis—one of many such boys, primarily fledgling homosexuals though including anyone there with a spark of artistic promise, whom he influenced and encouraged by his very example and his brilliant, almost demonic style of teaching—Burns became an important, even a unique, chronicler of gay life in the military, reminding us in real time how, in astonishingly high numbers, homosexuals—or "dreadfuls," as he called them in his typically camp code—were serving their country at a time when they were officially banned from the military, and long before another generation of traditionalists pretended they'd never been in there. Here, too, Burns's letters are as important a part of his legacy as his novels, offering forgotten snapshots of GI life—gay GI life—abroad, a life that seems quite inconceivable today. Without Burns's letters, how else would we know of soldiers performing Schumann, Brahms, and Gilbert and Sullivan for their fellows in the middle of the North African desert?

But I learned, too, of the peculiarly erratic combination of explicitness and evasion, high art and clumsy artifice, with which Burns wrote about his own sexuality in those works, and how he so often resorted to the subterfuges of gay men of his time. Burns's homosexuality simultaneously marked his greatest work, limited his artistic range, hastened his downfall, and, decades later, aided his reemergence as a literary figure of note. With breathtaking speed, he went from being one of the brightest literary lights of his generation—published by a prestigious house, much sought after for blurbs and speeches, photographed by *Life* and *Harper's Bazaar*—to an embittered drunk, living in exile, his talent eroded or blocked, his work brutally ridiculed or rejected, downing cheap cognac and soda prodigiously every night at the bar of a Florentine hotel until, at the age of thirty-six, under murky circumstances in an Italian seaside town, he died. His editor at Harper and Brothers, Frank MacGregor, summed it up best: "A lot of authors don't go anywhere, but you don't get the extreme that he was—from the top to the very bottom."

The drama created by *Lucifer with a Book*, I learned, was not confined to the Loomis campus: wickedly clever and singularly vicious, the work of a man emboldened by overnight success and beset by a lifetime of resentments, Burns's eagerly awaited and bitterly disappointing second novel had almost single-handedly sent him spiraling downward. That he was brilliant, talented, witty, caustic, and cruel would have been instantly apparent to me even as a fourteen-year-old boy in the Loomis library had *Lucifer* been allowed on the shelf. That he was so flawed and tortured—torn between proclaiming and covering up his sexual orientation, between his impulses to destroy and denigrate and, fed by the suffering he'd seen overseas, to ameliorate—would not have been. That was why, among those who remembered him, he was more loathed than pitied. "He was an interesting, even fascinating man," one of his former students, Thomas

Brush,* was to write, "but although he was usually very amusing, he was all but impossible to like—once you knew him—and I suspect that no one, woman or man, ever loved him in all his life. His cruelty always offended me, and after the publication of *Lucifer with a Book*, I really detested him."

But another former student of Burns's named Paul Barstow† felt very differently, for by his very example Burns had helped him and others like him come to terms with who they were. "He was a fine and greatly gifted man whom I liked and deeply respected—the only 'positive role model' during an appropriately appalling adolescence," Barstow wrote many years after Burns's death and, seeking to square away his accounts, shortly before his own. Speaking in the idiom of Dante—Burns, a brilliant linguist fluent in, among other languages, Italian, had translated Dante at Harvard—Barstow added, "I pray, with knowledge of his later days and end, that [he] has now passed through his *Purgatorio* and found some *Paradiso*."

That boy who, forty-six years ago, told me about Burns—I do not remember who it was—never mentioned Burns's homosexuality, and this was not surprising. Even in the late 1960s, in an all-boys school where sex was constantly and coarsely discussed and many of our teachers were gay, the subject almost never came up, except in offhanded, sophomoric ridicule. While we feigned a certain worldly sophistication about, and disapproval of, homosexuality, we knew next to nothing about it. In this respect, too, surprisingly little had changed since Burns's day. Only years later, as I started gathering material on him, did I even learn Burns was gay, and that revelation lent new impetus and meaning to my search: the gay world, to say nothing of the gay world in the years before, during, and after World War II, was a black hole for me.

---

* Later chairman of the Metropolitan Opera in New York.

† The longtime head of Wellesley College's Department of Theater Studies.

So what began largely as a sentimental story about my school and some ancient scandal there suddenly became something far more complex—and, for a straight man, unfamiliar, even treacherous. Burns proved to be a difficult man to know, to like, to write about. Readers may have to struggle, as I have, with his prickly personality: how much of it was innate, how much cultivated, how much a reaction to the predicament any gay man faced in that hostile era, how much he managed to overcome. But Burns was clearly a great teacher. And though he died the year after I was born, Burns would teach me, too.

2

John Horne Burns first laughed at the beginning of November 1916, when he was a very precocious twenty-four days old. According to his baby book, his father had been the one to hear it. Whoever recorded the moment—maybe his nurse, maybe his proud and hovering mother—was uncannily perceptive, even clairvoyant. "Jackie had as a baby the most hearty infectious laugh and the strangest things seemed to strike him funny," she wrote. "He gave promise at an early age to possess quite a sense of humor and to see quickly the ridiculous side of things."

Shortly before Harper and Brothers released *The Gallery* in 1947, it asked Burns to write, for promotional purposes, a short autobiography. For all his protestations—he insisted he didn't like talking about himself—Burns clearly relished the task, and what he produced was cocky and insightful, if selective. "The bee-ography will be a rather embarrassing piece to concoct because my external life is rather uneventful and because, although

I'm not modest, I hate to write down anything personal that may be used against me," he told a friend. And if he had revealed anything private, it probably would have been.

Burns was born, he wrote, in Andover, Massachusetts, at midnight on October 7, 1916 (as he liked to observe, the feast of the Most Holy Rosary), to "a gentle lawyer" and "a sprightly and realistic heiress of the Boston FIF's."* He'd been named after his maternal grandfather, John W. Horne, who, according to the *Boston Globe*, had amassed a fortune (worth roughly $5 million today) "by inventing a safeguard system of bookkeeping and fortunate mining investments," and whose estate had been contested. His paternal grandfather, William J. Burns, had been killed working for the Boston and Maine Railroad. His father, Joseph, who'd become a telegrapher at age thirteen, had, in a real-life Horatio Algerish twist, won a scholarship to nearby Phillips Academy after befriending its headmaster. That lucky break had spared him from a life in the textile mills of nearby Lawrence (though one of his brothers had also become wealthy, and *his* estate had been fought over as well). From Andover, Joseph Burns had gone on to Harvard and Harvard Law School. Burns's mother, Catherine, had graduated from Smith, where she majored in Latin, and never let anyone forget it. When Catherine Horne and Joseph Burns announced their engagement in 1914, at a tea held in her Roxbury home, the *Boston Journal* reported that among the guests was Rose Fitzgerald, daughter of the former mayor of Boston and future mother of a president of the United States.† For Joseph Burns, marrying one of the wealthy Horne girls was a great step up. Catherine, on the other hand, never got over the idea that she had married beneath herself.

---

* First Irish Families.

† Rose and Catherine were girlhood friends; sitting at a soda fountain one day, Rose had confided in her that she planned to marry Joseph P. Kennedy, though in fact, she confessed, he was really only her second choice.

The Burns family, 1922

She had little respect for Joseph Burns's family—she considered his brothers, who ran a clothing store in Andover, parvenus—and thought her husband ineffectual.

In October 1915, the couple's first child, named William after Joseph Burns's older brother, was born. He lived only a few days. Almost exactly a year later came another boy. That this one survived, and bore the name of Catherine Burns's beloved father, assured that come what may—including six more surviving children and a boy who suffocated in his crib at age one, John Horne Burns would remain his mother's favorite, a feeling that only intensified as young Jack absorbed, then mimicked and eventually outdid her peculiar brand of hypercritical intelligence. His siblings knew it: her mother was "just besotted" with him, one sister later recalled. From his mother he got his "mercilessness," Burns wrote in one of the more candid moments in his "autobiography": "she whetted her ambitions and her tenderness on me." For his

The Burns family, 1925

first two years—until his sister Cathleen came along—Catherine and John Horne Burns had each other largely to themselves. Even after the torrent of younger brothers and sisters, he remained separate. One can see it in a family portrait from around 1926 or 1927. Burns himself looks amused, but his laugher is more devilish than innocent. He looks older than his age and up to no good. His three younger brothers—Joseph (born in 1919), Thomas (1921), and Donald (1924)—appear almost like a different family, a separate and distinct unit of ordinary children, earnest and curious, sweet and placid. (Burns once boasted that as a boy, he liked to push one of his younger brothers into a hot radiator.) On the edge his sister Cathleen (1918) warily stands sentinel, ready to challenge anyone daring to take her older brother on. Of all his siblings, Burns was closest, chronologically and temperamentally, to her; they even spoke the same esoteric language.

Between Catherine Burns's inheritance and Joseph Burns's successful law practice—one of his clients was William M. Wood, potentate of the nearby American Woolen Company—the Burns family was wealthy for a time, with housekeepers, chauffeurs, and gardeners and an elegant house on Andover's main street, just down the road from Phillips Academy, better known simply as "Andover." When Catherine Burns needed to summon the kitchen help, she had only to step on the buzzer beneath the carpeting by her seat in the dining room. (Because several of the yardmen came from Scotland, young Donald Burns developed a burr.) But no matter how wealthy they were, as Catholics the family never fully fit into Yankee Andover. Catherine Burns liked to say that Andover's Catholics had nothing left to prove, but elite local institutions like the North Andover Country Club and the upper echelons of the local banks would still not have them. Oddly, the Burns family was equally alienated from local Catholics, most of whom were poor or working-class. Most everyone at St. Augustine's, the elementary school run by the Sisters of Notre Dame that Jack and his siblings attended, were the children of mill workers and domestics. *They* all walked to school; the Burns children sometimes had to fight their way onto the schoolyard after their driver—the family had two cars—had dropped them off. The isolation the Burns family already felt, Catherine Burns only intensified. Caustic and argumentative, convinced of her own superiority, she had few friends (apart from the woman who curled her hair). The family rarely entertained; caught between two cultures, scorned by the one and scorning the other, they'd have had no one to invite. "We came of immigrant stock different from the Yanks, and we dwelt in Andover partly in her tradition, partly aloof from it. We belonged to those intellectual sharecroppers who chose the town for the sake of its schools," was Burns's own, sanitized version of things.

Burns attended St. Augustine's from age five to thirteen. It was a proud and assertive place—forever rubbing its piety into Yankee noses by staging religious processions through the streets of downtown Andover—and strict, its sisters slapping wayward students with rulers. "This was my first—and until quite recently my last—contact with reality," Burns later wrote. "It was a long time there before I discovered that I must hit other boys with my fists to protect my own dreamy interests . . . [The nuns] inculcated into me a sense of mysticism, strife and terror, which has never left me. In the nuns' school I was a very bright little boy, possibly because my parents were the only ones in the town of Andover who were literate and thoughtful at home." (In a town synonymous with education, the claim was, of course, preposterous.) His years there gave Burns a great love of Catholic learning and theatricality, if not necessarily Catholic morality or practice. Its colorful rituals made other religions, particularly anything Protestant, seem pallid to him. Even when he got to college, he'd still come home Sundays to sing in the church. But Jack was the only Burns to graduate from St. Augustine's. Irate one May that Cathleen Burns wasn't chosen to lay a wreath atop the statue of the Virgin Mary—an award given annually to the exemplary girl in the eighth-grade class—Catherine Burns yanked all of her children from the place.

From there, Burns moved to Phillips Academy. He was only a day student at Andover, which made someone already at the fringes due to his rarified interests, precious temperament, and Catholicism even more marginal. "There," he wrote, "I suffered a little from the hazing, enough to loathe the American male

Jack Burns the boy: pious, introverted, impish

gregarious spirit, and I spat impotently to myself over the Fraternities. But I did make some good friends on the faculty and did receive a respect for urbanity and scholarship (useful) which still remains with me. At Andover I fear or I believe that I picked up the idea that an education should be liberal and should be for its own sake, not as preparation for a life of selling bonds."

An English teacher named Emory Basford, a homosexual himself,* who'd come to Andover around the same time as Burns and stayed on until 1964, recalled him as a chubby fourteen-year-old with effeminate mannerisms, a delicate complexion, and a nervous twitch. From an early age Burns had been extremely musical. Even before he could read, he could find any Victor Red Seal record that was called for and put it on the phonograph; at three or four, a recording of Donizetti's comic opera *Don Pasquale* had fascinated him, as all opera eventually came to do. At Andover Burns sang in the glee club, taught himself the rudiments of the violin, and became a gifted pianist. In a school dominated by well-bred WASP jocks destined for careers in law and finance, such interests pushed Burns even further out of the mainstream. (As Andover's official historian, Frederick Allis, later wrote, any boy in that era who liked classical music "was suspected of being a 'fruit.'")

Often, evenings as well as afternoons, Burns would visit Basford's dormitory apartment, where the two would play piano for each other. Basford also had Sunday teas in which students discussed writing and art, a tradition Burns would continue once he got to Loomis. Burns wrote short stories for Basford, who encouraged him to pursue a career in writing. In old-fashioned gay parlance, Basford was probably Burns's "auntie"—that is, a mentor, proving by his very example that nonconformity could

---

* To Burns's first biographer, John Mitzel, who interviewed Basford, he was "as gay as a handbag—the sweetest old queen I ever met."

be accommodated, even rewarded. A teacher of German named Dirk Van der Stucken, a man of mystery and overstatement, might have been more than that to Burns. He, too, was gay, and Burns spent lots of time with him; his family believed the two were having an affair. "To many of those boys who are the despised and sometimes persecuted 'odd-balls' of the academic commonwealth he showed enormous kindness and sympathy," an Andover alumnus was to write of Van der Stucken. It was from him that Burns might also have acquired his lifelong love for German *Lieder*, or art songs. Because of these men and others on its faculty, Andover gave Burns a great gift, extremely unusual for its day: he appeared to be at peace with, if not necessarily proud of, being gay, at least as much as anyone in that closeted era could be.

Burns had his share of gay experiences at Andover, hinted at elliptically in later years. For instance, he once recalled how his heart had been broken when he'd happened upon an assignation, presumably involving a boy to whom he'd grown attached. Precisely when this part of his life began isn't clear. In one wartime letter he claimed to have "come out at blushful seventeen," while in another he talked of expounding on the *Satyricon* of Petronius—an early, bawdy chronicle of gay love—"in our Turkish alcoves at 4:30 in the afternoon over our Dresden china shepherdess pots of bohea."* If his last published novel offers any clues, Burns quickly realized women weren't for him. "I'd resolved early in life that any true intimacy between man and woman must be essentially repulsive," the hero of that book remarks. "O, surely, the pleasure was fierce (for the moment) but the subsequent involvement of two people after the union of their bodies would be psychically too onerous to bear." But this was only part of a more general aversion to intimacy of any kind: the character describes how he couldn't bear spending entire

---

* A kind of Chinese black tea, to which Alexander Pope once referred in a poem.

nights *with anyone.* "The spasm never left any perfume behind it," he recalls.

While Andover left a major mark on Burns, Burns left almost no mark on Andover. When, on graduation in 1933, his classmates bestowed the usual superlatives on one another, Burns didn't win, place, or show in any categories, even in those—"most eccentric," "brightest," "wittiest"—in which, had he been better known, he surely should have competed. Fundamentally, Burns was a loner, though generally a contented one. His eldest sister, who came to be nearly as worshipful as his mother, once remarked that Jack carried "his own brand of bottled sunshine" around inside of him. "This is a sweet way of saying that I'm an egoist on excellent terms with myself," Burns was to write. "My nature is naturally a happy one until the world or other people get in my hair." Burns always considered himself good-natured, at least until everyone else spoiled things.

When did this isolation, this self-sufficiency, begin? To his wartime confidant Holger Hagen, Burns wrote that it dated all the way back to birth. "Shortly after my umbilical cord was cut I was aware that not much was to be hoped for from anybody, that I must live alone and die alone, and that just for my own satisfaction I owed it to myself to be as clever and as attractive as I knew how to be," he told him. With his mother, he placed it a bit later. "Since leaving the nest at 16, I've contrived to maintain the philanthropic modus vivendi of living by myself, cultivating the pose of solitude, possibly imagining I was some exquisite hermit—a cross between St. Francis of Assisi and the Buddha," he once wrote her. "I knew at fifteen I'd never be a Nice Guy or a Good Joe," his doppelgänger states in Burns's final published novel. "There were just too many things I simply couldn't put up with or excuse." Not until well into his army days did Burns even have a roommate. His pursuits were solitary. For a time, he considered becoming a concert pianist. (One story—from his brother

Donald, like Burns himself an occasional teller of tall tales—had it that Paderewski* once heard him play, and decreed that though he could be a great pianist, he would never be one of *the* greats, so Burns dropped that dream.)

For a time, his mother feared he'd turn into a Trappist monk. (Allaying her own frustrated intellectual ambitions through her eldest son, she never was one of those devout Irish-American mothers hungering to see such a son become a priest.) The two remained abnormally close, in one of those platonic mother-son love affairs known to other notable gay men, like the architect Philip Johnson. When, during Burns's days at Andover, Catherine Burns took a vacation to Point Comfort, Virginia, for instance, it was only Jack she brought along. Her crossed eyes became even more pronounced when she grew angry, but it was a side of her that Jack, unlike his younger brothers, rarely saw. His mother's ardent devotion nurtured an arrogance in Burns which would quickly curdle into a precocious cynicism, then nihilism.

After Andover came four years at Harvard, where, as Burns later put it, "I sopped up learning so rich and so thick as to make me precious and more than a little snide" and come "within an inch of going arty." He focused on his writing, turning out sheaves of essays, poems, and plays, alternately dazzling and frustrating his professors. Many had an archaic streak, like Burns's sonnet of October 22, 1934, subtitled "On Old Age," which began:

When eyes no longer laugh again to eyes,
And lips have sunk their magic in the years,
When songs dissolve in cadences of tears—
To die away from these, our summer skies . . .

---

* The Polish pianist and, for a time, prime minister of Poland.

"God help me! But this is as good as some of Shakspere's sonnets, sir!" wrote one of his professors, perhaps George Lyman
Kittredge—who favored that alternative spelling of the Bard's
name, as Burns himself came to do. But "this poem . . . is not
very good: rather musty and creaking," another professor complained about a different work. "You write more like John Keats
than any poet or potential poet I have *ever* read, but this has its
disadvantages as well as its virtues." In early 1935 he won the
dollar prize in a writing contest sponsored by the *Boston Traveler* for the following poem:

> *Beloved:*
> *Far nobler than the peacock and his train,*
> *That rule these many-pillared ivory halls,*
> *Art thou, Cathleen, my peerless starry swain,*
> *For thine is all the magic that enthralls,*
> *I sought strange sweetness far without the walls*
> *Of gray convention's shackling prison cell;*
> *I toyed with countless queens and waxen dolls*
> *Whose far-flung beauty oft had I heard tell.*
> *But never found the stars that in thine eyes do dwell. Thine*
>   *alone.*

The "Cathleen" was almost certainly his sister. Though all
his younger brothers did well initially—young Joe Burns went to
Yale (where he was a record-setting swimmer and qualified for
the 1940 Olympics), Donald to Amherst, and Tom to Brown—he
did not relate to them, nor did their own mother. The two were in
their own world. "I had always thought [Catherine Burns] knew
that my personality is quite a separate entity from the other excel-
lences of my other brothers, and that I do not live in quite the neat
groove that they do," he once confided in Cathleen. "And I can't
be any other way than what I am."

While at Harvard Burns also honed his extraordinary gift for languages, mastering French, German, and Italian, translating Gabriele D'Annunzio's verse play *Francesco da Rimini* and more than the first third of *The Divine Comedy*. Most important to him, though, were his novels. He was always writing one. Burns felt like a prisoner in his parents' house in Andover, known as "Sunnyside"; summer nights he'd flee to the hired man's room on the side of the garage, the one his father sometimes used as a law office, to get away and write. He worked at breakneck speed in microscopic longhand—he'd read somewhere that many geniuses had tiny handwriting, and seemed determined to emulate them—giving his works antiquarian titles like *Of Modern Grievance, Learn Valor, Child,* and *Your Quaint Honor.* Few in his family had any idea what was in them—and wouldn't have, even had they read them. When his night at the desk was done, he and his brother Tom would sometimes go down to the Andover depot, wait for the fast train for Portland to pass through, then walk back home, but never would they discuss what Burns had just written. Once, Tom Burns happened upon his brother grimacing into a mirror, his hands at his own throat. What on earth was he doing? "My principal character just found out what he was," Burns explained. What he was, Tom Burns assumed, was queer. The author, at least, found his early novels dazzling; that none was ever published seemed secondary. It's not even clear how hard he tried; some of them, at least, he tossed off for sport. "Practice novels" was how someone, probably Cathleen—who followed and encouraged, then curated, then bottled up, his work for decades—described them in a family scrapbook, simultaneously trivializing them and elevating their author.

Burns was also extremely active on the musical scene. He sang with the Harvard Glee Club—as a first tenor, his range was the envy of his colleagues—and participated when, on Good Friday 1937, Serge Koussevitsky and the Boston Symphony Orchestra

"Sunnyside." The "man's room" is in the building to the right.

joined the glee club in a historic recording of Bach's St. Matthew Passion. His musical preferences were akin to his literary ones; anything later than the seventeenth century wouldn't do. Burns may have known Leonard Bernstein, who was two years behind him, and in 1936 he wrote, with his schoolmate Irving Gifford Fine (who went on to become a noted composer in his own right), a musical comedy called *The Christmas Sparrow: Or Double or Nothing*, concerning parietal regulations on the campus. Both Bernstein and Fine were Jews, and along with still more Jewish students, they provided Burns an education, including an education in open-mindedness, which, as he later wrote to a reader, he'd never received at home.

> *I don't understand the feeling against minorities. I come from one myself which I find especially bigoted—the Boston Irish Catholic one. And they, who profess to such devotion to their worship, are especially virulent against Jews. It seems odd to me, since Catholicism was established by a*

Jew who was crucified—at least Holy Mother Church says so quite often. At Harvard, where my greatest love was music, all my friends were the brilliant Jews of the class of 1937. I loved them dearly; they had a spiritual quality missing in the blond sons of stockbrokers. Yet my father still passes remarks about kikes at the dinner table.

With some strange exceptions, like a repulsive character in his final published novel, Burns's philo-Semitism was lifelong; he once faulted the writer Irwin Shaw for not understanding Jews, even though Shaw was Jewish himself.

Perhaps because he knew they'd never be published, Burns the novelist wrote on gay and other outré topics with a brio and insouciance remarkable for his era. But aside from one oblique reference that he later recalled—"I remember Virgil Thomson* swishing around Lowell House in shorts when we were rehearsing his choruses to *A Bride for the Unicorn*,"†—Burns never wrote anything about gay goings-on at Harvard. Much of that life was furtive, and understandably so: only thirteen years before Burns got there, Harvard had convened a "secret court" to investigate homosexuality on campus, one that led to several expulsions. The proceedings received almost no publicity, but barely a decade later, their specter surely still hung over Harvard's homosexuals. At least once Burns got in trouble with the police, perhaps for cruising along the Charles, requiring his father to come in and fix things. Though he had certain odd gestures and habits (Tom Burns had never seen anyone hold a cigarette in quite the same way: between his first two fingers and his thumb, as if it were a dart; at dances he invariably went after the most unattractive women, as if to toy with them), Burns's emerging sexuality was

---

* The composer and music critic.

† A 1933 play by the Irish playwright Denis Johnston.

not discussed in the family. His sister Cathleen once remarked that she "hated what she knew about Jack," but that was about as explicit as it ever got. When Catherine Burns complained that one of her sisters was saying *"terrible* things about Jack," she did not specify just what these were, but she made it clear that these terrible things had to be terribly untrue.

For all his activities, at Harvard, too, Burns spent a lot of time by himself. The suite he had in Dunster House for three years, A25, he lived in alone, and it suited him. "I looked down on everything in the university as cliquish because in my own way I was the biggest minority clique of all," he recalled. "I dwelt in a delightful superhuman elegance—delightful for me. I laughed at everything because I was above everything. It was merely unfortunate that most of the world couldn't breathe the rarefied atmosphere that I daily inhaled." His classmates seemed perfectly content to let him stew in his own rarefied juices. "I say I knew him; I did not particularly like him, because I found him pretentious, egotistical, and not a little scornful of others who were not like-minded," a classmate named Sumner Willard, who went on to teach French at West Point, later wrote. "John had an original cast of mind and was not happy, not really comfortable, at Harvard." When Tom Burns later ran into various members of Jack's class, no one ever seemed to remember who Jack was. Maybe it was because Burns came home so frequently. And whenever he did, his mother made sure he had the honored place at the dinner table: alongside her.

It was at Harvard that Burns developed one more passion that was always to accompany him: alcohol. His parents were not drinkers. They kept a single bottle of liquor—Hennessy's brandy—in the house, tucked away on the floor of his father's closet in the master bedroom upstairs, but strictly as a necessity: Catherine Burns's mother was an alcoholic—when Burns told a friend she "tied on a beauty every five years" he had greatly

*Burns and his mother at his Harvard
graduation, 1937*

understated things—and whenever she visited her daughter, arriving in her chauffeur-driven Cunningham, she'd need a nip
or two to get her through the day. Perhaps out of deference to
his parents, during visits home Burns drank elsewhere, walking
three or four miles some nights to the bar at Shawsheen Manor—
the hostelry for mill executives in Andover—then walking all
the way back. Once, though, when he brought home a Harvard
friend, Catherine Burns actually had a bottle of White Horse
whiskey awaiting them. She appeared more eager to keep Jack
happy—and to impress his friend, whose family owned Boston's
famed Parker House Hotel—than worried about her family's
proclivities.

3

Sard, a handsome and hirsute thirty-year-old itinerant Gypsy, summons Tippie, a pathetic, heavyset man-child whom he'd picked up the year before in the Boston Common and bummed around with ever since, as he returns from washing their pots and pans in a nearby stream. "I have a gift for you, Tippie," Sard tells his companion. "Come hither, love[,] to me." In a minute, Sard holds Tippie by the neck, "gently throttling till the plump puss was baby blue." "His tongue poked out; his eyes jellied into pools of dark fear," the story continues. "Then he was lying in the grass and, fighting back to breath, stroking his abrased gullet. He was dead happy, he was."

This is a passage from *The Cynic Faun*, the novel Burns wrote in the summer of 1937. The title came from a poem written by Robert Hillyer, a Harvard English professor who had won the Pulitzer Prize for poetry, with whom Burns had studied Swift and Pope during his senior year. He'd dedicated the book to Hillyer.

"I shall never drink a highball mixed of drinking water but that I remember your own genial concoctions with cloudy Adams House water that did their share to engay (H'mm) those Tuesday afternoons," Burns later wrote him. Most professors would have been delighted by such a gesture, and maybe Hillyer was. But he would have been horrified to read the perverse tract, filled with assorted brands of violence and deviancy—incest, cross-dressing, murder, exploitation, nymphomania—that Burns had written in his honor.

Burns had put together an admirable record at Harvard. He was to graduate magna cum laude—only the C he'd gotten, in a government class his father had insisted he take in a vain attempt to make a lawyer out of him, had kept him from summa—and was elected to Phi Beta Kappa. That feat was commemorated in the white silk ribbons hanging from his robe in the graduation picture of Burns taken outside Dunster House with his mother. But as graduation approached in the spring of 1937, he faced a familiar dilemma: finding a job he could stomach. Too unconventional for a standardized profession, too undisciplined and omnivorous for academia, too intolerant and impatient to push papers somewhere to subsidize his art, too snobbish to mix with hoi polloi, pretty much his only option was teaching, preferably at an elite private school that didn't require the usual certifications. "I found myself such a perfection of attitudes and prefabricated architectures that there wasn't much I could do in life except mould young men in my own pattern," he was to recall. But where? In the New England of that era, he had a problem, one that trumped his multiple talents and the ten A's he had amassed: his religion. And he knew it, so well that he wasn't even especially indignant about it. It was just an obstacle to be negotiated. And Harvard wasn't helping him any.

Since he deferred to very few people, Burns rarely sought advice. But things got desperate enough that April for him to reach out to Andover's headmaster, Claude Moore Fuess, who'd been one of Burns's English instructors before taking over the place. "I find myself staring at 'after college . . . ?'" he wrote Fuess. "Because my training was in English, the most overcrowded, they tell me, of sports, and because I am a Catholic, I am getting rather panicky about what to do for a teaching position . . . Could you, at your convenience, suggest some course I might follow?" If anything, Fuess quickly replied, Burns was *understating* the problem: New England's finest private schools were rife with prejudice. That included not just his own, where the religious bias was institutionalized—Andover's founding document provided that "Protestants only shall ever be concerned in the TRUST or Instruction of this Academy"—but, whether by official proscription or unspoken tradition, many other comparably prestigious schools. "It is perfectly true that it will be hard for you to get a place in several of the schools which I regard most highly, including Hotchkiss, Deerfield, St. Paul's, Milton, and Choate," Fuess conceded. He suggested, essentially, that Burns stick to his own kind. "The public schools, however, particularly in Boston and vicinity, should be open to you if you care to move in that direction," he wrote. "Beyond that, of course, there lies the college and the university, in which the religious prejudice has less potency than in the schools. I can tell you frankly that if I knew any good school where you would be acceptable I would go to the headmaster personally and make a plea that he take you on." None came readily to Fuess's mind, but he pledged to leave "no stone unturned."* He evidently kept his word, for within a week, at least three schools—Kent, Loomis, and, surprisingly, Deerfield—were considering Burns. Deerfield indeed begged off (no openings, it claimed), and Kent, too, apparently demurred.

---

* Fuess himself was no great reformer in this regard: a few years later, when Jewish registration at Andover approached five percent, he pledged a return to a school as "predominantly Aryan as possible."

But infuriated by the anti-Catholic bias Burns had encountered, Loomis's headmaster, Nathaniel Horton Batchelder, invited him down for an interview. Unlike so many of its counterparts, Loomis was not a church school; its charter specifically barred discrimination on religious or political grounds. Burns came highly recommended. In a packet that Harvard put together, Hillyer called him "one of the most brilliant students I have ever had and I have no doubt that his teaching career will be unusually successful." Another of his Harvard professors, Phillip Webster Souers, called him "first rate in everything he attempts. He writes well, has a creative power, and at the same time is capable of applying himself to a severe, scholarly discipline." There was even a recommendation from one H. I. Brett, a banker for whom Burns had worked for the previous three summers. The only puzzling note came from Fuess, who sprinkled asterisks into his praise. He described Burns as "a satisfactory and gifted student" and called his scholastic record "excellent," but noted his grade point average was only eighty, and concluded with only qualified praise. "I know nothing whatever about his ability as a teacher, potential or actual, but I should suppose that he would do a good job," he wrote.

Batchelder snapped Burns up, telling colleagues he was probably the brightest young man he'd ever brought on. What would Burns have felt, apart from relief? Well, for someone who venerated old things and craved prestige, Loomis may have seemed a bit lacking: going back only to 1914, it didn't have the ancient lineage of Andover, Deerfield, and some of its competitors. And it was not only considerably younger than Andover, but smaller. True, it had come a long way in its short history: while not making *Fortune*'s list of "Twelve of the Best American Schools" the year before, it did rank among the six "logical additions" the magazine mentioned in a footnote. The status-conscious Burns probably felt he was making the best of a bad situation. He was also heading into something he never encountered at Andover: a one-man show. Batchelder (pronounced BATCH-el-der, and known to generations of Loomis students simply as Mr. B) had been Loomis's only headmaster, and, for better or worse, dominated the place in a way no headmaster at ancient Andover ever could have, at least since the Revolutionary War.

Burns's old mentor, Emory Basford, evidently feared that teaching, at Loomis or anywhere else, would thwart Burns's literary aspirations, and suggested that some form of hack work might be preferable. "Let me assure you that if I really wanted to write, not the Loomis Institute nor MIT nor CCC* can stop me," Burns replied grandiloquently. "If a school position numbs and enervates my goose-quill, why, then the world need never shed a tear on my grave, and all your sage and just warnings would have been spent on an ear that never needed to hear them anyway." Besides, he said, Loomis was said to be one of the best places for an aspiring writer; "Mr. B," he had been assured, "not only encourages, but insists, on [his teachers] having some outside interest," with writing especially favored. In any case, Burns went on, having a real job—and in the midst of the Depression—was preferable to the lives of those romantics in *La Bohème* burning their manuscripts to keep from freezing to death. "Don't you *really* think deep down that even the purest, strongest, chastest muse may die of consumption or undernourishment on the street corner or in the garret?" he asked. "You know me well, and that I am stubborn enough to find time for anything I want to do. Not sixteen hundred little boys can joggle my pen off the page, even if they peep and pule over my shoulder, and laugh at what I write all the while. After all, emotion recollected in tranquility can be set down at leisure. There

---

* The Civilian Conservation Corps, one of the many New Deal agencies designed to put Depression-era Americans back to work.

will, I say, always be emotion, always recollection, always some tranquility."

So Burns grabbed the job. Then, before it began, he set out to write one last novel. As usual, it came out in torrents, three thousand words a day, every day, in microscopic print, with few second thoughts. Between the Fourth of July and August 19, he got down exactly 107,951 words. He boasted to Hillyer afterward of having found "a new elegant simplicity" this time around, without all the exotica with which he'd bulked up his previous books. "I am very gay these days with the rich hope that perhaps I've produced something to repay you for your gracious helps to me all last year," he told him.

One might have thought that in the summer of 1937, with Europe in the grip of revanchist totalitarianism, the world needed no new specimens of evil, but Burns reveled in fashioning his own. "In my mind the new novel has become a symbol of the grandeur of wickedness," he wrote another Harvard student. "Sometimes (seriously) I am afraid to write it down, for it seems I have attained to a new logic of sin. The world can't be improved by it." That wickedness is neatly encapsulated in Burns's alter ego, Sard, who is not only dashingly good-looking—Burns was prone to falling in love with his own heroes—but erudite, gay (the female body "smells of fish"), pitiless, and ultimately solitary, someone who finds mankind laughable, companionship immature, and intimacy grotesque. "A body built for intensive copulation, stifled by a brain built for intensive criticism": in describing Sard, Burns was surely characterizing himself, or at least how he fancied himself to be. The world, in fact, need not have worried: the book was unpublishable. Its characters are two-dimensional and tiresome; its jokes—often directed at the physical and mental deformities of various risible characters—grotesque and repetitious; its prose, pompous and preachy. Burns isn't writing so much as playing with himself. But in at least a couple of instances it is brilliant— demonically so.

One comes when Sard recalls how, in a fit of pique at age sixteen, he deliberately lured his loyal and trusting best friend—a blind boy, also sixteen—into the water with him, only to let him drown, then worrying afterward only about concocting the right alibi. Then there is the misanthropic but telling soliloquy of another character, Francis, offered over repeated scotch-and-sodas at the famous Merry-Go-Round Bar in Boston's Copley Plaza Hotel. Its subject: the pleasures of drinking alone. As praiseworthy as solitude may be, Francis muses, it is only enhanced by drinking, "slumped degenerately back in your chair, scowling at the world," with "no censor at work plying the blue pencil of convention and the red pencil of materialism." Liquor "underlined" what was on your mind and "gave you a brief handicap in the Race for Truth."

> *He couldn't search for Truth when he was conversing,*
> *however passionately; nor could he get within walking*
> *distance of Truth when he was sober. (Then he concentrated*
> *too well on the wrong conceits.) Drinking alone made*
> *him diffuse his consciousness over many problems, like*
> *divine grace, and would let his intelligence slip away into*
> *highways and byways, where it found many a strange*
> *wedding guest to bring back to the feast, telling tales and*
> *thoughts too unorthodox to win a hearing at any smug sober*
> *symposium . . . Your solitary thinker sometimes saw a few*
> *good things at the bottom of his cup.*

Burns had not just begun to drink at Harvard, then, but had fallen in love with liquor. The acuity he thought it bestowed was a great asset to any aspiring writer, *and* it was an established part of the authorial persona, *and* it conferred a certain two-fisted manliness upon someone to whom that did not otherwise come naturally. (So, too, Burns may have thought, did smoking, which he had started to do at Andover, and to which he grew just as devoted, and addicted.) Justifying, even extolling, vice was a dangerous business. But whatever it portended for Burns personally, Francis's paean to drink—and a few other passages in an obnoxious and otherwise forgettable book—signaled the brilliance Burns was capable of once he opted to write more from conviction and experience rather than to show off and to shock.

It was September 1937. Now this exponent of wickedness and deviancy, still only twenty years old, made his way to Windsor, Connecticut—and to straitlaced Loomis.

4

Nearly every spring, when the Farmington and Connecticut Rivers overflow their banks and submerge the roads leading to it, the Loomis School is cut off temporarily from its surroundings. It's why the campus, built on twenty-one acres of land that the Loomises got from the king of England, had always been called "the Island."

As New England's prep schools went, the Loomis of Burns's day was actually less of an island than many, and not just because, even when the floodwaters crested, the roads were rarely impassible. Next to many of its counterparts, stuck on the fringes of small towns, Loomis was comparatively citified. Hartford was only a few miles to the south; a third of its students were "day hops," commuting from places like Bloomfield and nearby Windsor, giving the school an urbaneness and permeability more isolated institutions lacked. (That a goodly portion of those day students were Jews—at various "leading" schools, in even shorter supply than

Catholics—also aerated the place.) But nights and weekends, it reverted to the more hermetic model of its rivals. In a handful of brick dormitories built around a faux-Jeffersonian quadrangle, a few hundred boarding students essentially lived with their teachers, sleeping under the same roofs, eating and worshipping together. Their universe consisted largely of classrooms, a refectory, a chapel, a gymnasium, and the athletic fields carving up the land Joseph Loomis had been granted in 1640, and which, seven generations later, five childless Loomis siblings—named Hezekiah, Osbert, James Chaffee, John Mason, and Abigail—decreed would be turned into a school. On winter weekend afternoons, when there were no classes to dull the ambient loneliness, and the halfhearted sun set early, the place grew smaller and more somber still.

On September 22, 1937, bundles of the first *Loomis Log* of the new school year were deposited around the Quad. From the top of the front page, under the headline "Newly Appointed Masters," out stared John Horne Burns, six feet tall and roughly 165 pounds, his arms and legs crossed, wearing a dark jacket, chinos, saddle

Loomis in the early years

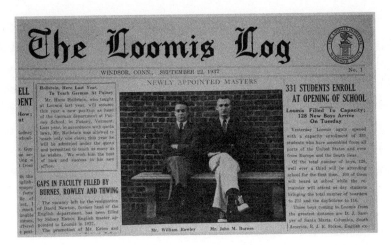

The school newspaper welcomed the new arrival.

oxfords, and an expression that was serious, skeptical, slightly dis-approving or even defiant. (A stickler for such things, he couldn't have been pleased to be called "Mr. John M. Burnes.") Burns was two weeks shy of twenty-one—he could have passed for a member of the senior class—and, for all his pretenses, a bit provincial. His face was mottled, perhaps from acne, and reddish. His nose was rather bulbous, his lips full, his eyes bright blue, and quick, darting, restless. To the many rich kids around the place, who had Brooks Brothers or J. Press as their haberdashers, Burns's wardrobe seemed meager and coarse. One well-heeled student described him as "a bumptious brilliant lower class boy [who] dressed abomina-bly—no sense of color, or bad combos of clothes and cheap suits"— just the type to wear white socks, as indeed, in the picture in the *Log*, he did. Burns moved into one of the small dormitory apartments the school assigned to unmarried teachers, at the end of a corridor of boys' rooms. Over his door he placed the famous words from *The Inferno: Lasciate ogni speranza voi ch'entrate.**

---

* "Abandon all hope, ye who enter here."

Once settled on the Island, Burns created an island of his own, an aesthetic refuge amid the prescribed daily grind of academics and athletics. Barely six months into his time at Loomis, he told Hillyer how pleased he was with his new situation. "As for my success here, I think it has been wide," he wrote. "After I became attuned to the 'classroom feeling,' I found teaching rather exhilarating." But the routine, he said, was of "a gentle grey Horatian sort"; he was counting on vacations and weekends away from the school, in New York or Boston or even Hartford, to supply some excitement.

The Loomis Burns found was going through tough times, buffeted by the Depression, an inadequate endowment, and natural disasters: not just the usual floods, but hurricanes. Scrambling to accommodate a growing student body and to make ends meet, it forced an onerous list of tasks on its teachers. Burns taught English and, occasionally, other classes, including one on poetry and another on "The Bible as literature." He revived the school's moribund literary magazine, the *Loom*, which proceeded to publish a good deal of homoerotic material. He also coached intramural soccer, but only because he had to. Like any unathletic person—he claimed to have played squash at Harvard, but that seems hard to believe—he looked slightly ridiculous with a whistle around his neck.

Music provided constant comfort. Compulsory daily chapel talks, normally dreary early-morning affairs, became lively whenever Burns delivered or performed for them. Speaking quickly and drolly, in manicured sentences and paragraphs, he'd introduce pieces not previously played in such an austerely New England setting: Copland's *El Salón México*, selections from *Porgy and Bess*. Or he and another young, gay faculty member, Douglas McKee,* would play pieces for four hands by Milhaud and Fauré. (So popular was their rendition of Ravel's *Mother Goose Suite* that in 1938

---

* Later headmaster of the American School in Paris.

they performed it for Loomis's annual alumni banquet at the Hotel Woodstock in New York.) McKee also accompanied Burns in a recital of songs by Poulenc. Once Burns performed two piano pieces, one vulgar and the other not, and dared students to tell them apart. He pitched in on productions of Gilbert and Sullivan, conducting so vigorously in the stifling theater that the sweat would drip off his nose, and he ran the "music club," playing selections from his enormous collection of classical records for campus aesthetes. (It was there that a student named Henry Breul* first heard Mahler's Ninth Symphony.) Probably as much to get off the campus and into civilization (and to find gay companionship) as to sing, Burns also joined the Hartford Madrigal Society. When his parents considered sending young Donald Burns to Loomis, and maybe having him share quarters with Jack, Jack said "Nothing doing," not just because he wasn't all that close to his kid brother, but also, surely, because he did not want him cramping his style.

Students grew accustomed to hearing symphonies and operas coming from behind the closed door of his apartment on the third floor of Warham Hall. Sometimes, though, usually on lazy Sunday afternoons when there was little else to do and, for teenagers finding themselves or aching for companionship, the pain of living away from home was most acute, Burns would leave that door slightly ajar, and the sound of music from his elaborate audio system reverberating down the dark corridor was an invitation for students to come inside. A few always did. Some, like a small, sensitive boy named David MacMackin, already knew they were gay; others, like Robert Purinton, would only figure that out later, though Burns clearly had them pegged. For the next forty-five minutes or so in Burns's small, sparsely furnished room, the boys would witness two performances. One came from whatever RCA Red Label records Burns had placed on his turntable;

---

* Later rector of St. Thomas Episcopal Church in Washington.

the other, more indelible one, was by Burns himself. It was an image that Purinton, who graduated from Loomis in 1942, never forgot. Even when at his most theatrically self-involved and self-indulgent, Burns was teaching.

It was an occasional thing. Two, three or four of us would sit down quietly on the floor, without speaking. We couldn't speak, because the music was so loud. No food or drink was offered. Burns never talked about the music or "instructed" us or even acknowledged us . . . it was kind of weird. We would watch him, standing in front of the loudspeakers with what appeared to be a baton in his right hand, "conducting" the recorded orchestra grandiosely and with great energy, his torso bending, his arms and hands and fingers waving wildly, communicating with the musicians, eliciting from them their most devoted, expressive performance, as if he were on a real podium, conducting a large orchestra. He put so much physical effort into leading the musicians that little beads of sweat would appear on his forehead. He went away to his own private space—he was not there in that little room; he was at the Met or Carnegie Hall—and we were just privileged observers. They were 78-RPM records he'd have to change periodically, but that didn't interrupt a thing. The music was gut-wrenching stuff like 19th century Italian operas and frequently featured sopranos on the verge, or at the height, of madness. There were no calm cerebral string quartets—it was always hordes of cavalry storming the castle. He was having great fun. It was a little bit otherworldly, mesmerizing to some extent, as if I were at the threshold of a huge, vibrant, pulsating new world and couldn't enter into it. I don't know why,

Burns conducting (L) and standing by his famed phonograph (R).

*but I always felt better after one of these sessions. I had a
sense of belonging to something, and not being an outsider.*

To Purinton, the other teachers at Loomis were relics; Burns, by
contrast, was smart, lively, opinionated, *original.*

Perhaps inevitably, students took to calling him "Horny Jack,"
but that was more a play on words and a description of his attitude
than an account of his actual behavior. "Burns himself had a reputation, much of which was his own fault," Tom Brush later recalled. "He liked to shock boys in his classes or at his table in the
dining room by confessing that he adored jerking off." Another
student recalled Burns, again in the dining hall, showing him
how to get his fingers to feel like a throbbing penis. Coming from
anyone else, the student recalled, it would have been shocking, but
from Burns, it was almost to be expected. But with him, unlike
with certain other teachers, there were no hints of impropriety.
"Hess has insinuated that Mr. Burney [*sic*] has made love to him,
but I don't believe it," wrote Alfred Duhrssen, who described his
years at Loomis in the late 1930s and early 1940s in his 1967 semi-
autobiography, *Memoirs of an Aged Child.* Whatever Burns was

up to in that regard seemed to happen off campus. That included not only sex but drink, though one Sunday afternoon, a student was shocked to see McKee and one of Burns's sisters propping him up as he left his apartment, drooling. To the befuddlement of some colleagues, Burns remained religious, leading a group of Catholics to Windsor for Mass most Sundays. Any institution that put on so good a show and that had lasted for two thousand years had to have something going for it, he figured.

As was then customary, Burns's homosexuality was simultaneously unknown to the oblivious and indifferent, and obvious to those inclined to care. For one class exercise Burns, naively or foolhardily or possibly provokingly, asked students to write down what they thought of him. "A homo" was among the things that a student named Michael Sudarsky listed. His essay came back with "homo" underlined—and "poor taste" handwritten alongside it. To Richard Johnson, two things gave away Burns's secret. One was his devotion to the poet Hart Crane, himself gay; the other came to him while watching Burns dash off to class one day, and noticing how his arms flopped as he ran. To use one of Burns's favorite words, he "flounced"; only a homosexual would run like that, Johnson thought. Like many of his peers, Batchelder didn't believe homosexuality existed anywhere, let alone at *his* school. Tom Lehrer, the songwriter and satirist who attended Loomis in 1943, tells of the time when Batchelder invited Burns and McKee to dinner. "What do you do about the problem of homosexuality here in the school?" a visitor from another school asked. "We don't have any of that here," Batchelder replied. "Burns practically choked on his soup, and he and McKee chuckled about it afterward," Lehrer recalled.

Lots of teachers at Loomis were closeted homosexuals, just as at Andover and comparable schools. The joke was that were you to give the small brown poodle belonging to one of Loomis's old French teachers a bone, he would suck it. But that didn't mean they related to, let alone liked, one another. Burns took a visceral dislike to one of the more popular and visible gay teachers on the Island: Norris Ely Orchard, also in the English department. Four years older than Burns, Orchard had graduated from Loomis and felt proprietary about the place; it was he who'd first shown Burns around. The two men shared a love for the intricacies of language and grammar; Orchard joked that he knew more about semicolons than anyone, and Burns admired him for it. Orchard, too, was interested in the theater—he'd written plays with names like *Lady Agatha Walks Again* and *Acme Paper Doilies*—and had a highly theatrical streak, making grand entrances into class by sliding across the newly waxed floors like a vaudevillian, then braking by his desk, sometimes quoting Shakespeare as he did. The two men appeared to get along, or so most people thought, and worked on various dramatic productions together. And they were neighbors: Burns lived upstairs from Orchard in Warham Hall.

In fact, for a variety of reasons, Burns held Orchard in contempt. There was the matter of Orchard's greater popularity. That he, too, had acolytes—many more than Burns, though generally less adventurous and zany than his—triggered Burns's lifelong competitiveness. Orchard was a patrician—his physician father had studied at Johns Hopkins—with a patrician's accent and bearing (he walked on his toes, his nose held high), triggering the class resentments of an Irish Catholic. Orchard enjoyed privileges denied Burns: while Burns had to coach intramural teams, for instance, Orchard was exempted due to his "other duties." Making things worse was an article Orchard had written for *Good Housekeeping* on how to get children, beguiled by movies and the radio, to read; Burns evidently felt Orchard had lifted the idea from him. But mostly, it was a matter of their stylistic differences.

Some who knew him disputed whether "NEO," as Orchard was known, was actually gay. "Orchard was not homosexual," Tom Brush later recalled. "He was somewhat effeminate and had numerous affected mannerisms that might lead someone to think him gay, but I believe that he never sexually touched another person, male or female, in his life and died a virgin, and I think I knew him better than anyone." (Of course, this hardly meant Orchard *wasn't* gay, and that he merely stifled whatever impulses he might have had.) So the somewhat more masculine Burns viewed Orchard as girlish and weak—the kind of homosexual who gave all homosexuals a bad name—as well as fundamentally dishonest: in other words, as both too gay, and not gay enough. Privately he ridiculed Orchard, declaring that he suffered from "tertiary epicenism"—that is, that he was sissified. "Jack, with his own homosexual tendencies, was suspicious of and antagonized by hint[s] of these qualities in others, unless they were in [*sic*] his approved list," the chairman of Loomis's English Department at the time, Sidney Eaton, later wrote.

At Loomis, too, there was something remote and inscrutable about Burns, to colleagues gay and straight alike. "As far as we all knew, he had no sex or love life at the time . . . he was very discreet about that whole area," McKee said of him. For five years the two men worked together, and yet, McKee recalled, "I never really felt that I had any idea what was going on inside of his head." Sometimes McKee believed everything Burns did was an act; there was "an unspoken barrier between what Jack really was and this sort of brilliant performance he was always putting on." Others felt that whatever else Burns was doing, he was simultaneously putting them down. "Perhaps I was afraid of him, afraid to be made to look like a fool," another Loomis teacher, John Dorman, later remembered.

Many, and maybe even most, of Burns's students—those who never penetrated his chosen circle—felt he patronized them. He could sometimes be cruel; one teacher recalled seeing a boy who, having stifled his humiliation in Burns's classroom, sobbed afterward in the corridor. In one of the papers Burns had students

write daily (which he promptly graded and returned), Samuel
Holmes suggested—presciently, it turns out—that the country
pay off its debts by setting up slot machines. Burns's only written
comment was from Coleridge's *Kubla Khan*: "For he on honey-
dew hath fed, and drunk the milk of Paradise." (It was, Holmes
surmised, Burns's highly literate way of saying he was nuts.) Another time Burns leaned on Tom Brush, then editor of the *Loom*,
to publish a student's sonnet. But the poem—to rhyme with "be,"
the student had concluded with the line "If thou thinkest so, my
dear, wrong art thee"—was *awful*, Brush protested. "Mr. Burns,
you *can't* do this to a boy," he pleaded. "It would make him the
laughing stock of the whole school. It's cruel." *"But it's so funny,"*
Burns replied. *Loom* meetings were held in Burns's apartment,
and when someone knocked on his door, Burns opened it only a
crack; if he didn't like the boy, he would turn him away.

"He always seemed to be amused by life," another of his
students, Peter Abel, recalled. "Not sardonic, not condescend-
ing . . . I don't know what the word is; it wasn't a smile of joy, but
'I'm just tolerating these folks around me.' Not that he was superior, but that he just understood better." To Ellison Smith, Burns
embodied a word he'd just learned: "nihilist." "He was someone I was always very cautious about having any direct relationship with, because I knew he'd put me down," he said. To others
Burns was simply puzzling. Elihu Berman was whistling through
a rolled-up certificate one night as he approached Burns. "Good
evening, sir, and up yours, too," Burns remarked as he passed.

But on those in whom he detected an artistic or literary or
musical spark or a gay sensibility or both, he left a profound impression. He not only accompanied Sebastian DiMauro when he
played Max Bruch's violin concerto in the Loomis chapel, but rearranged a portion of the piece too difficult for DiMauro to play.
"I can't think of any other teacher that really set me on fire. He
just opened the world to me," Henry Krotzer remembered. "He

made everything interesting," said Purinton "He knew everything about all the writers who ever were." The mission Burns
ascribed to his alter ego in *Lucifer with a Book* was really his own:
"to torture his students, to badger them into a little thought, to
shatter their complacency." And to a few, like Paul Barstow, he
illuminated a pathway they'd not previously seen.

Barstow attended Loomis from 1938 to 1941, until he was ex-
pelled, partly for academic reasons, partly because someone had
happened upon an entry in his diary describing a gay assignation.
In an essay he called "Tardy Valentines"—his attempt, written
shortly before he died in 2004, to thank those who had helped
him struggle with his own sexual identity—Barstow paid tribute
to the man he called "Mr. Casey." (So many years later, the instinct to conceal and to protect still ran deep.)

*Mr. Casey was a brilliant and inspiring teacher. His
energy was commanding and seemed almost explosive, as if
some chain-reaction were imminent. He ruthlessly mocked
ineptitude and inelegance but without condescension; one
damn[ed] well had to give a better answer next time or
finally write an essay which said something significant and
said it well. We aspired to his immense sophistication. His
classes were exciting; never tricked, we were astonished
into knowledge or perception. His literary enthusiasms were
infectious, and he shared his library with his students. It
was much more exciting to borrow a book from his cluttered
shelves, the flyleaf boldly signed, than to take one from
the cold, dry racks of the school's library, plated with the
school seal, and then meticulously sign it out after a hushed
warning of the due date.*

*He was one of only two good teachers I recall from what
was for me a vulgar approximation of Dante's Inferno,*

where not Pride or Avarice but Latin and geometry made
me feel stupid as well as wicked. When I pored over the
Doré* engravings, covertly marveling at the sinuous forms
so curiously de-sexualized, I thought of Mr. Casey as an
angel from across the great gulf fixed.

Mr. Casey was both more and less of a person than our
other teachers. We seemed to know less about the others
but to know all there was. With him it was the opposite:
we knew more but much less. Their private lives we could
imagine, his never. Beyond his apparent openness there was
profound mystery which frightened as much as it intrigued
our prurient minds. At least a few of us "knew" Mr. Casey
was homosexual, like us, if we, indeed, were. And that had
vast significance, at least for me, because he was a fine and
greatly gifted man whom I liked and deeply respected—
the only "positive role model" during an appropriately
appalling adolescence.

Somehow, the mere existence of, not to mention the
inspiriting contact with, a man "like that" who could
be unreservedly admired was, for me, a first glimmer of
redemptive hope, although too soon extinguished.

Could I have brought myself, ten years before I ever did,
to tell someone inspiring trust about what I struggled not
to be but could not help but feel I was? No, I couldn't then.
Perhaps, he might have been my Virgil, after all.

Burns was just about the only thing that stood between Taylor
Mead[†] and either insanity or suicide. "He taught us that Napoleon was a woman and Queen Elizabeth was a man and made

---

* Gustave Doré (1832–1883), French illustrator and engraver.

† The actor and writer Taylor Mead later starred in several of the films of Andy Warhol.

such bold and sassy statements about everybody, it was a tonic," he was to write. "But Jack was cruel also. I remember a midyear junior examination in English. It was 'write 500 lines of poetry from memory' and even though Jack told us that would be the exam and I wrote lines of some poems on my sleeves it turned me off poetry for thirty years or more." In his memoir, Alfred Duhrssen recalled how "Mr. Burney" invited him into his apartment and showed him the novels he'd written, one every summer. And how he gave him the key so that on weekends, when Burns was away, he could read his books and listen to his phonograph. He also described looking on one night when some boys hypnotized Burney. The teacher promptly went into a trance, sweating and trembling, whereupon a nervous student suggested asking him a question. *"Are you a fag?"* someone volunteered, and Burney confessed that he was.

Burns continued writing his novels, sometimes retreating into his bedroom to work on them even as students sat around his apartment. Summers, McKee recalled, Burns headed up to Provincetown, Massachusetts, and finished yet another. McKee was among the few who ever got to see them. They, too, were performances, he felt, "almost unreadable," "intellectual exercises, with no real human content at all." "He had a tendency to overdo it," one faculty wife remembered. "As someone said, each page was so full of brilliant wit that nothing stood out and it was all too much—a barrage." At one point, Burns actually submitted a manuscript to Blanche Knopf, wife of the publisher Alfred A. Knopf, who, as Burns later related the story, kicked him out of her office, telling him to come back in five years.

His few friendships were fleeting and fragile. Though he dedicated *The Cynic Faun* to Hillyer and tacked a photograph of him on the wall of his Loomis "cell," Hillyer had to stoke their relationship. "Not a word from you for many months, and I am wondering how you are getting on," Hillyer wrote him in 1938. Burns liked one faculty couple, Sid and Jessie Eaton, and dedicated his novel for the summer of 1941 to them—either *View the Corpse* or *Your Quaint Honor*, which may have been one and the same. Jessie Eaton later called Burns "a warm, caring, sensitive person and friend, an idealist, [with a] marvelous sense of humor, witty, brilliant, and like Jane Austen, amused by people's foibles." But Burns grew closest to the baby-faced David MacMackin, who enrolled as a freshman at Loomis in September 1939, just as Burns began his third year there. Such intimacy between a teacher and a student nine years younger was puzzling if not unseemly, though in some ways they were contemporaries: while Burns was immature for his age, MacMackin was unusually worldly for his. In fact, someone as steeped in English literature as Burns must have found MacMackin strangely familiar; the boy's childhood, after all, was something out of Dickens.

5

To some teenagers, boarding school is banishment. But to David MacMackin it was more like deliverance.

When he was eight years old or so, MacMackin's parents divorced. In the manner of the British, his mother took his sister, while young David went with his father—only his father never came for him. After some time had passed, a concerned neighbor contacted his father's older sister, Olive Templeton, a star of silent pictures. She and her husband took him in, but shortly thereafter—for how long, it's unclear—MacMackin's uncle began molesting him. Sometime after that Aunt Olive—who had an estate called Trailsend in Canton, Connecticut, not far from Hartford—sent her nephew to Loomis.

David MacMackin was eccentric, musical, precocious, and effeminate; in a poll the *Log* once ran for "Girls I'd Like to be Marooned on a Desert Island With," he had placed third. He won great fame on the campus by transforming his room, through

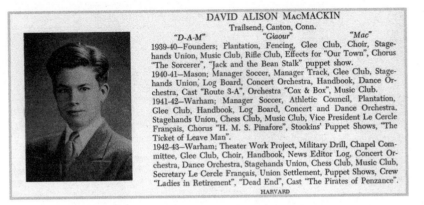

DAVID ALISON MacMACKIN
Trailsend, Canton, Conn.
"D-A-M"   *"Giaour"*   *"Mac"*
1939-40—Founders; Plantation, Fencing, Glee Club, Choir, Stagehands Union, Music Club, Rifle Club, Effects for "Our Town", Chorus
"The Sorcerer", "Jack and the Bean Stalk" puppet show.
1940-41—Mason; Manager Soccer, Manager Track, Glee Club, Stagehands Union, Log Board, Concert Orchestra, Handbook, Dance Orchestra, Cast "Route 3-A", Orchestra "Cox & Box", Music Club.
1941-42—Warham; Manager Soccer, Athletic Council, Plantation,
Glee Club, Handbook, Log Board, Concert and Dance Orchestra,
Stagehands Union, Chess Club, Music Club, Vice President Le Cercle
Français, Chorus "H. M. S. Pinafore", Stookins' Puppet Shows, "The
Ticket of Leave Man".
1942-43—Warham; Theater Work Project, Military Drill, Chapel Com-
mittee, Glee Club, Choir, Handbook, News Editor Log, Concert Or-
chestra, Dance Orchestra, Stagehands Union, Chess Club, Music Club,
Secretary Le Cercle Français, Union Settlement, Puppet Shows, Crew
"Ladies in Retirement", "Dead End", Cast "The Pirates of Penzance".
HARVARD

From the 1943 Loomiscellany

items picked up in local thrift stores, into a Victorian salon. At some point early on he fell under Burns's sway, becoming his most devoted disciple. And Burns was his devoted mentor. It's unclear whether they were ever sexually involved; their correspondence contains few such suggestions. But they visited one another often at Loomis, and on several occasions Burns went to Trailsend. The two devised their own patois, with code names for various students. They listened to classical music constantly, sometimes on MacMackin's fancy Capehart gramophone; they even recorded opera on Burns's state-of-the-art equipment. While apart, they corresponded continually. Their salutations and signatures were inside jokes: figures from poems, mythology, theology, operas, Gilbert and Sullivan. Their letters even came to sound alike. When Burns began a novel he called *What Wondrous Life!*—the phrase is from the seventeenth-century British poet Andrew Marvell—he dedicated it to MacMackin.

"I'm now at Loomis & shall be evermore," Burns wrote Mac-Mackin in one of the first letters of his to be preserved, from July 1941. But Burns was unduly optimistic: war had already enveloped Europe, and talk of war filled the American airwaves. Burns's family opposed entering it, largely because of his

MacMackin's dorm room

mother's rabid hatred of the English; when a girl came to Sunnyside to collect "Bundles for Britain," Catherine Burns threw her
out on her ear, earning Mother Burns scorn in much of Andover.
(She also refused to contribute aluminum to the war effort.) That
Burns himself, who had voted for the Socialist Norman Thomas
in the 1940 presidential election—a gesture that would have appealed simultaneously to his radicalism, idealism, isolationism,
exhibitionism, and nihilism—didn't feel particularly perturbed
by events overseas was evident that October, when the *Log*'s "In-
quiring Reporter" asked him, among others, whether America
should go to war. "Absolutely no," he replied. "Because: (a) If we

go to war we will come out bankrupt. (b) We are defeating a unifi-
cation of Europe which will come sooner or later anyhow. (c) I am
a pacifist. (d) I don't want to be shot."

But when, the previous month, Congress passed a law requiring men between twenty-one and thirty-five to register for a
draft, Burns figured he was a goner, and shortly after Pearl Harbor he was in fact called up. Within eleven days of the attack,
after entrusting his classical music recordings and manuscripts
to Aunt Olive and conducting one last performance of *H.M.S.
Pinafore*, he left the Island. He clearly wasn't unhappy about the
move: after more than four years at Loomis, he was feeling what
he later called "a minor and watery despair" over teaching students he didn't generally respect as well as "sipping tea and gossip
and nibbling secretly at my own foundations" and turning into
"something tweedy and bluff." Any return engagement there for
him must have seemed quite inconceivable.

Despite an ostensible ban on them, at least 650,000 and as
many as 1.6 million gay men served in the American military
in World War II, according to Allan Berube's landmark 1990
study, *Coming Out Under Fire*. Any of them could theoretically
have stayed home simply by declaring their sexual orientation—
"All you have to do is to tell them you're queer, and you're out,"
a gay character explains in Christopher Isherwood's novel *The
World in the Evening*—but few actually did, either because they
felt as patriotic, and as threatened, as everyone else, or because
they craved adventure and community, or because they wanted
to prove they were "real men," or because they feared being stig-
matized or blackballed (even among other gays) for staying behind. The screening was perfunctory and easily foiled; as the
gay scholar Donald Webster Cory was to write, "men who had
been successfully practicing concealment from families, employ-
ers, friends, and others for many years did not find it difficult to
continue the deception even before the eyes of a more discerning

psychiatrist for a period of five or ten minutes." Besides, many examiners didn't care and manpower was in short supply.

Restless and unfulfilled at Loomis, looking to see the world, less of a coward and pacifist than he claimed, in search of material and maybe more gay companionship than provincial Hartford could afford, off Burns went, first to Fort Devens, Massachusetts, then to Camp Croft, near Spartanburg, South Carolina. It was an Army Replacement Training Center, preparing troops to fill in for those soon to fall; thousands of soldiers were to pass through the place. It was, of course, an utterly alien existence to Burns, and he vowed to make the most of the experience. "This was to be the test of me," he wrote in his mini-autobiography. "I saw myself posturing, for I've always been a little Byronic, wondering if I *could*, in a crisis." Burns later claimed to have felt "brave and audacious" when he began his service. "I found that I wasn't as afraid of rifles and sergeants as many of the others who'd been living in a reality keener than mine," he wrote. In fact, he confessed to MacMackin that when he'd reached Fort Devens, he cried.

To comprehend and describe the experience, Burns turned to a new literary form: letters, which he now wrote even more prodigiously than novels. He was a natural at it, with an eye for the telling detail and a knack for the playful. He sent them everywhere; were he to have had to pay postage on them, he once wrote, he'd have burned through most of his salary. The majority went to his family, particularly to his mother; for long stretches he wrote her practically daily. (Though she soon had three other sons in the service, all of whom eventually went overseas, it was only Jack's letters she saved.) Burns wrote so many letters to so many people not because he had so many intimates, but because he didn't. He liked his own prose; in most cases, the recipients were almost secondary. Wartime needs and Burns's droll, aphoristic style neatly dovetailed: particularly once he went abroad, most of his correspondence was via V-mail—compact, lightweight aerograms that suited both military needs and Burns's pithiness. As many letters as Burns wrote, he wanted to write more: when, early on, the *Log* published a letter of his to the Batchelders—"If Mrs. Roosevelt can narrate her day, I guess I can, too," he wrote*—he included his address, just in case students wanted to write. Through MacMackin, too, he put out a call. "Will you spread my new address among the elect?" he asked.

From the outset Burns took pride in his letters—he was not one to doubt the significance of anything he observed—and thought of posterity. "I quite agree in my modest way with mother, that my letters merit publication," he wrote his father. "Hope she's saving them. She can get $50 for each a few years from now—just like a Shakspere autograph." He grew upset upon learning that his two youngest sisters had thrown out a couple of them, thereby cutting the thread in his historic skein. "Some of them say things never said before," he told Cathleen. But if he envisioned a published collection, it would have to appear in stages. The world might be ready immediately for his letters home, but years or decades would have to pass—a whole culture would have to change—before his letters to MacMackin could appear, and even then, they'd require extensive deciphering and annotation.

Burns set out to describe his new way of life and his new colleagues. With respect to the second, he now had another group from which he could feel distinct, and to which he could feel superior. "Two classes of personality manage to keep their idiosyncrasies in the washing machine of the Army; they are the officers and the imbeciles," he wrote the Eatons in early February 1942. "Everybody else is flattened either by his own consent or against it. I've Christily accepted all of Mr. B's thorny principles of

---

* Eleanor Roosevelt's column, describing her various activities, appeared daily in many American newspapers.

self-sacrifice and have cast my personality on the waters." Having scored well on an intelligence test, he was quickly shifted from thirteen weeks of basic training to a more streamlined six, followed by specialists' school. "At present I'm in the 'Intelligence' section, which may mean that I shall become an international spy, or just a scout poking his nose into machine gun nests," he wrote the Batchelders. Still, beginning at five-thirty every morning, his days, like everyone else's, were filled with roll calls, calisthenics, drills, window washing, and potato peeling. And learning how to handle Springfield and Garand rifles.

"The food is excellent, except for the coffee, with fine meats and three or four green vegetables," he told the Batchelders. Afternoons were as stringent as mornings; after an early supper, he wrote, "we are free till nine o'clock. Those of us who can still stand up go to Spartanburg, drink beer, read, or write letters. But if we have been naughty: a shoe out of line, a wrinkle in a bed, or failure to salute an officer, why then we get no free time . . . I need not assure you that I have been a Group I boy, other than knocking over a second lieutenant on the drill field when I slipped doing an about-face." He was too busy to help Sebastian DiMauro (the student for whom he'd rearranged that violin concerto in the chapel) to score Gilbert and Sullivan's *Patience* for a Loomis production, even though DiMauro had thoughtfully sent along some blank music paper. He assured the Batchelders, who had thrown him a farewell dinner, that he actually missed Loomis.

Still, Burns felt he'd lucked out. "I've heard that Croft is the favorite camp of the boys in Washington; everything new in the military is tried here first; it really is lovely here," he told his father in March. "Thank God it's not a hole like Fort Dix, with its over 100,000 men. I've no objection, you may tell Mr. Roosevelt, to spending the entire war here." Going into officers' training, he said, would be "silly": "They'll make me an infantry lieutenant, you see, and ship me into combat. I'll settle for corporal's stripes and my whole skin." Everyone wondered where they'd wind up; rumors were rife. "These are commonly thought to originate in the lavatory; hence the idiom 'shit-house intelligence,' or 'latrine rumor,'" he wrote the Eatons. "By May 15 I may find myself 'guarding' Hartford, or I may be on the Burma Road or in the Phillipines [*sic*]," he wrote DiMauro, whom he had not stopped mentoring. Nor had he abandoned his disdain for much of modernism. "What a chemistry of ideas has been brewing in your mind!" he wrote him a few months later. "I was afraid you'd hit on James Joyce and Freud sooner or later. Well, go to it; they're like an enema, and you have to wipe yourself afterward. The meat is very strong and you'll notice in a few years how much of it you'll have to spew up."

Four nights a week, girls handpicked by secret committees in the neighboring towns were bused into Camp Croft for highly chaperoned dances and other programs. Burns steered clear of all that, of course, and took refuge in music. At least for a time he mostly stayed on the base with other "chaste or timid souls," drinking beer and discussing "the golden age of operatic song." By late March, he'd moved to the "aristocracy"—the headquarters detachment, sparing him many of the indignities of army life. By May he'd made corporal and obtained a cushy sinecure, one for which his musical skills equipped him and which, incidentally, was to become a redoubt for gay soldiers everywhere: as a chaplain's assistant. For the Catholic priest on the base, Burns prepared the chapel—for instance, festooning it during Holy Week with irises, lilies, jonquils, and gladioli—directed the choir, and played the organ. He swelled with proprietary pride when seventeen hundred soldiers showed up for Good Friday services, the largest religious event in the camp's short history. "The Protestant chaplains can hardly hold in their bowels for envy," he wrote. The job helped induce what Burns called "a very strong Catholic revival," though never had his Catholicism lurked very far beneath the surface.

Of all the letters he received, Burns must have savored Mac-Mackin's most—"As soon as we got our hands dry and the 300 plates done, we wiped off our anticipatory saliva and bit in," he wrote him of one—and he answered them with gusto. Their well-established lingo, filled with the clues—or "hairpins"—through which gay men of that era winked at one another, was newly enhanced and personalized by an extended clerical metaphor originating in a Gothic horror story, set in a monastery, that MacMackin had written for the *Loom* shortly before Burns left Loomis. This obscure new language, filled with abbesses and priests, habits and soutanes, surplices and veils, appealed both to Burns's piety and his impiousness: Croft camp from Camp Croft. He never tired of the monastic images, as tedious as they became over several years of correspondence.

One particular neologism—a nun's horrified cry upon seeing one of her sisters collapse at the altar—became Burns's all-purpose exclamation, connoting excitement, revulsion, pleasure, resignation, or surprise: *Brwaugh!* It could also connote something more mundane: Brwaugh. And it could be a noun, appearing in midsentence to mean assorted gay activities, or just about anything else: *brwaugh*. But without a doubt the most crucial word in their private vocabulary wasn't new at all, but simply repurposed. It was "dreadful"—in this instance a noun, or more often an adjective, meaning "homosexual." Its origins were unclear. Maybe it emanated from Burns's vast storehouse of literary learning; in one poem Shelley wrote about "deeds too dreadful for a name"—code, some believe, for homosexuality. Or perhaps it was another of Burns's playful coinages. But it wasn't all play: along with the rest of their esoteric vocabulary, "dreadful" was a word that would elude priggish but unimaginative military censors. "My letters may be censorable, but not for military secrets," Burns confessed to the Eatons.

On matters musical, literary, religious, sexual, and interpersonal, Burns remained MacMackin's mentor, and MacMackin,

Burns at Camp Croft. His mother found religious significance in the aura around his head.

aka "the Abbess," his aptest student. "The Abbess polishes off people with a peculiar nihilistic love," Burns replied to what must have been one of MacMackin's more caustic letters. "We fear we watered such seeds for her." The level of intimacy between them is striking, and at times discomfiting. The two of them exchanged photographs, with Burns sending along a Kodachrome of himself in a field jacket with stripes and a "voluminous picture of me with 'tapestry finish'" that was, he warned, "subject to the rapine of sunlight, moths, and dreadfuls." (A copy of it also went to his mother, who thought she saw something miraculous in the aureole around her son's head, and hung it, like a portrait of Jesus Christ, in the parlor on Gainsborough Street.) MacMackin in turn sent down what Burns called "enough to eat, smoke, and bathe a whole regiment." Apparently playing matchmaker, Burns urged MacMackin to look up a "dreadful(ly) amusing corporal" working in the induction center on Asylum Avenue in Hartford. And to hop a train and visit him at Camp Croft. And when that failed, he invited him again, urging him this time to bring his "jools and minks," and to watch out for dreadful brakemen en route. When due for a leave, Burns asked, could MacMackin "gather a group of dreadfuls and delightfuls into some accessible cenacle against my coming into the nutmeg state?"

Officially, MacMackin envisioned a musical career for himself; after Loomis, he studied for a time with the noted conductor Pierre Monteux. But Burns had another role for him in mind: biographer. "The Abbess simply scares the shit out of us the way she emphatically enters into the spirit of Our Life and Works," Burns wrote him. "She seems to have thrown her saintly corpse into Our Mind with all the Recherche du Temps Perdu gusto of one who's sucked Proust and Bergson dry in Bushnell Park.*

---

* A park, alongside the state capitol, that was a prime cruising ground for Hartford's gays.

What we want to know is, is she our double or our Boswell? She seems to have such a firm grasp on our reality that we sometimes pause whether we're actually living our own life at all or whether it's some brwaugh *déjà vu*, whether we're existing merely in the Abbess's consciousness as most people live, move, and have their being in the mind of God."

Burns always traveled light, and did not save anyone's letters to him, at least long enough to matter; it would have been too unwieldy. But in MacMackin's case, it might also have been too dangerous; even with all the coded language, MacMackin was occasionally careless. Burns described reading one "hair-raising" letter from him—the topic was apparently a theoretical liaison between an underaged MacMackin and a colonel—with the chaplain for whom Burns worked looking desultorily over his shoulder. "If he ever saw that letter, I'd be court-martialed," Burns observed. Another time he wrote, "we rejoice that your letters don't pass through censorship as ours must; otherwise your v-mail of 1 December had certainly been in ribbons under the X-acto knife."

Despite the threat of immediate and dishonorable discharge, homosexual activity, while carefully concealed, was considerably more common in the wartime military than one might have expected. But to read Burns's reports to MacMackin, no doubt embellished at least to some extent, around Camp Croft it was open and notorious, omnipresent and incessant. Having been spared combat, he happily reported in May 1942, his military career had entered a new phase: "Dionysiac." There was a "raft of dreadful people" at the camp, Burns claimed, mostly higher-ranking than he. For Burns the action began even before he became chaplain's assistant, when he was "propositioned by an elegant slender Catholic sergeant" in the chaplain's office. The "great gathering place" for dreadfuls, he noted, was in the loft around the Hammond organ in Chapel No. 3. "Around the barracks a great deal of joke is made about ourself as 'corporal of the organ,'" he quipped. He described being awakened one night by *"dreadful* noises": truck drivers screaming "dreadfully" and making *"dreadful* insinuations" about other soldiers. A sergeant assisting Burns with the choir "has a beautiful voice, but shows rather *dreadful* feelings for incense, tapestries, & Romish liturgy," while a special services officer who'd once dressed windows in Macy's surpassed even MacMackin in "refined dreadfulness a la Victorian." The Seventh Regimental Medical Corps was "riotous & dreadful"; "twenty New York dreadfuls," calling themselves the "Mad Queens" and wearing their field jackets like "mink boleros," had just entered the Thirty-second Battalion; "all the chaplain's groups from corporals up wriggle their bums when they walk and use high-heeled talk": small wonder that in Burns's circle, Camp Croft became known as "Camp Crotch." "For pure and ecstatic dreadfulness," he told MacMackin, "civilian life is a hollow mockery beside it."

Some of Burns's bulletins were clear hype. How likely was it, for instance, that his only tears these days were "the struggling mists of orgasms, which are even more voluptuous than a London fog"? Or that the password used by most sentinels was "brwaugh"?

Burns broke Camp Croft's Catholics into three groups: "the slackers," usually boxers and conscientious objectors; "the duller Irish sort"; and the "elite," who were "either as dreadful as they know how when out of the priests' hearing or are just plain brilliant." He kept his distance from them all, he wrote MacMackin. While attempting to convert him to Catholicism, Burns conceded that the Church posed problems for dreadfuls. "I know so many dreadful people who are ardent Catholics ritually; but they are, of course, in a state of scarlet mortal sin because they refuse to give up their peculiar pleasures," he wrote. "Some are quite honest about it and don't go to Confession and Communion because they know they'd be committing a sacrilege. Others (and there are some here) keep up all the show of the most fervent Catholicism, but put their mouths which have received the Body and Blood in unlawful places. These, to use understatement, are in a very bad way." But for all its faults, he still held that the Church was "the only perfect thing I know in the world."*

To hear Burns tell it, to find action one needn't go into town, where, in any case, no hard liquor was served ("beer & wine only— this is Methodism"): he could find plenty on the base. "Last night at the Dugout I met a soldier who used to be a prize-fighter; he wanted at 10 o'clock to knock my block off, but at 11 he was suggesting that we go off somewhere to a little cave in the hills and find out each other's overtures," he told the Eatons in April. Only his departure three months later broke things up between them. "He wants me to come along," Burns told MacMackin in July. "I have his cap now, which is too small for me. Talk about double rings! He used to be welterweight champeen of New Guernsey, but he's a heavyweight with me, ha-ha. Everyone here is sadly and dreadfully decomposed, but at least the smell isn't of fish."

But it could not last forever. In two days, he complained in August, four WACs—"the real girls," he called them—were due to arrive at headquarters, threatening everyone. "What will happen is that we'll all be in the trenches by Xmas and the gals will have our juicy jobs," he griped. "Brwaugh."

---

* By contrast, Burns once described Protestant services as "glorified minstrel shows."

6

"G ood afternoon!"
It was how Burns began all his letters to MacMackin, at least those written after twelve noon. And like any of Burns's students, MacMackin would have immediately understood the reference, for it was with such sprightly but slightly sardonic exclamations that Burns had always begun his classes back at Loomis. "Good morning!" or "Good evening!" worked just as well when the circumstances warranted.

Burns's letter to MacMackin of August 21, 1942, which came after an uncharacteristic three-week hiatus, began in the same chirpy fashion, but the mood quickly changed. He explained his long silence with some lines from Gilbert and Sullivan's *Iolanthe*.

> *We apologize*
>
> *With humbl'd head [sic]*
> *And ev'ry hope laid low . . .*

*for our laxity in correspondence—but it's the first time in
our life we ever had a reason.*

*To thy behest,
Offended Queen, I bow . . .*

Three weeks ago while taking our dolce far niente at
4 A.M. in Spartanburg (and oddly up to no dreadfulness)
we were conked with brass knuckles by an assailant
incognito. Next thing we knew was three days later in the
station hospital. When we were brought in they thought
we weren't going to survive, in other words krepieren;†
they thought 'twas a mashed face and a fractured skull.
But we were very lucky. Yesterday we were released from
our bed of pain. 'Twas a mere concussion of the brain.
Our face is almost back to normal—no tusk is missing. Of
course, all the dreadfuls here have their own gossip on how
it happened. But we tell you the truth. We actually know
nothing. Three military tribunals have tried to scent out the
facts and have failed. Well, we are better now. The only
tragic news is that all people in this camp with delightful
jobs are going to be shipped to combat soon. Out of 4000,
that means about 3990 dreadfuls.*

After his startling disclosure, Burns quickly reverted to
form, discussing weighty matters like Gilbert and Sullivan's
Ruddigore.

"We tell you the truth," Burns had claimed, but there was
barely a shred of truth in what he'd written. The real story of his
injury and hospitalization, as contained in the records of what
was surely the only military tribunal so picayune an episode

---

* Sweet idleness.

† In German, to die a slow and agonizing death, like an animal.

would have warranted, was considerably more prosaic—and embarrassing.

No booze—not even beer—was sold at Camp Croft after 7:30 p.m. So, around ten o'clock on the night of August 4, 1942, after awakening from a five-hour nap, Burns had headed, refreshed but hungry, into Spartanburg. That much was fine; he had obtained the required pass, good until reveille at five-thirty the following morning. By the time he'd finished his dinner, undoubtedly supplemented by a couple of beers, at a local restaurant, it was 11:15 p.m.—too early to return to the base. Instead, Burns went to a nearby cafe, where, over two or three more beers, he struck up a conversation with another soldier. When the place shut down at midnight, the pair went to a local hotel, where they treated themselves to a bottle of rye. Then they went to a third restaurant, where a waitress brought them drinking glasses and three rounds of ice. Soon, and with some help from the waitress, the bottle had been emptied. It was now 2:00 a.m.

Burns remembered nothing after that, but brass knuckles had had nothing to do with his forgetfulness. As things came to be

Burns landed here after landing, face-first, on the ground.

reconstructed, a couple of hours later Burns and his new pal managed to board a bus back to the base, beating reveille by about half an hour. When the bus reached Burns's stop, he was so busy trying to rouse his drunken friend that he neglected to get off himself. Only as the bus began to pull away did he stumble to the front, head out the door—and fall flat on his face. The driver and two soldiers carried Burns to the dispensary, where he was bleeding, confused, and reeking of alcohol. "What happened to me? What happened to me?" he asked. Soon he was deposited in the base hospital. The diagnosis: a "moderately severe" brain concussion, along with lacerations on his chin, face, and scalp. When, five days later, a board of officers was appointed, its mission wasn't to investigate an assault, but to determine whether Burns had been wounded in the line of duty (in which case he'd qualify for disability payments) or as a result of his own misconduct. Needless to say, it was not a difficult call.

The panel convened on September 4. The proceedings were brief, consisting of testimony from a few eyewitnesses. Burns, by now sobered up and on the mend, represented himself, and was questioned as well. On the only real issue in the case—his drinking—he was unapologetic, almost flippant. He could have been Francis back at the Copley Plaza's Merry-Go-Round Bar, rhapsodizing on the glories of inebriation.

Q: Do you think you were drunk?
A: No, sir. I was only feeling good.
Q: Burns, do you drink seldom, occasionally, or habitually?
A: I would say that I drink regularly. When I go to town I have anywhere from six to ten beers.
Q: Do you often drink more than six to ten beers and become intoxicated?
A: I have been intoxicated once since I came to Camp Croft.

The panel quickly found Burns at fault. Had he known all the facts, MacMackin might have as well—for dissembling. There'd been no assault. Burns hadn't blacked out for three days. He hadn't known nothing. No three tribunals had investigated. No doctors had feared for his life. (Far from fearing Burns might not pull through, one doctor testified that his condition hadn't even been critical when he'd been admitted.) So why would Burns have concocted such a tale? Simply to excuse the long lapse in his correspondence, and to hide his chagrin over what accounted for it? To put a heroic gloss, of martyrdom and victimhood and even manliness—a fight!—over his boneheaded conduct? To impress MacMackin with his swashbuckling insouciance? Or was it simply that he was both immature and boastful—Burns came from a long line of embellishers, including his mother and a couple of his siblings—and simply couldn't help himself? With his brother Tom, at least, he didn't attempt any such stunts. He told *him* the truth.

There's no sign that Burns was penalized for his conduct, nor that he mended his ways in the slightest—continuing, as he put it a few months later, to "drink myself into atrophy" at regular intervals. Still, any head injury sending a man to the hospital for three weeks was no laughing matter, and the worst damage would not have been visible.

Though gay soldiers had to take care with those they propositioned, Burns evidently had no problems making connections. That September, for instance, he reported on the "horrible corporal in the 37th who calls me up on the phone and says 'I had it last night, but I've got to have something to chew on for breakfast.'" "On our next leave we will also bring our corporal from Mississippi who loves us dearly," he wrote MacMackin in October, "He says, 'You're mah boy, ain't ya?'" There was also the Irish-born magazine writer turned private with a "very broad wedding ring" with whom Burns exchanged letters daily, and drank nightly, whose gay wife—"a fragile Rosalind Russell sort with cloven hooves"—also came on to Burns. "We are amused to be courted by her in one post and her spouse in the next," he reported.

On August 31 Betty Grable came to Camp Croft, Burns related, "guarded by civilian press agents, a dozen M.P.'s, and 5000 panting soldiers." Predictably, he was not among those salivating; in fact, he found the whole thing exceedingly repulsive. "Quite the toughest-looking bitch I've ever seen," he told MacMackin. "This afternoon . . . she will make a personal appearance in our Rec Hall, where our office is. At a signal I and the station complement will let fall petals of roses on her platinum head [and] then two plaster cherubs, which will brain the hussy. In our office is the only bo-bo* in the hall. Should she decide to make use of it for her womanly micturition, I shall not usurp her position till Dutch Cleanser and the hopper have done their work many, many times."

But always, hovering in the background was the war. Soldiers kept arriving at Camp Croft, only to be quickly dispatched overseas, barracks bags and gas masks in hand as they marched to the troop trains. In September 1942 trained chaplains were summoned for immediate combat duty. Preparations for a European invasion were already under way; meantime, Allied troops had landed in North Africa. "The showplace of the South grows daily more lovely, what with landscaping and verdant grass on the red Carolina clay," Burns wrote DiMauro. "But the new cycles of men grow drearier apace. It seems there are no more young, attractive, fit, intelligent guys left to draft. We are getting now elderly tired men with triple hernias & eight children—or else ga-ga parachutists who've not passed puberty intellectually, if physically. Of course there are always Mississippians & Alabamans a la Faulkner, but they have six noses or become pregnant while at

---

* Lavatory.

camp. The only congenial folk left are the permanent (?) personnel of the camp, like myself. And they are being shipped to combat *come il vento d'autunno solleva le foglie.** The troop ships must be groaning at the rate battalions fly out of Croft into combat."

Burns hoped to embark from Fort Devens or Camp Edwards in Massachusetts, so that he could squeeze in one last visit to Boston and Hartford before, as he put it, "I sit in the lap of the sphinx." As war loomed ever closer, the sexual frenzy around the base only intensified. So close did everyone feel to Armageddon, he wrote, that "we do behave like Lucifer and his cohorts in their nine days' drop, when, the Angelic Doctor saith, enormities occurred."† Burns began to wonder whether such "enormities" would continue apace overseas. "Reports from North Africa (one from a friend now killed in action—which action we can't say) (in high-heeled language that the V-censors somehow miss) mention that the dreadfulness in the field beckons fire & brimstone that never comes," he related.

But Burns had picked his foreign languages well: in a war against Germany and Italy, he spoke fluent German and Italian. That he'd honed them the better to appreciate arias and lieder didn't really matter; they made him more valuable in intelligence than in the infantry. "We are doomed to a career of alcoholism and dreadfulness till we can screw our courage up to applying for the censorship classes of the adjutant general's office, after twelve weeks of which we shall emerge in the dreadful splendor of a 2d Lt.," he wrote MacMackin in January 1943. This he soon did. So, instead of being sent to the slaughter at Salerno and the other charnel houses Allied soldiers encountered on their way up Italy, in May 1943 Burns reported to Fort Washington, Maryland,

---

* As the autumn wind tosses about the leaves.

† In Milton's *Paradise Lost*, it takes Lucifer nine days to fall from Heaven to Hell, days filled with chaos, confusion, and anarchy.

where he learned the fine art of censorship. In *his* war, Burns's only weapon would be an X-ACTO knife. When off duty he frequented the bars of the Statler, Mayflower, and Willard hotels in Washington, all filled with other dreadful officers on the make.

Censorship: it was an odd role for a libertine, but it was also a nice fit: unsurprisingly for an intelligence outfit, Burns's unit was filled with highly intelligent people who, with their language skills, were worldly as well. "It was apparent that each of us was a genius in his own right," someone sounding suspiciously like Burns—he was on the committee that put it together—wrote in the outfit's yearbook. "The upstairs of 119 held seminars on Schopenhauer in the latrine. And 118 did the last act of *Tosca* between an upper and lower bunk." (Not all, though, were scholars; many were simply Italian-Americans who spoke Italian. Later, celebrating St. Patrick's Day in North Africa, Burns wore the green of an embattled minority: "My Celtic flame burns like peat among a bevy of greasers.") His sister Cathleen and MacMackin came down to Washington in June for his graduation from Officer Candidate School. Burns then returned the favor, and attended MacMackin's graduation from Loomis. It was probably then that, giving a chapel talk while in uniform, he told students preparing to enlist that they'd get a better deal from the navy than the army. As Tom Lehrer, who was there that day, later surmised, this was not the message that the superpatriotic Batchelder had expected from him. Burns just couldn't be controlled.

7

In eight short songs are encapsulated some of the most profound moments in a woman's life: love, courtship, marriage (symbolized by the golden ring on her finger), pregnancy and childbirth, old age and bereavement. Burns acknowledged it was hard for any man to inhabit Robert Schumann's song cycle *Frauenliebe und -leben—A Woman's Love and Life*. Perhaps because of its crystalline beauty, perhaps because of its classic Germanness (albeit from a far more enlightened time), perhaps because it depicted a degree of rapture, devotion, and domesticity he would never know himself—the piece touched Burns more profoundly than just about any musical selections he knew. Hearing it or performing it always brought him back to a few precious evenings he'd spent in an apartment on the East Side of Manhattan shortly before shipping off—precious because, for once in his life, he had actually been with friends. Thinking about it helped sustain him during the loneliest moments of his military service. It became Burns's "Lili Marlene."

In mid-July 1943, Burns got orders to proceed overseas "by the first available water transportation." While awaiting his departure, he was assigned to the censorship detachment of the army base at Fort Hamilton, Brooklyn. There he met two other American officers, Holger Hagen (brother of the actress Uta Hagen), and Robert MacLennan, who hailed from California. The three men quickly bonded. And though they spent only a few weeks together—maybe *because* they spent only a few weeks together—Hagen and MacLennan became the closest friends Burns had ever had. Neither was gay; MacLennan was something of a man's man—trained as an infantryman, he actually hungered for combat—which, for Burns, may have been part of his appeal: he was as ferocious, committed, and courageous as Burns was soft and indifferent. Hagen, meantime, was cosmopolitan (he'd been born in Germany) and highly intelligent. Many evenings that summer, Burns fled the base to drink and dine with Hagen and his wife, Beulah Wescott Hagen (sister of the gay novelist and essayist Glenway Wescott), in their apartment at 38 Sutton Place South, along the East River in Manhattan. There he would accompany Beulah, a mezzo soprano, on her Bechstein grand piano as she sang lieder. Often they performed *Frauenliebe und -leben*. Once, perhaps the first time they'd gone through it, Beulah stole a peek at Burns, and witnessed something few ever saw: he was crying.

How Burns's relationship with MacLennan progressed is unclear; their letters were lost. Holger Hagen later described his ties to Burns as the most intense he'd ever had with another man. But Burns's sexuality baffled him. "I was never really certain in my own mind: was he gay or was that, too, a 'mask,'" he later wrote. "His 'swish' way of talking certainly seemed to be deliberate play-acting. It was so very obvious. And God knows he never made a pass at me!" The two were to correspond throughout the war, addressing one another by Burns's most endearing sobriquet, one he bestowed on both himself and his closest friends, and which, not coincidentally, had a philo-Semitic ring to it: "Moe." (Beulah Hagen became "Frau Moe.") Hagen treasured Burns's letters "as documents of literary brilliance—always on the very edge of madness—and deep sensitivity to human suffering," and he put them aside, even once he got to Europe. Surely, someone would be interested in them someday.

On August 10, after enjoying with Douglas McKee the last good liquor he'd have for two months—"We got quite tight and celebrated his coming departure," McKee later wrote, "he was eager to go"—Burns left New York for the army embarkation port of Hampton Roads, Virginia, close to where he'd vacationed with his mother while at Andover. There it was more of "hurry up and wait." "All we do here is eat like dowagers at a White Mountain Summer resort, read bulletin boards, and go to the movies," he wrote the Hagens on August 12. But twelve days later, as a band played and a Red Cross girl served iced tea, Burns, carrying equipment weighing more than he did, made his way up the gangplank. Three more days would pass before his convoy was fully formed. Then he and his mates headed across the Atlantic, their destination much speculated upon but, at least officially, unknown, subject to zigzagging to avoid German submarines.

En route he wrote a collection of thirty-five sonnets he called *Nocturns.* "With only a faint blush and smirk I think they're the equal of anything in American poetry since Anne Hutchinson,"* he wrote home. "For the first time in my 27 years I'm convinced I've got something—something that will make my life the career I've planned for it since I was yelling for the milk at the age of a few months." (After three months of revisions he sent them off to

---

* Burns surely meant Anne Bradstreet (1612–1672), the first published poet in Colonial America and, for a time, a resident of North Andover, Massachusetts.

*Beulah Hagen, circa 1941, by George
Platt Lynes*

his sister Cathleen, with instructions to deliver them to the *Atlantic Monthly*. But first they had to be cleared; the local military censor had such trouble deciphering them that they were passed off to Allied Force Headquarters in North Africa for further analysis—scrutiny more serious, it turned out, than any scholar would give them. "They'll probably still be here ten centuries from now, rugged as the pyramids," he griped.) He also claimed, improbably, to have read three hundred books during the crossing, one of which, by Somerset Maugham, he'd thrown overboard in disgust.* Like his fellow soldiers, he survived on Spam. But his stomach proved strong, and none of his, like so much of theirs, had followed Maugham over the rail and into the Atlantic.

---

* Maugham's most recently published book, *The Hour Before Dawn*, is said to have been one of his worst.

As the convoy approached Europe it split up, with Burns's contingent heading to North Africa. For several days, he remained at a staging area on the northern coast of Morocco. And quickly he fell into a customary pastime: studying everyone else, relishing their idiosyncrasies. "The personalities here seem to be disintegrating," he wrote his mother. "My greatest enjoyment is to watch those who've got diarrhea from neglecting to scald their mess-gear rush past my tent door, tearing down their britches." For a brief time he led an infantry platoon of a hundred privates, training replacement soldiers for the Italian campaign, which was making its bloody way up toward Naples. It was an unlikely assignment for him, one for which he prepared very strangely: the night before one exercise he went through a bottle of cheap French wine that left him feeling like a corpse. "I'm on the wagon till the Armistice," he told his mother.

But he did well: "You're not the most masculine character I've ever known, Burns," a fellow officer told him afterward, "but when you were a platoon leader, you showed what an officer could be. They *loved* you." Just as he was about to accompany his troops to the front, a vetoing order came in from Algiers: instead of going into combat, he was to accompany his intelligence unit to Fedhala, a beachfront resort town twenty-seven kilometers northeast of Casablanca, a spot where American troops had landed the previous November. "All the infantry officers leaving today are beside themselves with envy," he wrote his father. "I was just getting fond of them when they were shipped to Salerno and shot," Burns later wrote. "The mercies of military intelligence saved me for a happier fate—perhaps to expire on a piano bench during a Schumann Lied," he told the Hagens. "Hope so, hope so."

Fedhala was lovely, and easy—"Eden," Burns called it. "The only rub in the beauties of this place—aural, visual, gastronomic—is that I'm afraid it may soften me up for any rougher place where the fortunes of war may throw me," he told

FEDHALA. — Hôtel du Commerce et rue Centrale.

Burns's first stop overseas

his mother. And the work was a cinch. Burns soon found himself sitting at a small desk in a converted convent schoolhouse, the text of the Geneva Convention at his side, reading the letters of homesick Italian prisoners. (They all said pretty much the same thing: that they missed home; that they were being treated well; that the American bread tasted like cake.) His unit's official name was Controlled Prisoner Information, or CPI, a rather "ghoulish" title dreamed up by a commanding officer, Burns wrote, "who wanted his wife to think he was doing something really heroic." His was what Burns called a "chair-borne outfit": the greatest peril he faced in North Africa came when a drunk soldier put a .45 against his head.

His biggest problem was boredom. "We live in what is certainly the most sybarite setup overseas—white hotels, good food, hot showers, sea bathing," he wrote the Hagens. "But nothing is ever completely perfect, except maybe a Schumann song. There is absolutely nothing to do in the evening after work; so

everyone goes softly mad, taking up solitaire, golf, or paper dolls."
And scrutinizing everyone else. "The people here are much like
those I knew at [Officer Candidate School]—some screwy, some
brilliant, some dull, some dangerous—but nearly all with some
Wertherian* cancer gnawing at their vitals," he wrote. "Consequently the cliques are many and tight. And there is always the
lunatic fringe who don't speak to anybody." To his mother, he
broke down his colleagues into similar categories: "the refugee
with his neuroses and constipation, the Italians with their vulgarity and lubricity, the *jeune homme exquise*, and the misanthrope &
hermit."† Casablanca—never identified by name, as per military
regulations—was grim and inaccessible: "Transportation cannot
be had even if I stood on the side of the road and revealed my
calves," he wrote the Hagens. "My body rejoices in health and
well-being, but my little soul is starved for books and music and
un-neurotic people. Even love here is bacillic and uninviting, between Arab cretins and French doxies." To his mother, he pegged
the rate of venereal disease in town at 99 44/100 percent.‡ "So
you find more than one hundred young men with nothing to do
of an evening except drink or read or gamble," he told her. "Consequently the tone here, while outwardly idyllic, is a little more
off the beam than a typical American town. Everybody is a little
mad."

To fill up all his time, Burns drank: when a buddy landed
him a bottle of good scotch from Algiers, he resolved to hoard
it for himself. And he wrote lots and lots of letters, including

---

* A reference to *The Sorrows of Young Werther*, Goethe's chronicle of the trials of a lovesick
young man.

† Apart from the last two, each of Burns's categories requires clarification: the "refugee" would
have been the Jew, who spoke German; the "Italians" would have been Italian-Americans; and
the "*jeune homme exquise*," surely the gay man.

‡ In its advertisements, Ivory soap famously claimed to be "99 44/100% Pure."

many at single sittings. Fueled by coffee, the fifth one could be as "Addisonian"* as the first. The ones home must have buoyed his parents, for they had fallen upon hard times: his lawyer father had lost his job—it hadn't helped that his principal client, the woolen magnate William Wood, who had once spontaneously peeled off a thousand-dollar bill and handed it to him as payment for services rendered, had shot himself—and the family investments had evaporated, developments for which Catherine Burns blamed her husband. The homestead in Andover having gone into foreclosure, in 1943 the family moved to a far smaller and more modest railroad flat on Gainsborough Street in Boston's Back Bay, in which some oriental rugs and ebony furniture were the only remnants of their former affluence. Burns began sending home fifty dollars a month, partly to pay for the education of his two youngest sisters, Connie and Anne. In what was a catastrophic comedown, Catherine Burns took a job selling underwear at R. H. White, a local department store, and renting out a spare room in the apartment to attendees of Christian Science conventions. Seemingly at her insistence—in order to buck him up—Burns periodically wrote separately to his father. Once, he sent him a ten-dollar bill for his birthday.

Burns mused in his letters on all manner of things: Hollywood (the film industry "has an inferiority complex about itself as an art form . . . smothered by bad judgment, stupidity, ignorance, and a spinsterish refusal to deal with reality"), the Red Cross, the scarcity of lightbulbs, street urchins, army dentistry, the packs of local dogs, the Moroccan maid who swigged his Aqua Velva, prostitutes working on Ash Wednesday, the flamboyant outfits of American pilots. "I don't usually talk about food," Burns wrote his mother, but sometimes it was *all* he talked about: food and service and wine and waiters. He detailed innumerable bills of

---

* A reference to the British essayist Joseph Addison (1672–1719).

fare, ranging from yet more Spam to glorious black market re-
pasts. Burns actually liked the army grub—"Put fricassee of
camel dung under glass, call it quail; and Burns will think he's at
Longchamps," the saying went. "The things they do with Army
beans are a revelation worthy of Ovid," he observed. There was
the "Caligulan spread" prepared one night by an alumnus of the
Waldorf Astoria. "Even the poor old C-ration that comes in cans
metamorphosizes under our chef's fingers," he once wrote. "In
the tin it's good old infantry hash, but on our table it becomes
something out of the cavern of Ali-Baba . . . As the hunter said
when he bit into the pie of moose dung a vindictive friend had
concocted, 'It may be shit, but it's good shit.' "

Burns tossed around all his languages, even with his mother:
"ingratitude" becomes "the nadir of *gentilezza.*" There were far
more references to saints—Rose of Lima, Therese of Lisieux—
than to pop singers. "Surely I've made the V-mail form as vi-
gnettish as ever Montaigne* could," he wrote her. His news
judgment was sometimes cockeyed; he'd fetched Marlene Die-
trich at the airport but had barely anything to say about her.
For all the usual flippancy, Burns was absorbing everything
around him, and it was changing and sensitizing him; it would
just take a while for his letters to catch up. "The African air,
the Ay-rabs, the odd behavior of Americans—all worked on me
strangely overseas," he later recalled. "My laughter shifted to
the other side of my face and finally died away altogether. For
the first time in my life I became touched, concerned, moved.
Sometimes I even wept. I discovered at long last that I wasn't
any different from anybody else."

Reading mail under nitrogen lamps alongside sixty other men
was enervating. There was nothing stimulating about clipping
the word "Casablanca" out of letters. Burns found his coworkers

---

* The sixteenth-century French essayist.

annoying, too. Sometimes the office seemed *too* gay; Burns complained of "a feminine and cliquish touch that before I could always flee, but we're bottled up." "The place is run by a small silky group of 'operators' who subjugate the majority to their ornery wills by spider tactics," he griped. "The politics are as dense as mercury. Marcel Proust would have loved the wheels within wheels. There's too much time to think and too little to do; consequently there's as much uproar here about moving a piano from one room to another as in the siege of Moscow. To fit the tone, I think I'll take up knitting and claw somebody's eyes out. Jane Austen would be amused; I seethe, because I'm not microscopic in my viewpoint, nor do I care for rocking chairs." His posting, he complained to his father, was like a sanitarium out of Thomas Mann. Slowly he came to feel indistinguishable from those whose letters he was reading: "Gradually my mind became that of an Italian prisoner of war, the same vacuum—good food, good treatment, the bedrock of despair," he later recalled. He still hoped to get to Naples, or at least Italy, before too long.

But he found ways to fill the time, and was soon feeling a strange sort of contentment in what he called "the alien corn."* He lost weight, as he always did when he was happy. He'd even come to appreciate that unidentified metropolis nearby, to which he'd go on weekends. "Strangely I've become fond of this city," he wrote his father. "Particularly in the evenings, once you are used to the foecal and Arab odor, it has a weird charm. The streets swarm with life. American troops, Arabs, Zouaves, French soldiers— all jostle one another on the jammed sidewalks." Burns lived, as usual, by himself, in a tent. The cold sea air—"insidiously it steals up through my mattress, and no matter how many blankets are on top of me, my *toccus*† gets the gust"—made a move indoors

---

* The phrase is from Keats's "Ode to a Nightingale."

† Yiddish for "rear end."

tempting, but not, he told his mother, given the choice of roommates the army was offering.

> One is a Viennese refugee whose mouth is never closed
> except when he draws a breath to tell the 1003d Ghetto tale
> of Finkel and Geschnitzel. The second is a hyperthyroid
> Eye-talian who looks like Groucho Marx and acts like
> a bolt of lightning that has never managed to get itself
> grounded. And the third is the slimey type of great lover,
> to whom his marriage vow is a Hitlerian scrap of paper.
> All I could say was a protesting 'Please!' to the billeting
> officer . . . 'Sir, if you order me to live with any of those
> three, I'll put my carbine in my mouth and pull the trigger.
> Then you'll have an investigation, which won't be nice.' I
> won.

Burns did make at least one friend: a "very lonely, intelligent,
comely Viennese" and fellow lieutenant named Paul Schonfeld.
He was, Burns wrote his mother, "one of the gentlest guys I
know," and the two became drinking buddies. Nor was this another of Burns's gay romances: he tried fixing Schonfeld up with
his sister Cathleen, urging her to write him. When, sometime
around Christmas 1943, he learned Schonfeld was being transferred, Burns grew depressed. "We were very close, with a kind of
studied intensity which wouldn't occur if we were leading a normal U.S. life," he told his mother. "He's oppressed too—even to
the point of saying when he gets tight, 'What shall I write on my
suicide note, Moe?'" Burns extended him a standing invitation
to visit his family in Boston "when the peace is signed in 1982."
But he later predicted Schonfeld would be sent home as a "psych
case," and in November 1944 he was. "Just before he cracked he
got a complete obsession on me, deciding that I was the quin-
tessence of all the evil in the world," Burns told Holger Hagen.

"He'd insist I get down on my knees in his room and pray that God would give me love for the human race instead of a vast Satanic hate that destroyed everyone who ever got to know me. Now I have my doubts. Was he simply projecting into me the things that drove him off his squash? Or am I really a walking Satan, instead of the lovin' little man I always thought myself to be? Don't answer these questions."

Once again, Burns's greatest solace came from music. As he told the Hagens, he'd turned into "a Diaghileff";* his letters are filled with details of the concerts, recitals, musicales, and jam sessions he organized, conducted, accompanied, or performed by himself—productions of unimaginable refinement and sophistication, particularly in a military outfit, particularly in so remote a place. Under his supervision, the music of Fauré, Respighi, Duparc, Handel, Palestrina, Bach, and Gilbert and Sullivan (and "some Victor Herbert for the rabble") filled the North African air. So did Burns's own compositions: once, he sang his own setting of the Edward Arlington Robinson poem "Richard Cory," the one about the suicide of a prosperous businessman (who, he claimed, was actually the father of a friend). According to the mimeographed program, the selections for the CPI's Fifth Musical Evening on December 2, 1943, featured Lieutenant John Horne Burns, baritone, singing two ardent and extremely difficult songs, Schubert's "Der Erlkönig" and Schumann's "Ich Grolle Nicht," along with an Irish air. Then, following intermission, Burns played Brahms's Hungarian Dances on the piano. But not all the performances were public, as he explained to Catherine Burns in January 1944.

What a war! If General Patton ever got wind of some of our evenings here . . . somebody's mother sent him two

---

* The Russian-born arts impresario and founder of the Ballets Russes.

*volumes of the Harvard University Glee Club Collection,
and tonight after dinner four of us—Charles Bacharach,
Bob Nuner, Reinhard Pauly—gathered for no good reason
to sing the entire two folios through at sight. This went
on for two solid hours over rappings of protest on the
walls from adjoining rooms. I think we covered most of
the choral music from Heinrich Schutz* to the present. I
was the first to collapse, on the whoops dearie! Falala's
of a Morley Madrigal. We simply knocked ourselves out
with the close concentration of sight-reading and that
bright close joy that comes of making music together.
Finally Charles Bacharach burst into hysterical tears
on the Crucifixus of Antonio Lotti. Then we all started
whooping and giggling like a bunch of dizzy schoolgirls.
The rat race broke up with oranges being distributed to
all of the quartet, and most staggered off to their beds. I
can't explain the odd mad fatigue except that we'd worked
hard all today, that it struck us funny to be creating lovely
music in a theater of war, that we'd enjoyed ourselves to
the bursting point.*

Officially, it was a scene that simply couldn't have been—three
gay officers, joined by a recent German immigrant turned
American officer, performing classical music on the outskirts of
Casablanca—and clearly would never be again.[†]

In January 1944, Burns told Beulah Hagen he was setting

---

* German composer (1585–1672).

† Nuner was a professor of French and Gaelic at Notre Dame, and Bacharach a recent graduate of the Eastman School of Music. "He has that gentle feminine wishy-washiness that besets
all Jews in the generation when they try to make the conversion from their strong religion to the
respectable mediocrities of Protestantism," was how Burns described him. (Burns later wrote
of spotting Bacharach in the bar of a North African hotel "full of depressed little people"
playing Chopin "with tears in his eyes.") Pauly had come from Berlin in 1937 to study at the
Manhattan School of Music, and stayed in the United States.

Five Préludes   Chopin (1810 - 1849)

Lt. Alexander Warner, piano

Sonata in B Minor
(Adagio-Allegro-Andante-Allegro)   Bach (1685 - 1750)

Lt. Reinhard Pauly, violin
Lt. Charles Bacharach, piano

Der Erlkönig   Schubert (1797 - 1829)
The Minstrel Boy   Irish Air
Ich Grolle Nicht (Dichterliebe, No. 8) Schumann (1810 - 1856)

Lt. John Horne Burns, baritone
Lt. Charles Bacharach, piano

Valse, Opus 64, No. 2   Chopin
Mazurka in A Sharp   Chopin
Mazurka in A Minor   Chopin
Valse, posthumous   Chopin

Lt. Alexander Warner, piano

INTERMISSION

Clair de Lune   Debussy (1862 - 1918)
Minstrels   Debussy
Le Vent dans la Plaine   Debussy

Lt. Alexander Warner, piano

Hungarian Dances   Brahms (1833 - 1897)

Lt. Charles Bacharach and
Lt. John Horne Burns, piano

Pavane pour une Infante Défunte   Ravel (1880 - 1937)
Kujawiak (Second Mazurka)   Wieniawski (1835 - 1880)
Andante and Finale (Concerto
            in E Minor)   Mendelssohn (1809 - 1847)

Lt. Reinhard Pauly, violin
Lt. Charles Bacharach, piano

What, indeed, would General Patton have thought?

to music the poem about Ann Rutledge from *Spoon River Anthology*,* and requested sheet music for some songs of Schumann and Hugo Wolf that he coveted even more than his American cigarettes. Later, he set a late Walt Whitman poem for her. (Trouble was, his compositions, like his letters, had to get past censors fearful that Burns was sending out details of the impending European invasion in musical notation.) He pledged to her that having sung *Frauenliebe und -leben* once—he felt he really should have tied two tennis balls to his chest to perform it convincingly—he'd refuse to do it again until he was sitting at her Bechstein on Sutton Place South. In February, he wrote his mother, preparations were under way for CPI's Seventh Musical Evening.

> *A corporal is checking the umlauts in the names of German composers and wondering whether it's Midsummernight's or Midsummer's Night. The prime donne of the evening have now forgotten that they are 2nd Lts in the Army of the United States—are rushing around scratching each other's eyes out—as though they were Tallulah Bankhead and Ethel Barrymore in the same play. The singers all secretly hope that the pianists will break a finger; the pianists that the singers will catch cold. Out of such vanity and pettiness are beautiful arts born.*

"Sometimes I think that the work that goes into these evenings, the high tradition of performance that distinguishes them, are a waste of the talent here," he told his mother the next day. "But then nearly everything lovely in this world fights its way up through Cenozoic mud." When he wasn't playing he was

---

* The 1915 collection of poems, each in the voice of an individual buried in the cemetery of a fictional Midwestern town, by Edgar Lee Masters.

listening to radio broadcasts from overseas, critically.* The incongruity and unfairness of it all became increasingly striking: around the same time, Allied troops landed at Anzio, thirty-three miles south of Rome; thousands would die in four months of fighting there.

---

* Toscanini's performances were "stinko, except in Beethoven," he wrote MacMackin after one such broadcast. "He lacks the touch of dreadfulness that makes a Koussevitzky glow and simmer." A concert by the Philadelphia Orchestra pleased him much more. "I was struck for the nth time," he wrote Beulah Hagen, "that the odious little race of vermin, to which we all belong, can also be heavenly lice on the body of God."

8

If music comforted Burns throughout the war, liquor fueled him. Even more than making music and writing letters, it was his most regular diversion abroad. And far from hiding it from his parents or anyone else, he flaunted it. Burns drank not only constantly but conspicuously.

Burns really didn't have that much to do in North Africa. He was caught up in a giant bureaucratic machine, one that became increasingly irrelevant as the fighting moved to Europe, its energies devoted ever more to make-work, "chicken shit," and self-preservation. He grew bored with his labors and impatient with the management, whose principal goal seemed to be staying intact and in place rather than being broken up and shipped to Italy—which was, of course, precisely what Burns wanted to happen. The only war wound Burns faced was hemorrhoids. What made things worse was that he remained lukewarm about the war itself, which he continued to consider pointless. He expressed his jaundiced take on it all on Armistice Day 1943. "I guess in the next war we'll have two Armistice Days—Armistice Day 'A' for the first world war and Armistice Day 'B' for World War II," he told his mother. "And in World War IV we'll have three different holidays to perpetuate the pattern of folly."

For a time he felt guilty about his indolence. "Sometimes my $158.05 makes me feel as though I'd put my fingers into the tax-payers' pockets—without giving them even a good grope for the embezzlement," he told Holger Hagen after returning from one pay line. The Moroccan air had a "Florida texture, whatever that may be," he wrote Beulah Hagen in March 1944. "I'll spend the summer swimming, drinking, sun-bahthing [*sic*], reading, writ-ing." Though all that primitive Italian handwriting strained his eyes, he managed to read books, many by gay writers. There was Thomas Mann's *Death in Venice*, reread between sips of ver-mouth at the local hotel (its "beauty, terror, and decadence" came through better for him than the first time around), and Lytton Strachey's *Eminent Victorians*. He also wrote—mostly poetry, which seemed better suited to his daily regimen than novels. He filled entire V-mails with them, one poem per. Most were to his mother; one can only imagine how crestfallen even she would have been to open up something from her favorite son, to find only opaque verse inside. A collection of ninety-eight poems, en-titled *Anatomy* and divided into sections on "Men," "Women," "Love," and "War," Burns wrote in mid-1944. (He sent those, too, to Cathleen, then spent the next two months worrying that either "the best part of me had gone to the bottom of the Atlantic" or that some censor "had gone mad deciphering it and had torn it to shreds.") "We see no reason why they aren't the best lyricism we've met during the war; they're not at all like Henry W. Long-fellow in combat boots," he told MacMackin.

It was still an era of ostensibly romantic vices—when you'd brag about smoking two packs of cigarettes a day to your own mother, and when that mother would actually supply you with them, lovingly: Herbert Tareytons, a carton a week. "We're cut to 25 packs a month, and I'm now hitting two packs a day," he explained to her in November 1943. That evidently worried her enough to demand an explanation. "[M]ost cigarettes are shorter than Tareytons, and don't give me my kicks," he told her. "Tareytons have 12 whole minutes of voluptuous languor packed into one. Chesterfields, PM's, and those I can get here last about 8 minutes. Consequently they make me feel like a lover whose mistress denies him his final rights. And I smoke more." In other words, send me more cigarettes so I can smoke fewer of them.

Catherine Burns couldn't procure liquor for her son, but this he managed to find, in one form or another, quite nicely without her. And here, he wasn't nearly so particular. Bored, homesick, naughty, still convinced of the clarity it bestowed and increasingly dependent on it in any case, Burns drank more than ever

Burns's most constant companion

in North Africa. References to alcohol in his letters, both erudite and juvenile, abound. One despair-filled night in Casablanca, he wrote the Hagens so drunk that he signed off not as his usual "Moe," but as "Jack (plastered)." (Never had he been "Jack" to them before. Afterward he did not remember mailing the letter.) He reported that the watch his parents had given him on his thirteenth birthday was ruined by swimming with it while similarly "plastered." In November 1943 he wrote his mother "drunk as a skunk." The cognac at the Hotel de France in Fedhala was as good for combating colds "as sitting on a can of Sterno." He split a bottle of brandy with "Moe" Schonfeld. Then there was the day in December 1943 when he tasted his first American beer—and then, presumably, his second, third, fourth, and fifth—since shipping out, giving him a contented glow he never got with "the more nervous French wines." "I can't quite see these keys, but I feel no pain about it," he told his mother.

For the first evening in months, he wrote Beulah Hagen in January 1944, he hadn't "sought solace in the grape of Omar Khayyam." But the next night, he confessed to his mother that after tying on "the worst one in my Bacchic history," he'd woken up in the military hospital minus his wallet and the thirty dollars in it. "I can only conclude that some Ay-rab rolled me while I had the blind staggers or was out cold some place," he explained matter-of-factly. As penance, and because he had but a dollar to his name, he'd resolved to go on the wagon until payday. But, predictably, his career as a teetotaler was brief. "Everyone has formulated a terrific WCTU* campaign agin me, telling me how well I look—the brilliance of my eye, the lucency of my complexion, the sparkle of my wit undimmed by hangovers," he wrote home. But "well as I feel without alcohol, I don't really feel any better than I am with it. Something tells me that when I collect my $168.50 on

* Women's Christian Temperance Union.

31 January, I shall, as usual, wire $100 home to you and repair at once to the bar of the Hotel de France." Within a few weeks, in fact, he was busted for taking the day off to get drunk.

Alcohol offered Burns the chance to do some travel writing. "One gets a little rationed rum at the officers' club and feels quite Somerset Maughamish drinking it," he told the Hagens in September 1943. "The native Moroccan Grenache is more lethal than marijuana, and far less pleasurable." "There's plenty of the wrong stuff to drink here; so I now have a 'rep' as unique as Sappho's*— the most quiet, efficient, habitual drunkard of CPI," he wrote two months later. "Burns, no germ could live in your bloodstream with the concentration of alcohol you've got there," an army doctor told him, and to Burns that was a point of pride. "Alas, and incense to Bacchus," he scoffed. "I've never looked better or felt better and happier. What'll I do if they ration wine and brandy here?" "The evening offers an embarrassment of riches," he told his mother in February 1944. "I can either go to see Mae West in *The Heat's On* (a great temptation—my 2nd movie in North Africa); or I may go to the Hotel de France bar. Which do you think will win?"

Nearly seventy years after serving, and singing, with Burns, it was his drinking—along with his "supercilious" expression, "slightly cynical mien," and effeminacy—that stuck with Reinhard Pauly, the last survivor of the quartet that sang its way through the Harvard Glee Club collection. That, plus how isolated he seemed, and the time MPs found him passed out on the side of the road. Burns came to feel drawn to Casablanca in part because it was more fun to drink there. Tiny, oppressive Fedhala reminded him too much of the boyhood home he'd fled; for people who came "to life after sundown, like a termite or a cockroach," small towns were oppressive, especially at night, no matter the locale. Or, as he wrote his mother, Fedhala was "a French Andover—only wuss."

---

* A lesbian lyric poet from ancient Greece.

9

By the time he went overseas, Burns had spent more than four
years at Loomis. That he barely mentioned it in his letters
shows how superficially he'd grafted himself onto the place. He'd
landed there by accident, stayed there under protest and through
inertia, seized the chance to leave, and probably wouldn't return.
But encounters with former students and colleagues at war, so
many of whom he had sold short, prompted surges of sentimentality and tenderness, and maybe some reflection and contrition.

True, there'd been one former student, now a sergeant in the
air corps, who "took great delight in calling me by my last name
and all that crap." But in Algiers in May 1944, Burns had encountered another Loomis boy, and it had been sobering. In fact, it
knocked him, at least briefly, off his pedestal.

*I kept looking at the little 1st Lt. staring at the bulletin
board in the Red Cross Club. I wanted to say, "aren't*

you Scotty Duncan?" but I held my peace until he turned around and said "you're Mr. Burns." He was wearing the sloppy open leather jacket and the wings of a pilot. I remember him a few years ago as a dizzy little brat with a cowlick, a puzzled grin, misspelled themes, and a constant chatter about Miss Betty Grable. He's not a dizzy little brat now; he made me feel quite humble to stand in front of him. I'd tried to teach him how to spell and punctuate, and here he was with more than fifty bombing missions. He talks slowly now; his air is that of a weary old man. There wasn't a great deal we could say to each other. To talk over the days when he was a lousy scatterbrained student didn't seem at all pertinent. So we shook hands, wished the usual luck to one another. I started to read Li'l Abner; he struck up a line with a Red Cross girl. It's odd what war does to people—how trivial little fellows instead of cracking under its stress like their self-styled betters change into something beautiful, timeless and dignified. I'll probably never see him again, but it did me good to run into him. Not so long ago I thought him a little silly. The last laugh isn't mine.

A few weeks later he encountered yet another former student, drunk and crying at the Navy Club. "It always hurts to see people I taught, to compare what they are going through now and the ideals I was handing out then," he wrote his mother. "He told me that sometimes on his destroyer he still reads Robert Herrick.* What could I say?"

As mean and deceptive as he could sometimes be, Burns was scrupulously honest about dollars and cents and civic obligations, and he grew disturbed by what he saw some GIs doing,

---

* The seventeenth-century British poet, best remembered for the injunction "gather ye rosebuds while ye may."

like selling subsidized, government-issued items to the locals for enormous profits. For twenty-eight dollars a pop, for instance, the *indigènes* could swath their corpselike bodies in GI mattress covers. All standards of decency were set aside and a new species emerged: the "operator"—a term, he noted, dating back to Al Capone. "Here you are an American soldier; you're fed, housed and you work—the rest is up to you," he explained. "This is where 'operation' sets in: it's up to each individual to provide himself a livable pattern of life. It's done with varying success, depending on how far one's personality has been removed from Darwin's Law. Operation in its simplest form consists of manipulating with French families; its climax appears in characters who become practically robber barons at it."

Over time warmth and compassion, whether toward other Americans, the locals, or even the enemy, came to wash over Burns's cynical soul. Small acts of kindness, like GI truck drivers offering him their field jackets after his own had been stolen, or letting him ride with them in the front seat, surprised and delighted him. "It's rather piquant to see that the principles of Jesus Christ are still in operation in the world," he wrote. "I guess a war submerges them in peoples, but not in people." After a couple of beers at the officers' club in Algiers one day, Burns sat down at the piano and began to play. "The spring afternoon was lovely and warm; so it called for some of the sweet stuff in *Tosca* and *La Bohème*," he wrote his father. "I hadn't intended to break any balls, but the [Italian prisoners of war] rinsing glasses behind the bar started to cry; so I stopped." Increasingly, his tolerance extended even to his much-derided "Ay-rabs." He admired how quickly a bar boy in Casablanca named Mucho picked up pet American phrases, without even a hint of an accent. "The first time I asked for a glass of wine, he smiled and knocked me for a loop by answering, 'The wind blew, the shit flew, and in come you,'" he recalled. "Which rather knocks our conception of an inferior race into a cocked hat." Such assaults on his snobbishness, such sudden fits of empathy and tolerance, such epiphanies about the virtues of common folk, seemed to startle him, as he confided to Holger Hagen.

Once I had quaint insular ideas that gentleness, delicacy of perception, magnanimity (in the Richard Coeur de Lion sense) were to be found only among the haves. I was at first horrified to find it among the have-nots—stunned as a Bishop of Trebizond* would be to find that the Zulus also bugger their choirboys. Now I'm soothed, as a drunk would be by having someone help him turn his coat inside-out-back. I've found a loveliness in little Ay-rab girls who beg for chewing gum and giggle when you ask them for American souvenirs, in the French aspirant who recites Wordsworth in an out of this world Algerian accent, in our own truck drivers from Chicago who say "I'm no fuckin' good, sir; but I'll drive you from here to hell." Am I getting like Aldous Huxley's St. Francis of Assisi, "a nasty little pervert who went around licking lepers' sores"?

This new understanding augured well for Burns's eventual next novel. He still harbored illusions about the old ones, directing MacMackin to move his manuscripts into Aunt Olive's basement for safekeeping. Maybe once the fighting stopped, these neglected masterpieces could be taken out of mothballs. "We still think they showed a most peculiar genius, more poignant than Djuna Barnes, Carson McCullers, and Ronald Firbank,"[†] he claimed. "The world should be ready for them in its postwar brwaugh." But

---

* A Christian heretic mentioned in some commentaries to Dante's *Purgatorio*, including Henry Wadsworth Longfellow's.

† Barnes (1892–1982) was a modernist writer and journalist; McCullers (1917–1967) was the author of many notable books, including *The Heart Is a Lonely Hunter*; Firbank (1886–1926) was a British novelist. All three were gay.

Burns also began thinking, more seriously, about the next novel. A couple of years had now passed since his last attempt, his longest interval since high school: he'd had too much new material, *good* new material, to process. But things had begun to crystallize, as he wrote his mother during a five-day leave in March 1944.

> *I've begun what has been bubbling in my mind for a long time—a novel about this outfit and the whole paysage about us with its myriad characters. It's very simple compared to my previous prose put-outs, but the flux of it is very un-simple, the flow of idea and strata of consciousness out-prousting Proust and out-joycing Joyce. For a long time it's been my feeling that one could write about this war and the people in it and its effect on the human spirit without being at Monte Cassino, because this war is so vast and so cumulative that one must treat it by examining a microcosm—say a unit like our own. And if the artist is good enough he could, by devoting his attention to the small, expand to the large. So a good novel about CPI would give a picture of what American soldiers were like, how Americans thought and reacted in 1944. Do you think I'm right? The scheme is both unpretentious and yet considerable in implication. By exploding the atom, you lay bare a whole world.*

Burns seemed delighted, even surprised, by his evolution from snobbery and despair to open-mindedness and decency. At times he also appeared worried by it, though he needn't have been; these two facets of himself would always coexist uneasily, with his newborn better angels forever struggling with the demons so many people spotted in him: as one of his army comrades put it, he was exquisitely considerate, but not at all kind. Burns not only knew his own limitations, but reveled in them.

He *liked* thinking he had some of the devil in him. A letter he wrote in July 1944 to his mother—whom he credited for his "merciless eye for everything"—was a ringing reaffirmation of a cold-bloodedness that not even war could cleanse. It was, he told her, "the most embarrassingly personal letter" he'd ever written. And he was clearly correct when he said that "it couldn't go to a more logical addressee."

Nothing and no one really satisfies me except myself and ideas—music, poetry, intangibles. I am a sensation-seeker of a fairly high order, and when there are no more sensations I'll probably die in a genteel but none the less jaded manner. By this token I can't help hurting people, of whom I always tire before they tire of me. They delude themselves into thinking that in me they've found some key, some secret, some be-and-end-all. Sooner or later I find that they're boring me or sucking me dry, and I have to make a clean break with them. It's impossible for me, like most soldiers, to have a "buddy," for my arc is too wide and too eccentric to admit of another's presence. This summation of my perversities, reduced ad absurdum, makes me a great genius, a fool, a misanthrope, an ascetic. Probably I'm some of all; there's a coldness and a cruelty and a logic in my reasoning that rather terrifies me . . . I've hardly ever failed to size up a character at once, on intuition; and later experience proves me to be right. I have moments of profound depression; my nerves are so sharp that I can reduce everything and everyone to a shamblesy zero. Then when I'm convinced I'm a cool ghoul, I have a moment of icy calm, like death; and the most exquisite fire and laughter glows in me, so that there seems to be between me and God a secret shared by very few.

The outcome of the war in Europe was becoming increasingly clear, but the war within Burns remained unresolved. He had no doubt, though, of his qualifications to write his new book. The war was furnishing him, and many like him, an apprenticeship. When a Red Cross girl newly arrived from the States played him the latest pop tunes from there, he was shocked at how "feeble and sterile" they were. "Then," he wrote home, "a consolation dawned on me: that possibly the men and women who will write the music and the stories of tomorrow are at present out of their country, learning the thing which causes great art to be born: sorrow. I *know* that the post war period will be a horrible one for Americans, but out of it will come for the first time music and painting and writing that will be on the same level that Europe has already given the world because Americans will no longer be dizzy children." He knew his couldn't be some blood-and-guts book; that had not been his war. While others in his unit, "fat bespectacled neurotics" who'd never fired a rifle, traipsed around in combat boots, he still went about in low shoes. As he later wrote Holger Hagen, his lot had been "simply to see the effects of war after the wedge had gone through and left nothing but splinters and pain." And that, presumably, would be what he'd write.

Repeatedly, Burns predicted that the war had unleashed in millions of GIs forces that would be very hard to contain once they got home. "The only thing that bothers me is the madness that must follow this war," he wrote his father. "You cannot live through one unscarred. And the effects on the young men may be quite frightful. If the twenties were a period of post-WWI insanity, I predict a much higher index this time." Then there were the broader social upheavals the war would cause, particularly for oppressed groups that had enjoyed their first whiffs of dignity. A fellow officer, a Rhodes Scholar from the South, predicted an exacerbated "negro problem" following the war—"He did have a certain Georgian bias against the black race, which no amount of education seems to extirpate, just as a German summa cum laude may be an excellent Nazi"—and a resurgence of anti-Semitism. "I hope the country can cope with them," he wrote his mother. "If not, I don't know what good winning the war will do."

The colossal waste of man-hours behind the lines, the very ennui among all those festering soldiers, would bring its own set of problems. "We can only pray that it doesn't leave the hundreds of thousands of dogfaces so completely demoralized that when they come home they'll be good for nothing nobler than sitting on the front porch and eyeing the girls with a glassy stare," Burns wrote. But he was sure he would avoid any such crack-up. "There is something polyplike in my soul which will always sidestep or seem to yield or give just before the crash comes," he explained.

10

When it came right down to it, Burns's war had but one goal: to get to Italy. Strategically it was something of a sideshow, and as such, a poor place to be: intent upon drawing German soldiers away from the Russian front and France to ease the impending invasion in Normandy, the Allies there were short-handed, and faced high casualties. But Burns would risk no such perils. Practically anywhere there would do. "I'll probably end up in some jerk Italian town, working for the Army of Occupation," he wrote his mother. "But even then I'll avail myself of the Italian sentimentality and the grappa,* which ought to have matured by now." For months he'd been dreaming of things Italian: hearing Signor Oliviero De Frabritiis† conducting the Verdi Requiem at the Teatro Reale in Rome on a Sunday afternoon; the melon

---

* An Italian brandy.

† Italian conductor and composer (1902–1982).

flowers; Neopolitan kissing; a quickie on the grave of Elizabeth Barrett Browning* in Florence. His heart was especially set on Naples, which happened to be the closest to North Africa. But he couldn't get there—because, he came to feel, he was too competent, and tolerant, and, he suggested, manly. All around him, it seemed, nearly everyone smelled of fish.

That he remained very much by himself Burns readily conceded. "I move in no particular clique, hearing the secrets of all, who hates whom, and laughing to myself like a smug chambermaid," he wrote his mother. His mind, he said, "just watches and listens and weighs." Demolishing his workmates, especially the "famous personalities" among them—like the pompous, fussy, and obese former history of religion professor at Columbia, for instance, or his section head, an Italian-American he likened to the mobster played by Edward G. Robinson in *Little Caesar*— became his "favorite indoor sport." "I get those with reputations to talk, sitting demurely by; then slowly I proceed to turn them upside down and shake all the psychic change out of their mental pockets," he wrote. "It gives me a Mephistophelian feeling of power." He watched with disgust as fellow officers moved up the ranks for reasons having nothing to do with their merits, then strutted their stuff. "To use an Army vulgarism," he told his mother, "they think their shit doesn't stink." But while he regularly disparaged his colleagues, *he* held a peculiar fascination for *them*, or so he seemed to think. One supposedly wrote General Eisenhower himself to say that Burns was the greatest genius in the European theater, while another (evidently Schonfeld) had "decided I was the essence of all evil, like Goethe's Mephistopheles."

In January 1944, while still mired in Fedhala, Burns voiced

---

* The British poet (1806–1861) who lived in Italy and is buried in the English cemetery in Florence.

his frustrations to Holger Hagen. "So far the only fortunates who got themselves shanghaied at least as far as Palermo were those who fucked up their humble little jobs here, and were shipped up on the line to where they could do more harm; or those who made such cunts of themselves that they were put on the first requisition," he wrote. He circled "cunts" and wrote in the margin, "If you don't"—here a few words are missing, presumably, something like *understand my use of this term*—"please don't ask any of your friends what it might mean. Some day I'll explain all." Burns's choice of epithets was no accident. Invariably, he depicted his colleagues as women. And weak women, if that wasn't already redundant. And Victorian women, fussy and insular, commissioned directly from civilian life, spared the rigors of training. "[T]he war to them was an unfortunate interruption in ruffling through old manuscripts," he complained to his mother. He called them "The Girls," or "aunties and Elsie Dinsmores,"* gossiping over their knitting, quibbling over their church picnics, fussing over their acrostic puzzles, tittering over thimblefuls of illicit (at least for them) brandy. "All they need, instead of OD's,† is an old-rose tea gown," he wrote. They "should have been baptized Alfretta or Emma."

"Perhaps I'm the last of the Victorians, but I can't yet see my way clear to move up the line by fair means or foul," he told Hagen. "Perhaps I may go berserk by St. Valentine's Day and find myself in Rome as a Lt Col in charge of bordelli of castrati to serve the lusts of pederastic Cardinals." In fact, he *did* resort to foul means, getting himself busted for drunkenness in what he confessed to be a "puerile" attempt to get transferred. It didn't work, but it sure did entertain the ladies. "All the old maids of

---

* Elsie Dinsmore was a priggish, religious young girl who appeared in a series of children's books between 1867 and 1905.

† Olive drabs, i.e., army uniforms.

CPI who've been dying to get something on me are today going about gloating with pleasure at my extra-duty for misconduct," he wrote his mother in February 1944.

By that point, "having hit almost the bottom of the Biblical pit," Burns was officially depressed. "Can't decide whether it's the pip coming on, or too much perusal of war news, of *Time* and listening to Nazi radio programs, or utter ennui with work and being abroad," he theorized for his mother. "I've gone around with a painted grin on my lips; my frame of mind has been one of bitter misanthropy, distrust, and probing." In what he called a "catalepsy of despair," he set to music (for baritone and piano) François Villon's "Ballade des dames du temps jadis"—the melancholy medieval poem that asks, "Where are the snows of yesteryear?" "It's caused quite a sensation here, particularly among those who think I'm awfully snooty: either a prick or a genius," he wrote. To Hagen he added, "they tell me it has an almost intolerable ache, plus a certain musky quality of smegma* and such, possibly superinduced by smelling the Ay-rabs as they swish past in their veils to and from the Casbah." In addition to his own compositions, he led the CPI chorus in Brahms's *Liebeslieder* Waltzes, witty and sentimental songs of love. "The nostalgia of them here is almost insupportable," he wrote. "After each rehearsal we have to change our OD trousers, which become enmired on the front with a sticky smear, depending on whether we carry left or right." In March he was disciplined again, probably for more drinking. "I'm just passing through a fucking-up stage I seem to have missed at puberty, when I was just all sweetness and light," he told Hagen.

Even his badinage with MacMackin turned darker. "We pass about in a fervid dream, with frequent excursions into drunkenness and dreadfulness," he wrote. "The world seems a greater shambles

---

* The cheesy-smelling secretion that gathers under the foreskin and around the clitoris.

than the Loomis orchestra. In general we derive a ghoulish sport from it all, but also our high-impedance ear detects the surface noise of death and mayhem." With Hagen, typically, he was less flippant and more pointed. "I've suffered no hardship whatever— physically," he wrote. "But constantly I feel a heartbreaking malaise, a decomposition of all that I've known. Can't tell you, Moe, whether it's an added heightening of my senses of reality (or the reverse), or closer contact to the bacteria of war, or a sudden paralysis of my brain from some kind of paresis. But we do all live in a kind of cocained dream, on a level quite different from anything I've known outside of surrealism and the novels of the Brontë bitches."

Such brushes with the fighting remained rare. "The only thing that convinced me I'm overseas is the Arabs and their foecal smell, and the amount of French I hear," he told his father. Even glancing references to the war are so scarce in his letters that they're almost startling when they appear, as they did in one from January 1944 to his mother.

We listen carefully to the cultivated Italian announcers, spraying German propaganda into the night. They're incredible programs: excellent symphonic music, corny 1922 jazz, and the wildest blurbs you ever heard about American atrocities. But what we hear and what we know makes us smile at the wishful thinking in the United States. The papers that we see from Boston, New York and Chicago give us the impression that we are wrong and that this war certainly should have ended at least a month ago. But it hasn't. The other night I met some Army Air Force pilots fresh back from Foggia* for a rest. I can't tell you any of their tales until the war is over, but we're all pretty well

---

* Site of a major American airfield from which planes took off for bombing runs over Germany.

convinced that the war's end is not yet. There's so much life yet in Jerry.* The invasion is going to be frightful.

Burns's allusions to the war were more likely to be triggered by something inconsequential, making him appear sometimes shockingly callous. "Your shirts probably went down with that boat, the casualties of which were today released," he wrote his mother in February 1944. "My shirts can't be weighed in the balance against a thousand American lives. But next time you dispatch me a package, please enclose some Palmolive soap, since as I told you, we're cut to two cakes a month on our ration card." When Burns finally mentioned Hitler, it was only out of fear that a U-boat had sunk the ship bringing him some precious sheet music. The fighting seemed as futile and imbecilic to Burns from North Africa as it had from Windsor, Connecticut—maybe even more so, since he now saw it closer up. "In the end we'll have gained nothing—except maybe another war; and so on ad infinitum," he wrote. The very idea of moving up in these ranks repulsed him. "I really don't care," he told his mother that June. "Since my eyes have been opened and I've seen actually what is going on and the senseless waste and meaninglessness of war, I'd almost be ashamed to have it or its machinery confer any honor on me; it would be like the kiss of a prostitute."

He cast an absentee ballot for Roosevelt and quickly regretted it; but even the Republican alternative, Thomas E. Dewey, was no better. Maybe he should have voted Socialist again. His politics remained the same half-baked soufflé of pacifism, socialism, internationalism, isolationism, and cynicism he'd shared with the *Log* before shipping off. The war was all a capitalist plot, with Americans at least as culpable as Germans, maybe more, since a disproportionate chunk of the "world's goods" lay in grubby

---

* The nickname given to the Germans during World War II, particularly by the British.

American hands. At times, even he seemed to realize how silly his amateurish redistributionist theorizing sounded. "I shall make an elegant figure in Moscow circles around 1950," he once wrote his father.

But if the war itself did not stir him, the disasters of war did. Remarkably, though there was a bullet scar near Burns's desk, it took a visiting colonel—who'd landed in North Africa in November 1942, then gone on to Sicily and Salerno—to convince him of the horrors American soldiers were encountering. "We couldn't speak for [a] full five minutes after he had left," he wrote. Along with "a deep cool pity" for those GIs, what stuck with him was "a shame at the human race." Burns also heard from a Japanese-American— a captain from Hawaii, "slim and sloe-eyed as a geisha"—who'd been wounded in Italy as a member of the legendary 442nd Regimental Combat Team, the first unit made up exclusively of Japanese-American volunteers, many of whom had been in internment camps or had families there.

> *He was weary and heavy-hearted, alternating between laughter and tears. He's of course completely Americanized, but under his pretty, slant-eyed mask I felt a quite Occidental horror and fatigue. And he adds fuel to my feeling that the best thing for the selfish, the unruly, the hypocritical is a taste of the cold Italian earth and rocks around Monte Cassino. But I suppose that in this war, as always, the good and the true are up there getting their heads blown off; the future Hitlers are some other place with their feet on a desk planning a new Armageddon.*

A few days later he met a major and a captain, normally confined to a military hospital for shell shock after seeing action in Italy, but allowed to go out occasionally (in the company of a doctor or two) for a drink. They filled him with foreboding. "They were kind, but they were in a different world than I," he wrote. "I suppose they'll always stay that way—on a numb plateau of experience, wisdom, and sorrow, a confraternity of pain and of being pushed farther than a human being ought to be pushed."

Burns constantly complained that the war as portrayed for domestic consumption in *Time* and *Life* and in the "subtle corn" of the syndicated war correspondent Ernie Pyle (who, as Burns later put it, wrote of "sentimental Americans just wanting to go home to Oklahoma") had been sanitized. He saw and praised John Huston's searing documentary *San Pietro*, which chronicled a battle in December 1943 sixty miles from Naples but had not been shown in the States because it was "almost more than any heart can stand."

The greatest indignity he could describe to his father concerned the family of sparrows that had moved into his latrine, defecating on those defecating below. Still, in his six months abroad, he wrote, he'd lived more than in his previous twenty-seven years combined—and changed. "I know that lots of strange things have scarified my brain and heart," he wrote. "In many respects, it's done me good—the loneliness, the homesickness, the contact (if not with bullets and foxholes) with the misery of a very sick world." His mother had put her finger on it: "I think I have more compassion and tenderness."

A new world had opened up to him: "I'm fond of characters here that I could never have talked to as a civilian," he wrote his mother. "The things that used to enchain me: wit, perception, kultchah—no longer seem to matter much; they're an accident of birth and money. The closest friendships here—and at the beach-head—are founded in tenderness, sacrifice, courage, humor, kindness." He'd gone abroad as what he'd always been—"a very clever boy, attractive when he chose to be, palming off beautiful manners for a lack of heart." But at some point, he wrote, "I became aware that there are millions of other people in the world, and that really they're very much like me." No longer, he vowed, would he live on a "beautiful little peninsula all my own." With Rembrandt-like regularity, Burns monitored the changes in his face, and must have thought his new worldliness and wisdom were apparent from a photograph of himself he sent to MacMackin and various other people, in which he stares sadly up and off somewhere, his cap rakishly askew, the ubiquitous cigarette dangling from his lower lip. "The abbess is *priée* to put this on the Mary altar, light a vigil lamp, and decree a day of fasting and abstinence," he wrote MacMackin.

By May 1944 Burns had inched closer to Italy: specifically, to Algiers. It was, he told his father, the most glittering city he'd seen overseas, with "the same out-of-this-world hysteria of pleasure that must have distinguished Paris 25 years ago. Babylon and Sodom and Gomorrah were Peoria compared to it." Now the war was just a short hop across the Mediterranean, and one sensed it: the city was "constantly in a state of frenzied dither, the way a party would be if it were thrown by young men who knew they would die tomorrow . . . We swim in a lather of despair, joy that isn't joy. The science of semantics disappears altogether." To MacMackin, Burns described belonging to "a rather agreeable-looking bunch of zombies in the uniforms of all nations." All, he said, were "puzzled, hurt, nostalgic; they've a feeling that they've lost their pattern of life and their raison d'être." True, there was still dreadfulness, but "without the old unholy giggling glee." It was in Algiers that Burns had his first roommate ever—actually, a *tent*mate—a Southerner named Lou Drezek. The two were combustible—Drezek got "very violent when drunk," while Burns tended to "stew in my own juices over fancied wrongs"— and the buttinskies in his unit predicted disaster. They were wrong. Besides, living under canvas instead of in some ritzy hotel catered to his "hair-cloth tendencies": it was penance for being his former self. Burns hadn't made any postwar plans as yet; no one had. Like everyone else, he knew he might go back to the United States by way of Japan, or could remain in Europe as part of an army of occupation.

It all depended on events, whose unpredictability made them ripe for wagers. "There's a pool on the invasion-of-Europe day, a pool on the end-of-war day (with bets ranging from 25 to 100 years from this date)," a pessimistic Burns had reported to his mother in March. D-Day finally came on June 6, 1944, but, characteristically, Burns took no note whatsoever of it. ("The embarrassing cleavage between the actual and theoretical wisdom seems to be one of the things we've inherited from the Victorians," was how his letter to his mother the following day began.) Of apparently greater moment, as of D-Day Plus Five, was the news he shared—carefully—with MacMackin: he'd fallen "dreadfully in love," he declared—with whom, he didn't say—but wasn't quite sure how to handle it; it wasn't as easy as it had been in college, when, as he put it, "our brilliance blinded

324   ALGER. — L'Hôtel de Ville et le Boulevard de la République. — LL.

Burns's second stop

us as to just what we were up against." Being gay, and half of a gay couple, wasn't as easy in the army abroad as it had been in the more sheltered and tolerant Andover or Cambridge.

By July 1944, a year had passed since Burns had been ordered overseas. In his universe it was, he told his mother, "a date commensurate with that of the invasion" (his first comment to her on it); in that time, he wrote, "I have lived more, seen more, and cried more inside (tears being verboten to all Aryans) than in all the other 26 years put together." Or, as he told Holger Hagen:

> *I'm used now to being overseas, and so much calmer than I was. The sorrow and the loneliness that I thought would eat my life away did a beautiful job of erosion on me: as a matter of fact I guess I came face to face with myself and life and death. Now the chemistry is being extroverted; I see so much that I didn't see and love before. I was living in a beautiful world, but it was selfish; there was no one to share it with. I was a beautiful and finished gentleman, but my manners were only a shell to hide something that wasn't there. It's coming now, gradually; but the hand of God almost annihilated me with* ungenügender Selbstsucht *till I saw what a beautiful comedy I was playing.*

Ungenügender Selbstsucht: it is a phrase Burns would have known well, both from Goethe's poem "Harzreise im Winter" and the *Alto Rhapsody,* in which Brahms set a piece of that poem to music. It means "insatiable self-love" or "narcissism," and it is why Goethe's young traveler, having "sucked hatred of mankind from the abundance of love," finds himself so bleakly and bitterly alone. Goethe asks God whether, somewhere in his book of psalms, he has something to "quicken" the youth's heart and "reveal to his clouded gaze the thousand springs by the side of the thirsty man in the desert." What divine inspiration could do for

Goethe's misanthrope, Burns suggested, the war was now doing for him; the question was what *he* would now do with the extraordinary second chance he'd been given—and if, if he used it properly, he, too, need no longer stand perpetually apart.

"Now in my hand is a key that I never used before—or used for others' undoing," he told Hagen. "Don't I sound just like a revivalist?"

11

In late July 1944, Burns's fondest wish came true: he finally got out of North Africa, where "pianos and nerves are forever out of tune," and headed to Italy—and to Naples. Bombing, first by the attacking Allies, then by the retreating Germans, had reduced much of the city to rubble; hulks of ships sat like rotting teeth in the famous harbor. Chaotic and teeming even when intact and peaceful, the occupied city was a swarm of hunger, theft, debauchery, and desperation, its inhabitants doing whatever it took to survive. "A flytrap of bustle and efficiency and robbery in the midst of ruin and panic," was how Burns later described it. Rival parties vied to replace the Fascists, whose presence had been reduced to the tattered, hortatory posters still plastered around the place. "There's something buffoonishly tragic about Musso's purple utterances eulogizing the courage of the city—some pasted on the side of a house with two walls standing," Burns wrote. "I especially like the atrocity ones of a wild-haired mother holding a mangled child

Burns's third—and most important—stop

to her breast while bombs drop in the background, captioned: *Le mamme d'Italia non dimenticheranno!** No one can blow up a whirlwind like the Italians, as Dante knew."

And yet, beneath the debris, the city remained vibrant. Overlooking the bay, with Vesuvius looming in the distance, the setting was as spectacular as ever. Its people, determined and resourceful, were rebuilding their lives. Even the famed San Carlo Opera House was up and running: resurrected by the British, the company was performing daily, principally for soldiers, many of whom had not known *Tosca* from Tulsa. Burns soon found himself settled into a palazzo—"everything tonier than a shack is a palazzo"—a block from the main drag. On three sides were churches and on the fourth a whorehouse, open around the clock; in front, on the curb, sat twenty demure little girls in black bombazine dresses, newly deloused, always hungry. For all the degradation, Burns was enchanted, as he explained to his mother.

---

* "The mothers of Italy will not forget!"

It's no use: that ole black magic is upon me. I keep
telling myself that the country is dirty, and the people
superstitious and mercurial. Yet I love Italy the way
nothing has hit me since crossing the Atlantic. The place
casts a spell pure and simple; I keep telling myself that it's
a purely historical and snobbish inebriation—but 'tis there
just the same, just as the drunkard's pink elephants are real
to him. However much you may laugh rather scornfully at
the Italians (I did, too), I assure you that you'd only have
to have your own fine sensibilities brought into juxtaposition
with The Best and you'd go haywire, too. The spell is
insidious, but by no means unpleasant, like a junket to an
art gallery after three martinis.

Burns described how he and a French *sous-lieutenant* named
André Colombier drove to the top of the city shortly after he had
arrived and beheld the magnificent harbor at sunset. "It's one of
the loveliest sights in the world, and I melted," he wrote. "The
port was a little misty, and the many islands off the coast looked
like a surrealistic dream of space. The city is flung around by
hills; and you can't see it without a gasp. It was the happiest afternoon I'd spent overseas." The pestiferous air actually restored
Burns's health; his hemorrhoids shrank, his sore throat cleared,
his creative energies returned. "Wonder if there's something to
Christian Science?" he asked his mother. "Nearly all of our unit
are going around looking like grey zombies, and the rest have
sandfly fever. I alone bounce around and am about as popular as
Polyanna [*sic*] at a wake." "Italy—the warm womby nights, the
persistent armpit odor of a jump-joint—has brought a Renaissance in my arid soul," he told Hagen.

When he wasn't living Naples, Burns wrote about it. In their
eloquence and insight, his letters from there create a portrait of
the city rivaling Norman Lewis's classic *Naples '44*. They contain

thoughts and observations on assorted topics: the rakish deviations from standard GI dress ("The general effect is one that would cause the Secretary of War to drop dead on Massachusetts Avenue"), the bric-a-brac—bomb bits, little gold balls— atop soldiers' heads ("If the war goes on much longer, I look for Carmen Miranda hair-dos and fruit"); the dreams of the Italian POWs ("big plates of *pasta asciutta** and a soft brown wife to sleep with"); the half-destroyed city streetscapes ("You can see skeleton rooms where people once lived and loved and fought and died"); the clothing of assorted Italian panjandrums ("The streets are glutted with various Italian petty officials in their ridiculous uniforms, Mussolini's compromise between grand opera and the grandeur that was Rome"); the effect of the heat on his appearance ("It's impossible to look like anything in a cotton uniform. If you go out crisp in the evening, you're sure to return a wet sack"); the virtues of various opera stars, like the "dumpy" but still moving Beniamino Gigli and up-and-comers like Ugo Savarese.

He described to his mother how the occupants and occupiers of the beleaguered city each waged their very different struggles to survive. Daytimes, on its impossibly crowded streets, "the city goes about its tasks like a million sleepwalkers in the heat": "palsied old women in black" pick up cigarette butts or beg for handouts, little boys make "various offers for the bodily needs and hungers." Then, after dark, when all the Italians had to be off the streets, came the desperation, and loneliness, and madness, of the soldiers. Lost in the giant rooms of their ornate clubs, the din of competing pianos and hot orchestras behind them, hordes of officers knock themselves out with gin or cognac at fifty lire a pop. By nine-thirty or so the tension has grown unbearable— and the bars have closed anyway—and everyone drunkenly heads outside tearing about "in a last minute search for someone to

---

* Dry pasta.

sleep with—sex, color, or nationality being irrelevant." By eleven o'clock "they have either found someone or go wherever they are going and sleep it off, to repeat the process the next night. Much of the lurid tempo of the city is from the stark raw sex hungers that stalk it as a natural ghost of the roughness of war."

In another letter, Burns bridged the social chasm dividing the city, leaping from the "lousy hungry pawing children" speaking the Neapolitan dialect in its center to the "handsome, exquisitely mannered, and generous" patricians in their hillside villas, the serene and beautiful white-haired matriarchs who "can cope with any situation simply by sitting back in a tall straight chair with their wrists dangling." With them, the conversation "was conducted gently and musically, with none of the screaming and gesticulation associated with Wops." He touched on topics like the Neapolitan drinking water ("marvelously cool and mineral-tasting . . . the same stuff that put hair on the chest of Caesar's legionaries") and the war-scarred visages of the locals ("all Italians, even the handsomest ones, resemble the heroes of movie executions, with an ageless grief on their faces—all without benefit of touches from Max Factor") and the Italian susceptibility to kindness ("I use the *Lei* form on a lovely girl and she practically has an orgasm on the spot").

Burns's letters could be ruminations on a single person or place, theme or experience, each exquisitely tailored to the four corners of a single page of V-mail, with just enough space to tuck a cursive "Jack" into its lower right-hand corner. V-mail was "conducive more to brevity than to eloquence," Burns once wrote, but like the sonnet, in the proper hands its very constraints became a virtue. Burns's best resembled his beloved lieder: compact and lyrical. That most were perfectly typed made them look as elegant as they read. His letter of "fri 16 mar 45—Italy" is, to use another of those mangled coinages Burns so loved, a "jool"—part vignette, part travelogue, part feuilleton, part rumination, part plea, part diagnosis, part nocturne, part prose poem.

By the sea there's a long escarpment which the Italians have thrown a railing round and planted trees to make a little park in the best classic manner of attempting to improve on nature. Nobody looks at the park, but you can lean on the balustrade and peer out into the Mediterranean and give yourself up to the luxury of melancholy. On warm evenings there are several hundred people occupied in this inoffensive pastime, looking out into the night and living in anything but the present. Some want to be alone because it's about the calmest escape you can find in this city; but most welcome being talked to. An Italian sergeant lolling next to me up and said: "How the stars must laugh at us." It wasn't very original of him, but I allowed how he was right. He had that dark feline quality of looks that I like so in the North Italians. He was in that strangled position of many prisoners of war whose families have been blockaded by the line of war across Italy, hadn't heard for two years from his family in Milan, didn't know whether they were alive or not. He had that quality of despair that the Italians walk around in, absolutely bottomless, without any ray whatever of future hope. I suppose intelligent Germans have it too. Since he asked for nothing, made no cracks whatever against destiny, the Allies, or God, I shared a cigarette with him. He had a marvelous automatic smile, something carried over, I suppose, from the times when he smiled out of happiness. Later on I met a British officer not nearly on such good terms with the world: "I don't see how Americans can possibly be unhappy. Such pay! Such clothes! Such food!" I preferred the Italian.

Burns continued to censor letters, though now they were ones written by American soldiers. It was tedious, but it was the price of admission. And, above all, it was safe, as he noted to his mother on August 15, 1944.

*I met so many of the guys who are taking part in the
newest invasion today. They rested here before being
jammed into the landing barges. Most of them were pitifully
desperate; they'd been through Africa and Sicily and
Cassino; and they didn't see how they'd miss getting theirs
this time. Consequently the city was like a plague-town of
the Middle Ages: the wildest merriment to drown the steps
of Death. I knew some better in an evening than I do many
of my friends. Urgency, sorrow, confusion, annihilation of
everything they'd known in America.*

*Well, the death-rattle can't go on forever. And there's a
cool wind this afternoon. Augury?*

Once they had departed, Naples was bereft of GIs; on the
dance floor of the officers' club in the stately and stolid Fascist-era
Banco di Napoli on Via Roma a pair of nurses danced drearily to
an Italian band playing "Lili Marlene." "I've always hit a new city
just as it's about to lose its wartime excitement," he lamented to
his mother. To his thirteen-year-old sister Connie, of all people,
he reflected on "the maddening contradictions of this war" and
the relative merits of Italian and American music-making. "On
the same peninsula where Americans are still dying, I spent the
last two afternoons at the opera—gorgeous performances of *Rigo-
letto* and *Tosca*," he told her. "The orchestra, chorus, and sets are
superb; the singers are above average. For 150 lire ($1.50) you get a
far more honest, more integrated, and more artistically acceptable
performance than you'd see in America for $7—especially at the
creaky Met, where everything is subordinated and cheapened by
million-dollar voices and Missus Astor's poils."

Sometimes, he raised those same contradictions inadvertently,
as when he celebrated the first fresh meat he'd had in Italy. "The
new invasion had so snaffled up the harbor that for 3 weeks we've
been living off canned C-ration," he griped. "Italy is preferable to

Africa, even though I'm closer still to death and want and sorrow," he told Beulah Hagen a few days later. "In spite of the rubble from bombings and the cold anguish of Americans just coming out of, or just going into, combat, I feel much less pickled in [the] formaldehyde of ennui and irrelevancy than I did in Africa . . . If I'm not happy I'm at least in a froth of perpetual stimulation."

Stimulation there was aplenty, but the elegant signora in the cool villa in the hills above town who tried marrying off Burns to her eldest daughter was wasting her time. As Burns told MacMackin, for gay soldiers Naples was an outsize candy store. "No American city has the brwaugh-extraordinary which is the daily run over here," he reported. So fetching was the place, he wrote, that combat veteran friends of his who'd been sent home were clamoring to come back. He described the night in early August 1944 when he and an audience full of soldiers—"the corridors echoed to the click of infantry boots"—heard the British conductor John Barbirolli lead "one lovely sibilant giving" of Frederick Delius's "On Hearing the First Cuckoo of Spring" at the San Carlo, then ventured outside.

> We felt our way into a blacked-out giardino by the port, flickered over only by a bombing moon . . . As soon as we'd lit a cigarette, we were aware that the place was flea-thick with nuns and prioresses on other benches, or whisking around the santieri fioriti with their wimples twittering. Many were in pairs (as virtuous religious walk, eyes downcast, giggling over their maiden jests.) But quite a few mystics were alone in contemplation. Several plumped down with us to share their apperceptions of the ultimate. We maintained a pious distance between ourselves and their holy habits, though a couple of over-zealous pushed us right off the bench. At last, in holy ecstasy, we went to the cell of a novice who had a bottle of Lacrima Christi, and passed the night waiting to Matins together. Brwaugh!

To his mother, too, a few days later he spoke of a monastery, but of a very different order. As teeming as Naples was, he told her, he had spent his past several months there in "monastic contemplation" over another war—the war within himself. And, he told her, he had made "a myriad of delicate adjustments" to his soul. He could see the changes in himself on his own face as he brushed his teeth—something "quite sad and quite calm" that became him, mesmerized others, and would serve him well in the very different postwar world to come. "I realize that to live in the most disjointed period in the history of the world, one can become either an idiot, a maniac, or something very great," he wrote. "I'm not quite sure what the greatness will be, but myself will find the answer to that too."

Maybe, but there'd be a slight detour first. Burns's ventures into Italian dreadfulness soon exacted a steep price.

12

In the late 1930s, on the outskirts of Naples, Mussolini built himself an enormous modernist campus to trumpet Italian accomplishments abroad over the centuries, tout his own newly reconstituted Roman empire—extending across the Mediterranean to Libya and down to Ethiopia—and salute Naples's glorious role as Italy's gateway to the world. He called it the Mostra d'Oltremare, and he placed it in Bagnoli, a few miles from the center of town. Along with dozens of exhibition halls, an arena seating 15,000 people, and various theaters, it featured a swimming pool, amusement park, fountains, gardens, and its own aquarium. This was no "fair in papier-mâché," Mussolini sniffed, but something built for keeps, filled with Fascist exhortations in words and statuary. Barely a month after it opened in May 1940, however, Italy declared war on France, and the complex was shut down. Then it was damaged by bombs. And then, in late 1943, when the newly arrived Americans needed a gigantic hospital for their war wounded, they took it over. White coats replaced black shirts; the Mostra d'Oltremare became the Twenty-third General Hospital, dedicated to dismantling everything Mussolini had put together, there and beyond.

On any given day, as many as three thousand Allied soldiers were housed there. Most came from abattoirs like Anzio and Cassino, where thousands of GIs were killed and wounded, but a certain few had fallen more ignobly to a different enemy: the Twenty-third also handled cases of venereal disease. In fact, as fighting on the Italian front slowed down and the hospital prepared to close—it moved to France in the fall of 1944—Neapolitan women posed more of a threat to American men than German soldiers, and VD patients constituted an ever-larger percentage of the hospital's population; because men with venereal disease could be put back on their feet and sent into combat more quickly than those with more serious injuries, penicillin earmarked for battlefield casualties was redirected to them. Their brand of combat was concealed from the American public; back home, distinctions weren't made among the "wounded."

Military authorities had placed all prostitutes except those in licensed brothels off-limits to soldiers; that got them off the streets, which was why so many young boys—often the young women's kid brothers—pimped for them, thereby becoming an enduring image of wartime Naples. None of this mattered much to gay soldiers, who traveled in very different, and presumably safer, circles. According to one 1945 study, their figures for venereal disease were lower than among soldiers generally. But some of them, too, wound up at what Burns later called "Mussolini's fairground at Bagnoli."* Neatly removed from the city, it was perfectly situated to become the Dantesque place where sexually wayward soldiers could simultaneously be banished, hidden, humiliated, curbed, and cured.

---

* Burns was mistaken: the complex is actually in the Fuorigrotta district of Naples.

For all the tobacco and alcohol Burns consumed, he had for the most part remained healthy overseas; while others got sick on the Atlantic crossing, he had held his Spam; when colleagues got the "GI shits" following a dinner of wild boar, his constitution had remained "unimpaired." Periodically, prophylactically he'd ingest vast amounts of water, just to flush himself out. But in mid-August 1944 he told his mother he'd not written her the previous day—a Tuesday—because "I felt so godawful that anything I'd have to say would sound like my own obituary." "Like an umbrella turned inside out and stuck upside-down in a grave" was how he put it. At four-thirty that afternoon he fell onto his cot "and prayed for [a] speedy and merciful demise." Perhaps it was a local specialty called sandfly fever, he speculated, or else he'd "been bitten by that party-girl mosquito Ann Opheles." On Wednesday he rallied, and was "only half a corpse." But by Sunday the fever had returned: his joints ached, he thought someone had placed an iron band around his head, and, as he put it, "I felt good only for the garbage can." He feared he'd keel over getting out of bed. He thought of going to the hospital, but instead revisited *Tosca*. The people in his box noticed his "exquisite shade of grey"; later, at the mess hall, it looked more like gangrene. His French *sous-lieutenant* friend proposed some nightclub hopping. "This was too much; so I just put my hot head down into my plate and wept deliriously," he wrote. He started another water purge, then wrapped himself in three blankets and went to sleep. When he woke up, he was his old self, or thought he was. That is, until reddish chancres began popping up on his body, most likely in the vicinity of his penis. These could not be cured by excursions to the San Carlo.

On August 31, the letters home suddenly ceased. Had his parents known what had happened to him the last time he'd gone silent, they might have been alarmed. The flow of mail resumed only on September 10, when Burns wrote his father to say he'd just emerged from a week in the Twenty-third General Hospital, without saying why he'd gone there. "I felt too awful to write during the incarceration, but now I'm in better shape than since I left the States," he told him. "I felt something hanging over me for a long time, but now I've done had it out under expert medical care. I look about ten years younger, they tell me. All that remains is the good old overseas depression, which nothing will ever cure but a gander at the Statue of Liberty." End of discussion. The family thought he'd had something wrong with his kidneys.

With MacMackin he was, as usual, more expansive, abandoning most of his customary posturing. And this time, unlike with the "brass knuckles" episode at Camp Croft, he told MacMackin the truth—either for the sheer shock value of it or because, after all, MacMackin had now become his Boswell.*

Since the Abbess has been chosen to write our biography, we see no reason why we shouldn't give her the reasons for our sequestration, which have been hushed as effectively as the pregnancy of a nun. It seems that the dreadful life here isn't as free of consequence as it is under the gonfalon of the Statue of Liberty, and that in the course of our Italian brwaugh some of the sisterhood infected us with a spirochete or two. In due time these produced their fruit on our so far immaculate body and we went screaming to the dispensary to show various medical officers our now maculate skin. After a round of Kahns and Wassermans [sic]† we were immured in a venereal ward along with other burnt Ayrabs, French, Italians, and Americans. We can truthfully say now that we've seen everything. The new treatment for

---

* It was not MacMackin's first connection to the subject: his aunt Olive had appeared in *Damaged Goods*, a 1914 silent film about syphilis.

† Tests for venereal disease.

*syphilis is drastic, but it takes only eight days, having just
been proved in the land of the free. Sixty hypodermics of
penicillin were forced into us subcutaneously, once every
three hours day and night. The results are more miraculous
than anything Bernadette Soubirous* saw at Lourdes;
we now propose a statue to Professor Penicil on the Abbey
Grounds.*

Just how much infected soldiers endured in Bagnoli can be
gleaned only from what Burns later wrote about it in *The Gallery*; though it was a historic enterprise—penicillin, which had
gone into mass production a year earlier, had only just begun to
be administered for venereal disease—a stop in the venereal disease ward at the Twenty-third General Hospital was not something very many soldiers would have written home about or later
wanted to memorialize. Burns's account is undoubtedly the best
there is.

In it, he describes arriving at "Mussolini's fairground," and
how it could have passed for one of the high schools built back
home a few years earlier by Roosevelt's Works Progress Administration, but for the "plaster statues of ripple-thighed naked young
men in Fascist attitudes of victory" scattered around the place.
He describes the multiple layers of reproach and ridicule meted
out to every VD patient entering the premises, be they officers or
grunts, whites or blacks, Americans or Ay-rabs, from the gloating puritanical sadists working there, be they smug Americans
or lowly Italians. The patients were placed behind barbed wire
and segregated from everyone else, though not segregated among
themselves: black patients, too, were in the ward, macabre har-
bingers of the integrated military to come. Each was forced to

---

* The young girl whose repeated visions of Mary in a nearby grotto gave rise to the famous
pilgrimage site.

wear fatigues with VD plastered on their backs and legs, "in letters high enough to be read half a mile away."

Burns depicts the brutalizing exorcism of what one doctor called, oddly enough, "the dreadfuldreadful," but which was also known around the place simply as "It." Those with "the clap"—gonorrhea—had it relatively easy: four injections over a single day. But because no one was quite sure how much penicillin syphilitics required, the doctors erred on the side of excess: eight full days of injections: every three hours around the clock. Patients were jabbed with primitive blunt needles in a grim orbit around their bodies, rotating from one shoulder, and then one cheek of the buttocks, to the other. As the days passed, and with their skin reduced to hamburger, the injections of the precious, yellow, viscous fluid became even more painful. In between jabs, the soldiers slept restlessly, ate listlessly, exchanged gallows humor, and wandered catatonically around a courtyard—"a chain gang without chains." As in Dante, jaded veterans—those a few days into the cure—explained things to neophytes. In what Burns called the "freemasonry of penicillin," a certain camaraderie developed. At last came the final injection, followed by the "baccalaureate sermon," when hardened doctors warned departing soldiers not to fuck up—and come back—again. Some listened, though many did not.

There were regular reminders that any officers in the place would automatically be busted. But Burns, for some reason, was spared. He was merely docked nine days' pay, and then—this was undoubtedly more of a hardship for him—faced ninety days of sexual abstinence. He returned to his palazzo on Via Medina to find letters from nearly everyone he'd hoped to hear from, plus some precious Tareytons from Beulah Hagen. His life had been saved. And in at least one other respect his adventure had been worthwhile: it was all material he could mine. The day before his letter to MacMackin, he'd fashioned a poem about his ordeal, and he would not stop there. As mortifying, and embarrassing, as the experience had been for him, it was just too good not to use.

Tom Burns, then a navy ensign, hadn't a hint of what his brother had just endured when, a few days after Jack had been sprung, he hitchhiked to Naples from nearby Pozzuoli, where his ship had just docked, to look around the place. He'd thought his brother was still in North Africa; the two were not corresponding, and he hadn't gotten any word from home of his move north. Inevitably, he found his way into the Galleria Umberto I, the once-elegant cross-shaped Victorian arcade which, to occupiers and occupied alike, remained the heart of Naples. Between all the broken glass and debris he spotted a photo studio, and in the window was a picture of a seemingly generic GI, wearing the same khakis as millions of other soldiers. Then he looked a little closer. It was Jack! The owner told him it had been taken just a couple of days before.

Burns as an officer

The two brothers were soon reunited and, joined by Jack's roommates in his palazzo, they raised glasses fashioned from the bottoms of brandy bottles and filled with *eau-de-vie algérienne*. "All thought [Tom] quite nobly mad in the best Burns tradition," he reported home. Over the next few days they saw each other several times: on Tom Burns's ship (Jack came aboard with a friend who, though wearing a wedding ring, struck Tom Burns as gay); at an outdoor club once belonging to Mussolini's son-in-law, Count Galeazzo Ciano; at the opera; and at the officers' club on Via Roma, where, between drinks, Jack gave an impromptu recital. "The rest of us were absolutely fallen on our faces," Tom Burns later recalled. "He'd sit there, never lose that marvelous voice." The man just had a hollow leg. To Tom, Jack simply seemed two years older; he got no sense whatever that he'd just survived some ghastly medical ordeal.

After so chastening an experience, Burns was more selectively dreadful. Still, he soon informed MacMackin of a new Neapolitan lover: one Enzo, "who sells it for L200 to *simpatici* dreadfuls"—or *had* sold it. (Enzo, he reported, "has been getting a wide berth from the clientele because they're getting ornery about forking up when back home they got it for love," Burns explained. "But the Italians in general don't understand the British and American *punti di vista*. The Saxon phalanx is thinking of inviting John L. Lewis* over to get a little unionism in the ranks.") Then there appeared Lino Russo. His name began popping up in Burns's letters in October 1944—even in letters to his mother. Lino had served seven years in the Italian army, fighting with the Germans, and was now "shitting green" at the prospect of being recalled. As Burns, who had clear geographical preferences in such matters, put it, he was "the typical North Italian type—handsome without being greasy, supple as a black panther."

---

* The leader of the United Mine Workers union.

At first, Burns felt Lino was crowding him—"European men have a feminine streak in them, a sort of elegance and catlike intuition that you don't meet with in the States. In friendships they're almost like a woman in love—they throw jealous scenes and expect you to give them all your time. In return for this you get a really extraordinary devotion and sacrifice from them"—but he quickly made room. They spent hours together going over *For Whom the Bell Tolls*. "I improve his English, and he my Italian," Burns explained. "He's a wonderfully alert mind, with that pathetic eagerness of all the sharper Italians to make up for twenty years of self-deception and chicanery by the acquisition of wisdom. And there was a time in Africa when I feared I'd never be happy again." So happy, in fact, that were it not for his family, he would now consider staying in Italy once the fighting stopped. "I've always sniffed at expatriates as people who were unable to take it in their own countries and had to get out," he wrote. "But there is something in the air here that I've never in my life experienced before—an absolute peace, a feeling of walking on air all the time. It's probably the way heaven is supposed to be—disembodied ecstasy, in which your heart doesn't pound or your hand shake. But anyway I feel like a man born blind who suddenly sees the beauty of the world and life for the first time. But don't worry; I haven't gone nuts; I'm not writing from a psych ward. I'm just h-a-p-p-y."

By November, he'd sent a picture of Lino to his mother, who, prone to look the other way on such matters regarding Jack, would have seen him as a boy and a friend but never both. He'd also given Lino a cake of his precious Cashmere Bouquet (which, starved for such luxuries, Lino would periodically take from his pocket and smell), and shared with him a slice of "Pierina Pederast's aphrodisiacal fruitcake cooked in grapefruit rind," a confectionary creation of David MacMackin. ("Our Love's verdict: '*È dolce. Così dolce come una bocca americana su un corpo italiano,'"** Burns wrote him). By Christmas, they'd exchanged engraved rings. *"Oltre la gemma, fino a ricordo,"*† each declared. "The whole fuckin' place swims in brwaugh," Burns told Mac-Mackin, but he seemed to be confining his activities. And taking few pains to hide them. "In a time of loneliness and selfishness and death, God has been good to give me a friend of such sweetness and unselfishness," he wrote his father in January 1945. "He never asks for anything but to be with me. You'd love him too." "I wish I could send you a phonograph record of Lino's pronouncing your first name," he wrote Cathleen two months later. But within a few days, trouble: Lino's father was pushing him to marry his boss's daughter, "an ugly girl of 30." Lino apparently fended off both fathers, at least for the time being, because the two men continued to see one another.

Burns, who'd been promoted to first lieutenant on November 7, 1944—"I'm touched that Mister Roosevelt thought of me even on election day," he wrote home—had fallen not just for *Italia*, but for *gli Italiani*. While some were treacherous, he told Holger Hagen, "the majority are gentle, tender, marvelously vital." He felt himself becoming one of them. Part of it was his proficiency in Italian, a language in which "trivialities take on a grandeur beyond themselves." As part of his newfound populism, Burns now derided what he called "the appalling attic of useless lumber" he'd amassed during his education. Whether he really believed this or not, that education had furnished him with skills that had opened up the entire country, and culture, to him. "Perhaps the reason that Italy has smiled on me is for my accent[,] which has been likened to a wisp of smoke across a 14th century Florentine horizon," he wrote his mother. "My French has always been pretty good, but the effect of a stream of Tuscan on a warm Latin

---

* "It's sweet. As sweet as an American mouth on an Italian body."

† "Beyond the gem, to the memory [of my beloved]."

is astonishing: doors fly open, rare wine pours, stately ladies appear like Beatrice* on the bridge at the Arno." He wondered what good this talent would do him in the more homogenized world a world war produces. "The French are always calling everything *feeneesh*; the Italians are all yelling *ochei* at one another; the British and Americans say nothing now but *non fa niente* and *beaucoup* of this and that," he wrote. "And even I have been known to start a sentence in English, middle in French, and end in Italian."

"For months now I've been getting more Renaissance by the minute: assuming Giotto[†] attitudes, talking Italian with my hands, making love with a faint reek of onion on my breath," he wrote Beulah Hagen. And the Italians took to him, largely because he treated them respectfully. In November 1944 he described the scene in the transient officers' mess to his mother.

It seems that when you don't wish a dish, instead of shaking your head, you must shout in English at a little man who doesn't understand a word of it. Italians are high-strung anyway and it's easy to get them so upset that by the end of a meal they're crying and serving you with shaking hands. I get marvelous service in a joint where nearly everybody else complains that it takes an hour to eat. When I go in, the head waiter seats me personally. I ask the waiter how his wife is. On my plate appear extra little somethings; a second on dessert appears without my asking for it. I was touched the other night when my cameriere *helped me into my jacket and said:* Che piacer di [sic] servire una persona così gentile come Lei.[‡] *I'm telling you this not to show what a marvelous guy your son is, but to*

---

* Beatrice Portinari, the young Florentine woman who became Dante's muse.

† The Florentine painter who helped usher in the Renaissance.

‡ "What a pleasure it is to serve someone as nice as you."

*show that even here in war kindness goes so much farther
than harshness.*

"If everyone were like you, there wouldn't be wars," Vincenzo
the barber, on whom he bestowed matches and chocolate, told
him once in the middle of a shave. Then there was the *sergente
maggiore*—the one who, whenever Burns gave him a shot of whiskey or a cigarette, burst into tears—who, hearing of Burns's recent promotion, left off a small present at his door. "It meant more
than all the handshakes I got," Burns wrote. "I have never seen a
people more tortured and more good-hearted than some of these.
It is difficult to watch them without one's eyes filling up and deter-
mining that humanity must never go through this again." "When
Abraham Lincoln spoke of malice toward none, with charity for
all, he was surely looking beyond the present days," he wrote his
father on Lincoln's birthday 1945. "I see a lot of the malice and its
fruit, and very little of the charity, except when some American
not carried away by mad dreams of promotion or gain does some
exquisite act of kindness. And I see those, too, which gives me
hope." Critics would one day fault Burns for excessive sentimentality toward anything Italian. But his letters reveal this was not
some after-the-fact affectation.

It helped that with his recent promotion, "the Italians ap-
proach me as if I were Lorenzo de' Medici dispensing largesse."
A large retinue, including a black private, a British sergeant, and
a small Italian girl of five, followed him through the street, he told
his mother; "practically everyone I have ever been decent to in
this city waits on street corners till I pass[,] and joins. I'm thinking
up a Sermon on the Mount, but all I could say is that human love
is a touching thing." Sometimes, though, the adulation got to be
too much, like the American warrant officer who insisted—rather
ambiguously—that Burns reminded him of his wife. "How am I
to take that?" he wondered.

About Americans, his feelings were considerably more mixed. The GIs "evince an almost stifling bitterness, homesickness, and disillusionment," he wrote Beulah Hagen. "Particularly interesting are soldiers and officers returned to rest camps here from combat. They fall into three groups: a) those who have been made purified and integrated personalities by the experience; b) the dazed; c) the disgruntled, who feel that the experience of battle has put them in a class by themselves, rather like the deification of American athletes." To know the first group, at least, was "ennobling and touching." In some ways, Burns thought, Americans were actually *more* civilized than Europeans: "They don't *hate* anybody; they have no desire for revenge." They really did represent the world's last best hope. But he also saw what American soldiers were doing to exploit a decimated people. In his own small way he refused to participate: he wouldn't sell the precious five-dollar bill he'd gotten from home—with its seal blue rather than occupation gold—on the street, where it would fetch twice that. "I don't wish to share in the guilt which is prolonging the war and the sufferings of so many on the earth," he explained. "Or perhaps I may save it for my first drink in the States." "The world falls into two categories: those who hate the [war] because they are getting killed in it or because they were happy as American civilians, and those who are having the time of their lives out of it," he mused to Beulah Hagen. "The last are the true enemies of the human race."

Gradually, as moss began growing on the rubble, the Americans and British moved north, leaving Naples largely to the *Napolitani*. "The tidal wave into Northern Italy leaves us as usual like crabs in a pool after the tide has gone out," Burns observed. And changes ensued: Burns watched, "with a mental footnote on the economics of the war and the law of supply and demand," as Italian girls propositioned impoverished Italian soldiers. ("*Non* *sono Americano,"* the men would tell them. *"Eh! No fa niente,"** the girls would reply.)

Listlessly, begrudgingly, he continued to do his work. "Burns is a moral ruin—not to say a cancer—down in Italy," his pal from Brooklyn, Robert MacLennan, wrote Holger Hagen. Eventually he wore out his bosses, and in January 1945 Burns was promoted to a "semi-executive" position, entitling him to sit at a double desk and do next to nothing. Now, as he told his father, "I can indulge in my usual fantasies without rows of Italian script dancing before my eyes." He'd been relieved of at least part of "the white man's bureaucratic burden": "The squirrel has been taken off the treadmill, put in a deluxe cage, and his eyes bandaged. The sound of the typewriter, after all, is the basic rhythm of modern life—even in war; the machine gun is simply a more explosive orchestration."

Next to prayer, music had been his most potent balm. But between his new humanity and the ambient Neapolitan melodies, his taste had evolved: no more stuff "written to prove something or to give some intellectual cult a titillation like a crossword puzzle," but only compositions "which stir me inside the left part of my chest." (The sentiment was not entirely new. "I got through Stravinsky, Copland and all the other angular emotionless horrors when I was still in college," he once wrote.) That invariably meant opera, especially Puccini: someone he could like only surreptitiously while still in snooty American musical circles he could now embrace unabashedly. By March, he'd seen *Tosca*—"my favorite opiate"—with Maria Pedrini and Beniamino Gigli twenty times. He became something of a Pedrini groupie, even dining with her once in her *pensione.* While other GIs posted pictures of Betty Grable and Rita Hayworth, he tacked up a shot of her.

---

* "It doesn't matter."

Some operas he found revolting; *Lucia di Lammermoor* was "like sticking your nose into a cedar chest and going into ecstasy over the mothballs"; *La Gioconda* was "certainly the worst opera ever written." And even some productions of beloved operas like *La Bohème* disgusted him, like the one in which the diva playing consumptive Mimi, Pina Esca, must have weighed 240 pounds. "As a little seamstress dying of pthisis [*sic*] she's as convincing as [Lauritz] Melchoir* as Peter Pan," he griped. With MacMackin, he was coarser still. "She has no conception of musical style whatever, and resembles a bright fat schoolgirl who suddenly after coming in her jeans over Frankie Sinatra finds herself the possessor of a beautiful voice."

For all the comfort it provided, sometimes music only heightened the pain. With a soldier friend named Michael Patrick, Burns went to the San Carlo to hear the familiar operatic twin bill of *Cavalleria rusticana* and *Pagliacci*. The very next day, Patrick was returning to the front, meaning these might be the last operas he would ever hear. "The performance was extraordinarily fine—brutal and nervous, so that an English sergeant behind us, sent by the drive and richness of Italian music, turned to his companion and said 'You can take your Wagner and you can shove it up your arse,'" wrote Burns. But several times, as Burns tried to follow the action on the stage, Patrick placed his head on his shoulder—and wept. Afterward, at the apartment of a friend with a piano (for which Burns paid half the rent), Patrick asked him to play the dreamlike "Im wunderschönen Monat Mai," the opening song in Schumann's song cycle *Dichterliebe*, celebrating young love in springtime. "I thought at first he was going to cry again and think about going back to the front," Burns later recalled. "All he said was, 'what hope for the human race when somebody can write a song like that.'"

---

* The Danish-born opera star (1890–1973) known principally for his Wagnerian roles.

13

*

Burns, too, was writing—mostly poetry. It "kept me from going off my trolley for good," he told Holger Hagen. The poems were often ostentatiously obscure, though to MacMackin they were much better than the "centrifugal whorls of frou-frou" Burns had written previously. But in one of the more accessible ones, called *Mister Mars* and written in September 1944, Burns railed against their common enterprise.

> *Rósters of philanthropy*
> *rate me high as Carnegie:*
> *different deeds did I in breeze*
> *piker Mephistopheles;*
>
> *and a monument to war*
> *ought to rise in every square.*

Lincoln's name is known to all—
I am Lincoln grown more tall;

emancipations I have worked
Honest Abe, I fear, would shirk;
from faith, from love, from life, from limb,
after cream remains the skim.

Mary meant to be a nun:
Mary's veil has popped a run;
patriotism had her give
virginity she'd kept alive.

John was married brilliantly
Till he came to Italy;
what a girl has given John
generations will pass on.

Roy was gentle as the grass,
As the shadows evening pass:
Now a loneliness of Roy's
Makes him lie with other boys.

Helen was a loving nurse:
But I smiled to hear her curse
when the Anzio Express
screamed to rest beside her dress.

Michael was a parish priest;
Foremost-looking, not the least:
his battalion did for him
more than a Gregorian hymn.

O America, you owe
debts to me you'll never know;
raise the monument I rate
by subscription in each state.

But it was another poem, *In the Galleria Umberto*, written five
weeks earlier, that best captured the larger project taking shape in
his mind.

She loves the sun:
she loved her mother's milk two years ago,
warm in diluted run
and trickling slow
like this same lymph that trickles down the panes.
She is so young
she cannot reach a rung
and plays in loneliness among the stains.
She wants the flies for friends
and waves them down invitingly;
when one descends,
she grows alarmed at his temerity.
And in her hair
a phalanx walks that prickles on her scalp—
she would not care
except an itching quivers on her lip.
At two years old
she does not comprehend her rags;
she will be told
her gown is modish bag
that carried mail or brown potatoes when
her turn came to be born,
and it is worn

not wholly clean.
She thought she had a friend—a soldier passed,
Falling against the walls;
the gallery stalls
echoed his calling-out that he was gassed.
He gave her sweets,
a roll called Lifesavers; she peels
the crystal rings off one by one and eats;
the sweet fruit flavor and anneals
a dryness in her mouth.

Her friend has gone
when she had planned to play;
and now upon
the stone crevasses stay
her tears,
a wretchedness she wears,
her fears.

Once, when the building was intact and its pavement clean and polished, feet would glide over the marble and mosaic floor inside the Galleria. But now, with its protective glass canopy shattered by war, the tears of starving children merged with the rain and pigeon shit, and the spilled vermouth, and vomit, and pee of the drunken soldiers. Then the grime and dust that had descended on Naples— microscopic historic fragments of the pulverized city—bound together the brew, which stuck to the stones. Burns knew it all well. He was always in the Galleria: it was close to his palazzo, and right next door to the opera house. And he wasn't alone. From the moment it had opened in 1892, most everyone who lived or ever found himself in Naples went there.

A huge chunk of the cholera-infested city had been cleared to build the Galleria. It had been designed not only to clean up, but to *lift* up, Naples: the city aspired to help lead newly unified Italy, and craved an arcade to rival Milan's Galleria Vittorio Emmanuelle II, erected a few years earlier. Shoehorned into a smaller site, the Galleria Umberto I looked less stately and imposing from the street, but that only made it more surprising and stupendous inside. From the beginning, though, there were limits to what even something so formidable and lofty could hold back: before long, Naples's intractable problems seeped in. "The arcade has become the attraction of beggars, pimps, street urchins, idlers," went a report from ten years after it opened. "It should not be allowed that a beautiful and elegant meeting place, such as our arcade, continues to be the refuge of the filthiest derelicts of our Neapolitan life. Those people must be pushed back into the darkness where they belong." So the Galleria had always represented Naples at its most elevated and most degraded, embodying both its elegance and tawdriness, its high aspirations and grim reality. And with the war, and the Germans, and then the Americans, its incongruities had only grown more stark.

Like most GIs, Burns would never have encountered anything like the Galleria before and, like those loners who secretly crave activity all around them, who'd leave Andover for Boston and Fedhala for Casablanca, he found it thrilling. As one of his characters to come put it, the Galleria was "the tiniest yet the greatest city in the world," one that "enraptured him as a circus does for a child." For Burns, its appeal went beyond the craftsmanship, and the ready availability of cheap booze or temporary companionship. His was the fascination and envy of an American accustomed to a more atomized existence, in which like-minded people come together only evanescently, for something colossally and continually communal. Everyone came to the Galleria. If anything, war and adversity had made people cling to it even more tenaciously. Alongside vendors of primitive paintings of Mt. Vesuvius and pillows with MOTHER (often misspelled) stitched in them were the

Napoli *Interno della Galleria Umberto I.*

Galleria Umberto I

local burghers sipping espresso, and old men scavenging cigarette butts, and *scugnizzi*—street urchins—seeking handouts, and the soldiers of every Allied nation, and the bartenders and prostitutes who served them. And it never stopped, at least until curfew. In fact, life in the Galleria only intensified as the day wore on. By sunset, its air "had a thick swooning texture like tired gold melting"—or of that amber-colored penicillin in the syringes. The sounds, too, thickened as evening approached. "There was the pad of American combat boots on the prowl, the slide of Neapolitan sandals, the click of British hobnails out of rhythm from vermouth. There were screams and coos and slaps and stumbles. There were the hasty press of kisses and sibilance of urine on the pavements." By moonlight, shadows singly and in pairs chased from one cavernous corner to another.

For Burns the Galleria became a faithful, undemanding companion. It had almost a religious feel to him: as one of his characters was to note, it was as spacious as the Vatican, and even shaped like a cross or a cathedral. And it grew all the more dear to him because, for all its degradation, it somehow maintained its dignity—like Italy and like Naples themselves. So the Galleria elicited from him a set of emotions—love, respect, gratitude, sentimentality—he'd accorded very few of his characters or friends or relatives, or anything else he'd seen or experienced or written about. And it bestowed one more blessing on him: a canvas broad enough to capture something as enormous as what he had been witnessing.

In December 1944 Burns moved from his palazzo to a fifth-floor room at the Hotel Terminus, near the train station. His "cell"—he made it sound like something out of Loomis—had a real bed rather than the usual canvas cot, as well as a dresser *and* a mirror; it was, he wrote, "a cleaned-up version of such flea traps as the $1-a-night Hotel Dixie, just off Times Square." It even had a semblance of heat, though "it's as cold as the ramparts of Elsinore here all the time," he griped. Visiting Americans passed through; picking up his room key one day, "a rather lovely creature" in a USO-shows uniform, wearing a powder blue bandanna on her hat and reading *Stars & Stripes*, bade him good morning: it was the actress Annabella, in town for a production of Noël Coward's *Blithe Spirit*. "She's not quite so ravishing as when Tyrone Power married her; she has circles under her eyes, but she's still quite an appetizing salad, especially against a bombed building," he wrote. But his personal turbulence continued. "The essential flavor of being overseas is that you're living in a dream, walking around under cocaine," he wrote his mother in January 1945. "You keep saying, 'All this can't be happening to me; I shall wake up soon.'"

He enjoyed "an orgy of reading," as if to liberate the great novel he believed to be encased inside himself. Most authors then writing in English he found hopelessly vacuous; he gravitated toward the Russians, especially the short stories of Chekhov. "In these stories," he told his mother, "I get the impression of human beings wandering around lost—not the slick little marionettes of a Somerset Maugham, but real human beings, drunk, convulsed with crazy despair and joy, and aware of their own littleness— while the author himself is aware of their greatness." The dog in one of them "becomes so humanized and sharp in her knowledge of human beings that you end the story almost in tears, knowing that the dog knows a great deal more than Ginger Rogers does."

He was eager to see his family, Burns insisted—"you're the only ties I have in the world, the only loyalties"—but that seemed a bit forced. His three brothers, also in the service, faced dangers he'd never encountered, but he never asked after any of them. Even Tom's visit to Naples warranted only a few lines home. Really, he was in no rush to return. He now had a more important mission: to describe, and explain, what was happening before him. He couldn't "bury myself from the hugest tragedy the world had ever seen." The world had been smashed into pieces and, so disassembled, could be more easily understood, particularly with his new "cool empathy." "In Africa I found truth in myself and in the cognac bottle, which must be taken sparingly," he wrote. "In Italy I have it in a completer understanding of what is really happening in the world, and in music, which was almost lacking in Africa." Making sense of it all was something he actually felt divinely ordained to do.

All my life I've had an uneasiness and discontent with the status quo—not through any inability to cope with it, but perhaps through some dim inkling (much stronger now than two years ago) that I was born for some purpose which has not yet been achieved. I think without bragging I can say I possess certain gifts of understanding and penetration which are not being used to their fullest, but I also believe that they will be—if each of us is truly an agent of God in some vast scheme we can't pretend to understand. So at 28 I'm still in a state of suspension of faculties. Outwardly I smile and am charming, but my ear is listening very hard for something!

The great conflagration had produced a whole raft of new data to explore. Burns thought he'd figured something out, discovered something no one wanted him to know, and he needed to say it. "I think I've penetrated through a night that only I know to some sort of understanding of what the world *is*, not what people would like me to believe it is," he told his sister. "I have lived in the middle of a colossal myth that so many other Americans are still caught in and believe in." Word of his ruminations reached his friends. "Burns I hear from now and then in a rather chastened mood, stripped of all that old frivolity, and contemplating the eternal verities," Douglas McKee wrote Sebastian DiMauro in May 1945. Reading John Dos Passos's *The State of the Union* made Burns want to see the United States again, and determine his role in it. Then he read Dos Passos's *U.S.A.*, and it provided a different sort of inspiration: "He did for the last war what I would like to do for this one," he wrote his mother.

On May 1, Burns picked up the latest issue of *Time*, which included a three-page photographic spread from Buchenwald. For half an hour afterward, he told his mother, he sat in a kind of "frozen fit," his hands shaking so badly that he couldn't light his cigarette. Maybe the Germans should be sent off in labor battalions for the next twenty-five years, fixing Europe, he suggested. By and large, though, epic events still went unobserved. Only two months after the fact did Burns mention Franklin Roosevelt's death on April 12, for instance, and even then, only to note how shocked the Italians were to hear jazz blaring that day over the loudspeakers outside the Red Cross Theater. When, in early May, Burns learned of the Nazi surrender in Italy—one million German soldiers laid down their arms that day—it was, characteristically, between acts of *Tosca*. He seemed considerably less moved than the personnel at the San Carlo.

> The curtain went up on the second act, Scarpia's apartment in the Farnese Palace. But instead of Scarpia at dinner the stage was filled with every last employee of the opera house—electricians, carpenters, and my favorite fat soprano of the chorus in her civilian house dress and her Wedgies. Well, they sang about every national anthem except the Horst Wessel* and then it was announced that the German armies in Italy had surrendered. So I went out into the night and after one act of my favorite opera . . .

---

* The anthem of the Nazi Party.

We're still doing our work today, although it makes no
sense whatever. I wonder where the catapult will hurl me next.

The end of the European war five days later produced other
celebrations, like a festive meal at the British officers' club. "We
sat down to an Allied dinner: Consomme a la Churchill, chicken
patties Roosevelt, and Vegetables a la Stalin," Burns told his father. He celebrated the next day by sleeping until noon. His plans
to see *La Bohème* at the San Carlo scotched, he marked the occasion by playing chess (badly) on a ship in the Naples harbor.
He then went with Lino to the sulfur baths of Solfatara, where he
scalded himself, then to the beach at Baiae (which he knew from
the poems of Shelley), where he ate huge Sicilian blood oranges and
went swimming. Too much sun left him, as usual, with burned
skin and a stinging sensation all over his body. "On returning I
looked at my cooked flesh, drank some cognac and aspirin, and
put my fevered corpse between sheets," he wrote afterward. But
before long, talk of Lino ceased; it's unclear whether the affair had
run its course—with Burns, these things had never been long—or
whether Lino succumbed to the pressure and married the boss's
ugly daughter. Burns was resilient: by late May he had moved on
to a soldier from New Zealand—or, as he called him, "my Kiwi."
   Burns maintained a pretense of heterosexuality, though
never very strenuously or persuasively. He once told his father
he'd decided not to marry an Arab girl after all. To his mother,
he described the crush that the head of the Hartford Madrigal
Society—the middle-aged spinster daughter of the late Episcopal
bishop of Connecticut—had on him, plying him with "elderly
mash notes" and expensive sheet music. "Don't be surprised," he
wrote, "if I marry an heiress who looks rather like Dante's bust
with a red wig on its skull, and you have a lot of little nutmeg-
staters calling you grandma." Later, Burns reported to his father

that a twenty-three-year-old Italian woman at the Red Cross named Gerarda de Bernardis "has been nibbling at my heart." "She says she will never marry an American, because they live in a different world than hers," he went on. "But she has bewitched me, *la soave strega!*"*

By then Burns had been sent to the headquarters of the U.S. Army in Italy in Caserta, twenty-five kilometers outside Naples, to start going through the personnel files of Mussolini, captured only the week before. "I know more about the inside of the Fascist party than most people living today," he wrote afterward. But nothing was holding Burns's interest for very long. "I had hoped to go to Paris until they got hold of Mussolini's files," he wrote Holger Hagen. "Now I'm running for Librarian of Congress." Even Italian opera was "getting to be like a sucked orange" to him. Still, when the German-speaking remnant of his intelligence unit went to Austria, he'd happily stayed behind; for all his love of the language, he loved very few of them, and was pleased to see them drive off with their "enormous numbers of jeeps and toilet paper." Additionally, he had no desire to be among a different vanquished population.

In fact, his love for the Italians, even those who filched his money, his watch, his cigarettes, his cans of meat, only grew. And he soured further on America and Americans. All he had to do was pick up *Time*, and American materialism, arrogance, and provincialism came crashing down on him anew. Just compare *Rhapsody in Blue* to a Hugo Wolf song or Fauré's *Requiem*! Attempting to keep the officers' club on Via Roma from degenerating into a "men's dump," he'd set aside a small room with a piano for his own recitals, but some Texas yahoo major fresh off the Dies Committee† had summarily moved the piano out to the

---

* The sweet witch.

† An early incarnation of the House Un-American Activities Committee.

dance floor. "It's not so much fun to stand at a bar with a lot of disgruntled Americans when you'd rather play Brahms," he told his mother.

Burns found his fellow GIs brutal, bitter, self-pitying, exploitative, and contemptuous of everything Italian. "But since I love the language, the people, and the music, my pleasures are more varied and subtle than the idea that every Italian woman is to be had and that every gentle and dignified Italian is to be called *Paesano*, preferably in a shout," he told DiMauro. "Italians who have nothing somehow or other touch me more than an American officer bitching away because he has had to take Raleighs instead of Chesterfields," he wrote his father. To him, American officers were "thuggy people with jeeps and mistresses for the first time in their lives," living in "villas which a catastrophe outside themselves has hurled into their paunchy laps." American boorishness even extended to "Frankie" Sinatra, who, having neatly dodged wartime service with a perforated eardrum, gave a concert in Caserta in early July 1945. Burns was sitting at a nearby table when the singer and his entourage arrived for lunch. "He looks like a corpse in an ill-fitting suit of the most sumptuous tweeds," he wrote his father. "He had with him three American actresses who looked more whorish than anything I have ever seen on Via Roma of starving Italian girls who have to make a living.* What pissed off the whole mess hall is that the Voice's party got coffee while we were drinking GI lemonade."

Worse even than American boorishness was American bigotry and stupidity. Yes, Burns wrote from time to time about "Wops" and "pickaninnies" and "boogies" and "nigger's eye" shoes, but that was the carelessness of the time; as a Roman Catholic "mick" and a "queer" to boot, he had an instinctive sympathy

---

* Two of the women touring with Sinatra were the singer Fay McKenzie and the dancer Betty Yeaton.

for anyone similarly oppressed. In various letters he detailed the flak he'd gotten from other officers for bringing a black colleague or Lino to dinner, even though he paid the twenty-five-lire tab. "I was made the object lesson because our major objected to my sitting there with Lino and jabbering in Italian all the time," he told his father. "Ho hum. I think there's enough sadness in the world that I at least may go all out to make some one happy when I like him as much as I do Lino." Just to stick it to his narrow-minded colleagues, he made plans to bring a Japanese-American soldier friend who, for all his bravery in battle, was still suspected of spying for Tojo, and "plant him right under the major's nose."

Another episode involved an American officer and the soprano Caterina Jarboro,* in Naples with a troupe of black performers for the USO. Afterward, Burns wrote his mother, he couldn't stare into the eyes of the Italians who'd witnessed what he had just seen without shame.

A drunken parachute officer was feeling ugly and looking for someone on whom to vent his hate. The negress Caterina Jarboro took what he drunkenly thought to be his place at the bar and ordered a drink. Since you do not lynch negro women, no matter how much you loath[e] the black race, he stormed around to find a colored man to pick on. He found a little negro, since now the hotel is full of colored USO units. He thrust his face into the poor little guy's, and out came a flood of choice vulgarity and abuse. He told the little colored man to tell that nigger bitch to go home and learn her place. He said this in various degrees of shouting and obscenity for fully five minutes and charged off like a spent bull, leaving the little colored man in tears. There is

---

* Jarboro (1903–1986) is said to have been the first black singer ever to appear on a leading American opera stage, two decades before Marian Anderson.

a frightful commentary on modern life to see a small black man in a smart US officer's uniform standing beside a Tom Collins and bawling. Even those at the bar who don't care for negroes were embarrassed and silent. I was so angry that without any pretense at being little Joe Jesus I had to go up and tell the little negro how sorry I was that any American officer would behave so. The expressions on the faces of the Italian waiters showed that they saw little difference between this and an SS trooper clubbing a Jew. We have glass windows in our own house, I fear.

In February 1945, a group of enlisted men, all wounded in combat, joined his unit. "Several are Jews, which should give the lie to the famous barb that the Jew does all in his power to stay out of a rifle company," Burns told his mother. "Almost all are what would be called 'superior people' in an academic society; they put to shame the laziness and selfishness manifested by some of our other GIs and by some of our officers." They were the exceptions, though: apart from members of persecuted minorities, Burns's sympathies lay far less with Americans than with Italians, "who make our own despairs seem like a child crying over a sawdust doll."

His conviction that the American press was whitewashing the war was only strengthened when, in May 1945, he was interviewed for two hours by an ABC newsman named Ted Malone. Malone's broadcasts focused on "the human side of war"—"as though," Burns told his mother disgustedly, "warfare were made by something else than human beings and as though a dreadful fact of our time had to be reduced to something sweet and simple." Burns often found corroboration for his scorn in a person's physiognomy; Malone, he noted, had "the build of a pouter pigeon," along with "thinning hair, a tummy, and a face that seemed porcine and indolent." He'd shared some of his writings with Malone, which turned out to be a mistake. "About the little girl in the Galleria Umberto, crying for her poverty and the war and picking the lice out of her head, he wanted to know whether she actually existed and whether I'd had a love affair with her," he recalled bitterly. "Live and learn, I always say. And the vulture is an integral part of nature's economy."

Burns nonetheless insisted he would not stay abroad. "I have only to resist the snares of European life enough to remember that I must go back to America eventually, that for all our crassness, immaturity, and bad manners, we still live under the best government (or scheme of it) in the world," he told Hagen. He worried for his Loomis friend Douglas McKee, who'd written from Germany to say he might not go back. "That is death," Burns told his mother. But he remained in no rush. He foresaw a period of disillusionment, recrimination, bitterness, and readjustment—a *Best Years of Our Lives* scenario, in which officers used to authority and autonomy and respect found themselves jerking sodas and pumping gas. The lost generation that would follow this war, he predicted, "will make F Scott Fitz G look like a child in her party dress," because this time there wouldn't be an economic boom to prop them up.

"From tricky little symptoms I have seen over here, our war is just beginning when we go home," he told Hagen. "Now that we have made a shambles of the world's yard, our own stands to blow up in our faces if we return with a thankgodthat'soverwith attitude—and nothing else." America was not invulnerable to "our own home-grown Fascists who blithely mouth shibboleths as vicious as any in *Mein Kampf*." His wartime experiences only confirmed his pessimism. "Until now without reservation I indorce [sic] Dean Swift's sentence* about that odious little race of vermin and the glorious pessimism of that great Wop poet

---

* From *Gulliver's Travels*.

Leopardi,* who even a hundred years ago found the human race going backwards at a great pace," he wrote Hagen. But Burns still thought himself an idealist. He and his friends "have no other desire in life but to purge themselves of hate and to live like human beings—enough but not too much to eat, enough hooch, lots of ·music, kisses on the right mouth. Otherwise human life means absolutely nothing. I choose to think that it does or *can.*"

---

* Giacomo Leopardi (1798–1837), the supreme Italian poet of pessimism.

14

Burns began his new novel on June 18, 1945. He already knew
its title, its themes, its superstructure. It would be called
The Gallery, and rather than centering it around a single military
unit—his own—as he had once envisaged, it would focus on a
single place: the Galleria Umberto I. And it would contain another, separate gallery—a gallery of characters passing through
it. Burns had always written quickly, and perhaps because he'd
not been drinking, at least as much, he now moved even faster,
and was soon showing portions of it around. It was more accessible than his other books, not clotted with pretense and obscurity,
and it was "causing a sensation," he reported, "flooring everyone
here from male whores to uneasy Lt. Cols." Fueling it all was his
newfound pity. "I have it now," he told MacMackin, "though not
in the sense of Greer Garson weeping in Technicolor over the lot
of illegitimate children." "They tell me it is very fine," he wrote
Hagen. "James Joyce had to resort to private symbols, but I can

use English wrenched in the anguish of the world." A month later, he dropped more literary names with Holger Hagen. "My novel, which is like Dostoievsky, Andrew Marvell, and Voltaire, is called *The Gallery*," he told him. "It is a huge affair . . . It's so good I can't believe I'm writing it. Just hold on to your 20-20 vision and your *cristal eien** will see every fuckin' word."

"I had a large reading public in Naples who waited for each page as it came hot from my typewriter," he later told his mother. While Americans thought it "too strong"—that is, presumably too strongly anti-American—Italian readers were moved and pleased. The fledgling novel wasn't obnoxious or perverse like *The Cynic Faun*. And it wasn't mannered like so many of his letters, lacking the pretentiousness of those to Beulah Hagen, the self-indulgence of those to his mother, the flippant campiness of those to MacMackin. Burns was no longer writing for himself, or for a select few. He wanted to be heard. He'd grown serious.

A letter to MacMackin suggested how he'd sobered up. Suddenly, it was no longer "Dear Giaour"[†] or "Mon très cher Priapus," but "Dear David." Then he went on to lecture MacMackin on the various foibles of dreadfuls, whom he now—and for the first (and only) time in their correspondence—called "homosexuals."

Speaking of the army of belles that Plato suggests in the Phaedo,[‡] Konrad Heiden[§] has a stinging sentence to the effect that the 20th century homosexual is rarely completely

---

* The phrase is either an inside joke or German gibberish.

† The Turkish word for "infidel" and the title of a famous poem by Lord Byron.

‡ Burns probably meant Phaedrus, who suggested in Plato's *Symposium* that because of their devotion to one another, an army of lovers would be the mightiest army of all.

§ Burns had evidently been reading Heiden's 1944 book *Der Fuehrer: Hitler's Rise to Power*. In it Heiden, a German-born Jewish journalist, discussed the homosexuality of several early Nazis, notably the head of the SA, Ernst Röhm, and wrote that "assuredly the pressure of public censure has distorted more characters, weakened more moral resistance, created more dishonesty toward oneself and others among modern homosexuals than among other people."

*honest with himself. Even if he ever arrives at the point of
accepting his bias as merely an incident in his personality,
he sets up all sorts of pitiful little compensations. Camping is
after all the essence of the tragic spirit contorted into a leer
no Greek mask ever knew. He sets up for himself a tinseled
world that has nothing to do with any reality, believes himself
a golden and divine spirit, gifted beyond other men, and
frequently goes over into the realm of art, which soothes the
feminine ganglia in him. Unless he has a first-rate mind,
merciless self-appraisal, and honesty too large to force
his world on a larger one he becomes an artist as warped
as his own psyche; and you get ugliness, negation, and
nonessentials substituted for the blood of great art.*

In *Sodome et Gomorrhe,** he went on, "Miss Proust" had also
exposed the dishonesty of modern homosexuals. "It was a pose
which used to irk me in you," he scolded. (Only once before had
he shared his ambivalence about gay culture with MacMackin; it
happened a year earlier, after describing his hyperactive dreadful
existence in the army. "With a few exceptions," he wrote, "the
life strikes us as "centrifugal, horrifying, and deathmaking." Still,
Burns suggested he had become a kind of guru to other gay soldiers. "Our sense of empathy is said to be just out of this world by
the many dreadfuls who for some reason or other look to us as to
an obelisk," he wrote a month later. "They believe that we've happened upon some secret of life lost since the Ptolemies.")

A presumably angry response prompted Burns to concede
that his young protégé's rage was "perfectly justified," only to fire
back that MacMackin had zeroed in on what had "attracted and
repelled people" to his mentor "since I began to walk"—that is,
just how rare and special a creature he, Burns, really was.

---

* The fourth volume of *À la recherche du temps perdu.*

I have known a few people to whom I didn't have
to condescend, against whom I didn't have to shut off a
sensitivity and a penetration that fascinates and horrifies
you. There is no need for me to justify myself. I have been
lonely because I have been excellent, and you know that
you pay a price for everything in this world, as the Irish
washerwoman says. Posterity (if there is any alive) will
pass judgment on me. That's all I want of life because the
rest has come and always will come easily. My perfection,
which is sadly lacking when it comes to small talk and
anything else more earthly than good manners and a certain
meekness, is not of the same rhythm as most of the people
you frequent. Otherwise you wouldn't be compelled to
turn to me so often, as though I held the answers in my
palm. Perhaps I do. Naturally I have often to isolate my
consciousness because I can't waste too much time of that
allotted to me.

Dazzled by his new self-knowledge, Burns was trying to throw his old self overboard. Learning from Holger Hagen that their dear friend from the Brooklyn Navy Yard, Robert MacLennan, had been killed in Germany in the final days of the war could only have fortified his resolve. "I just sat there numb for a long time, without even the American compensation of saying 'oh, shit,'" he wrote Hagen. "Then I went out and got drunk, the first time I've had to anesthetize myself in a long while." Burns said he loved MacLennan "with a special flame that will never flare for anyone else." In fact, the two were virtual strangers, or, as Burns put it, "except for our furious exchange of letters, we saw so little of one another. Yet the essence remains far more perfect than almost any other more protracted rapport I've had with anybody." And it was true: proximity and duration had little to do with Burns's notion of friendship; if anything, they were inimical to it.

The writing slowed down in July, when Burns flew up to Florence to be interviewed for a job at the new University Study Center being set up there for restless American soldiers marooned in Italy. After "malevolent and nerve-wracking" Naples, Burns suddenly felt repatriated. From the moment he'd stepped off the plane and cleared his eardrums, he wrote Holger Hagen, he'd been "in a trance of delight"; it was "as if Firenze had been waiting for me since Dante died in 1321." "I simply stand by the Arno and muse on a canto of the *Paradiso*, and the most incredible things start happening to me," he went on. "The Florentines and I seem to have some sort of atavistic understanding. You know that as an American I don't hold with this expatriate shit. I'm aware of the Joyce-in-Paris James-in-London brand of escapism. But I'm happy here for a while. And after 2 years of probing and malaise, I think I deserve my small orgasms." "We realize for the first time in our 28 years here what complete uncloying delight is," he told MacMackin. "We're going to buy ourselves a bicycle and settle down *per sempre*." If she ever expected to see him again, he told his mother, she'd have to come there.

For two years I wondered if there was any dignity left in humanity. Here it has been nobly re-affirmed for me. Just to see these handsome people in the streets, talking quietly among themselves (they never shout, as in Naples), the proud tranquil faces, the immaculate beautiful women with never a veneer of brittleness, and above all the exquisite manners and the quiet laughter have given me such a lift that I'm again finding in others the solace that I always had within myself. I seem to have lived through an ugly dream, to emerge unharmed into a sunlight that vitalizes but does not burn. The tempo of Florence is indefinable—brilliant without being tense, warm without being sticky.

"I'm now completely Italianized," he told her. "They tell me I look just like Dante Alighieri when I lean against a column. Met Beatrice Portinari by the Ponte Vecchio. She sends you her love."

Hanging out with other English-speaking expats at the bar of the once-luxurious Excelsior Hotel—even while much of Florence starved, string quartets still played there—or strolling along the river nearby, Burns seemed to meet everyone he'd ever known. Then, on his second day in town he met the newest closest friend he'd ever had. His name was Orlando Pennati, the son of a lawyer with a beautiful home on Via Maggio. Orlando, too, had survived a stint in the Italian army. The two men even looked alike. They passed their time sunbathing, walking, listening to music. "At midnight I took a jeep ride along the Arno feeling so delirious (without benefit of alcohol) that if the jeep had hit a bump, I'd have gone right on up and kept going, like Beatrice in the *Paradiso*," he told his father. If it hadn't meant risking court-martial, he'd not

Burns beheld Florence with much the same rapture as Dante beholding Beatrice.

have bothered returning to Naples for his bags. And until the U.S. Fifth Army came to town, "strutting and yelling like a basketball team," there were "few Americans around to thrust their drunkenness and bad manners on the dignity of the place."

Burns did repair to Caserta, cadging a ride south with an English paratrooper and a laconic Scotsman. Viewed from the ground rather than from a few thousand feet, traveling through Viterbo, Poggibonsi, Formia, and other ancient towns destroyed less by combat and retreating German troops than Allied bombs, he wondered whether Italy could ever be rebuilt, and whether the war had been as "clear cut as the newspapers would have you believe," and if it had all been worth it. "[O]ver the heaps of dust people are still picking their way around in what used to be their homes," he wrote his mother. "I cannot bear the expression in their eyes."

Burns was torn between Florence and Naples, which he saw as a battle between the past and the present, between escapism and engagement. Anyone so unsure about who he was, was, unsurprisingly, unsure about where he should go or what he should do next. He clenched his teeth and, as he explained to his mother, at least for a short while, he ate his spinach.

I recognize so well the urge to retreat into the beauty of Tuscany, and I know that if I ever yielded to it, anything good I might do with my life would be smothered. However much my sympathies are tied in with the calm and exquisite life I lived in Firenze, the fact remains that I'm an American living in 1945. I am not a Florentine and I am not an escapist. It's so easy after all the things I've seen and known to desire to crawl into a beautiful hole and cover one's burrow with tapestries. My instinct, which I trust profoundly, tells me I mustn't do this.

But suddenly, without a war hanging over them all, those *Na-politani* he'd so praised—all those street urchins clutching at his trousers—had become hard to take. And, for all his new "cool empathy," he was ready for a relapse. "I can't walk through some of the streets . . . without holding my nose and wishing that the poor squalid overcrowded people would leave me alone," he wrote. "In a sense it's something of a relief because for a long time I was so full of [the] mystical milk of human kindness that I had to keep checking on myself to make sure that I wasn't catching the paranoia of Paul Schonfeld, to be sent home in a straight jacket imagining that I was Jesus Christ." That job at the GI university in Florence looked increasingly tempting. As for after that, when he learned the State Department was looking for Italian speakers—a position that would let him stay abroad even longer—he vowed to apply.

15

One historic event to which Burns was *not* oblivious was the atom bomb, the first of which went off over Hiroshima on August 6. It disturbed Burns profoundly, more than any other aspect of the war; he returned to it repeatedly in his letters. In one, sent to his mother a few days afterward, he envisioned a postnuclear remnant retreating to caves with pianos and cooking utensils, procreating a new and more humane human race. "The first of the progeny who invents so much as a slingshot will be pushed off a cliff," he told her. To him, the bomb revealed yet another unpalatable side of American culture. "Even more fiendish than the invention itself is the callous joy with which it was greeted in the press, surely an indication of how far humanity has dropped in six years of war," he wrote. It only intensified his belief that America's essential impulses were dark, leaving it in no position to lecture anyone. "I see no further point in Americans babbling about atrocities, since it depends on who commits them, doesn't it?" he asked. It also strengthened his vow to make things better, or at least to explain the bad things he saw happening. "I am kept going by an antipathy to almost everything I see, by your letters, by music, and by my novel *The Gallery*, which has 'em in the aisles here, even in typescript," he wrote Holger Hagen two days after Hiroshima. "No second of my life must be wasted in non-essentials, sez I."

A few days in Southern Italy had him once more longing for Florence, and wondering whether he'd ever get back there. "Ten years from now I shall still be deciphering the handwriting of Benito Mussolini and compiling lists of his mistresses," he lamented. There was five hundred years' worth of work in the Fascist party files, and all of six people going through them. Equally formidable was the heat. "The amount of water, GI lemonade, iced tea and coffee I throw down daily is sufficient to float a Liberty Ship," he wrote. He also passed the time writing song lyrics in Italian, even though, as he told his father, he'd no desire to be "the Ira Gershwin of Italy."

But Burns finally got his walking papers, and in the wee hours of August 14, 1945, with Vesuvius still shrouded in the darkness, he flew back to Florence. Halfway up from Rome, the copilot stuck his head in the cabin. "War's over!" he cried over the rush of the motors and the wind. Thanks in part to the very bombs he had denounced, Japan had surrendered; he could stay in Florence for a while. Burns checked into the Excelsior for a night, then moved to the Majestic ("the perfect place for an old maid to die"), settling into "a drowsiness that is yet quite keen and perceptive, the way a dog sleeps." With its soothing air, its softness, its wisdom, its moderation, Florence was a place where nervous breakdowns were inconceivable. Even its ditchdiggers looked noble. But Burns still recognized the peculiar perils the place posed. Expatriates there became "enervated, as though some vital force had been sucked out of them," he conceded; he could see it in those

American women who married Florentines, then "lost their vitality and settled down to a gentle dream-like life of opium eaters. They produce the prettiest blond doll-like children you ever saw, and seem to have stopped living altogether, except in a trance."

He ventured to his new school and its 2,200 students. Some had been wounded in combat, some craved culture, some had fallen in love with Florence, some were simply in no rush to go back to that farm in Iowa. "I saw Brooklyn Jews eager to get home and start in the dry goods business, but also eager to get whatever the army was offering educationally," he wrote later. "I saw bright soft Japanese of the 442nd Infantry who are our most brilliant students. I saw negroes who are taking a little Italian because they have begotten themselves Italian children during the peninsular campaign." Collectively, they kept him more on his toes than the boys of Loomis ever had. Waiting tables and tending the grounds were German POWs, who were occasionally beaten up by ex-infantrymen. The buildings, in a former Italian army installation featuring a swimming pool and tennis courts, were given names like "Harvard" and "Princeton." Burns taught three classes a day (of French and Italian) five days a week, but with no Mr. B piling on the make-work, there were unaccustomed chunks of free time. Burns enjoyed touring Florence which, having already returned to its traditional rhythms, had emptied out for August, though without the tourists who traditionally took their places. The town was bathed in that golden Tuscan haze of Renaissance paintings.

Burns set about to cut *una bella figura* around town, instructing MacMackin (the two had evidently made up) to buy him both a fur-lined traveling cloak and a tippet at "Abbie, Dabbie and Bitch's."* After he told them he'd gladly be buried in Florence, his students joked about raising money for a plot alongside Elizabeth Barrett Browning in the old English cemetery. One

---

* Presumably Abercrombie & Fitch.

Sunday Burns stopped by the Church of Santissima Annunciata, and was "scandalized" by the shoddy casualness of Italian observance. With three Masses, their starts slightly staggered, going at once, parishioners came and went "like trains leaving Grand Central." Besides that blemish, for two weeks Burns was too entranced by Florence to return to his novel. But before long, he told MacMackin, he was retreating nightly to the Hotel Maestoso to write, from there to "sally forth for iced coffee and watch the dreadfulness of the evening." He planned on staying put, especially since, after the A-bomb, this world didn't seem long for this world anyway. And besides, he kept reading about how scarce jobs were back home, and had images of standing in breadlines with other veterans.

Nearly a year earlier, Batchelder had informed Burns that he'd continued contributing to his teacher's annuity, and it was a measure of Burns's new humanity, perhaps, that he'd actually been touched. "I probably sha'n't go back there to teach, but the gesture was a kindly one," he told his mother. It was also a sign that at least one job awaited him stateside. But as dire as the situation was, Burns couldn't see returning to Loomis or any prep school: "I now know too much of the world to work on the souls of rich and stupid adolescents who waste four years because their families desire it," he wrote. He'd take a month to see his family, then return to Europe for the State Department. He filled out his application; certainly few candidates were better qualified. The form was exhaustive, going into such issues as whether he'd ever had a nervous breakdown. Asked why he wanted to join the foreign service, he boasted to his mother, "I concocted a bit of English prose which for pithiness, eloquence, materialism and spirituality, deserves to rank alongside of the Gettysburg Address."

Burns the novelist hadn't retrenched: by mid-September, *The Gallery* was already half-done. In Florence, too, its composition was a quasi-public event: "*Caro poeta, come si tira avanti [con] la*

No.

To

JOSEPH L BURNS
89 Gainsboro Street
Boston (15)
Massachusetts

From

01 003 087
1 Lt John Horne Burns
(Sender's name)

Hq University Training
(Sender's address)

Command-MTO- APO 49

sun 26 aug 45
(Date)

(CENSOR'S STAMP)

Dear Daddy,   Quella Firenze di Toscana

I heard Mass this morning in the church of Santissima Annunziata. I was
scandalized. The church itself is a huge thing hung with crude red tapestries,
vulgar offerings in the form of precious medals hung in cases like collections
of trophies of the hunt, and paintings all over the ceiling. Many of the
women came uncovered - not so much as a handkerchief on their hair. It was
the 'SocietyMass' at 1100 hours. At the main altar a high Mass was in progress,
which I vainly tried to follow. All about me there was constant motion, because
at the two side altars low Masses were being said one right after the other,
like trains leaving Grand Central. It was like a sacrilegious three ring
circus. In twenty minutes three consecrations occurred in various parts of
the church, so that I didn't know where to look or where to do reverence.
The nave in European churches is constantly clear - no chairs or pews: the
congregation stands throughout the service. The congregation is in constant
ebb and flow because of the difference in timing of the three simultaneous
Masses. No one seemed to be paying any attention to what was going on. I felt
that I was in an art gallery at tea time. The conversation was like a courtesan
reception - everyone discussed everyone else audibly: who was whose mistress,
etc. For the solemn Mass, which I futilely tried to follow, there was a
huge organ and a choir of men hidden behind a chancel screen. They sang
well in the chants, but the music for the Mass itself was a tawdry and noisy
operatic affair. I was certain of having been in church only when Renzo
touched my hand with holy   water as we left.
                                                        Love,

V-MAIL

A typical Burns V-mail, pungent and snug

Sua Galleria?"* artsy Florentines would stop him on the street to ask. "I thought at first it was going to turn into something many-volumed and Proustian, but by much brooding and UnThomaswolfeian pruning and planning it now stands in my head at about 800 printed pages of gorgeous marble to the end of an era," he wrote. A "behemoth," yes, but an *accessible* one: "I think I can be better than Mother Joyce and not caviar to the general [public] because I have decided to write definitely in this world and not out of it, which seems to have been the disastrous track of art in the last 50 years," he vowed. There'd be chapters on individual characters, interspersed with streams of thought from a composite American soldier. "I think it is very good, and without any twin in any language that I know. But there I go in the megolamania of the Artist a la Mann and Goethe," he wrote Holger Hagen. He'd decided to dedicate it to the two Hagens and the late Mac-Lennan, each of whom had given him more than anyone else ever had. The Hagens must have found his ardor flattering, and more than a little perplexing.

For the first time since grade school, Burns's weekends were free. Rather than take the usual day trips to Siena and San Gimignano, he stuck around town. Thousands of the unemployed stood along the Arno, their ranks swelling as veterans returned. The situation was combustible, and would grow worse as the Americans began to leave. Their livelihoods disappearing, Italian women made their futile pitches to Burns. They were more subtle than the "Wanna blowjob, Joe?" of Naples; a rich countess in Fiesole, a former Fascist, wanted to turn him into a kept man; the blond switchboard operator at his school sat down beside him one day while he played Liu's song from Puccini's *Turandot* and declared, *"Ah, che bocca squisita che c'ha, Lei!"* "I rushed screaming out into the night," Burns told his mother. "I know I have a

---

* "Dear poet, how are you progressing with your *Galleria?*"

nice mouth, but it surely isn't that nice!" But some Italian women maintained their dignity, as Burns discovered one night at Florence's main train station, and recounted afterward to his mother.

Last evening after supper I mosied out into the Piazza della Stazione for a shoe shine. The station itself is a gorgeous affair of the noblest Fascist modernism. Now no trains run out of it because it is a GI rest camp. I couldn't find any little boys at sundown. Instead a fairly young woman motioned me to sit in her chair. I thought twice about having a woman shine my shoes, but thinking she could use the ten lire and the cigarette tip, I sat down and watched her thin blond hair bent over my shoes with polish and buffer. She's the mother of two small boys who each take their turn on the stand. Her husband is a prisoner

Florence's train station was without trains.

*of war in California, and seems to be the best off of all
the family by the provisions of the Geneva Convention. I
know enough about the Prisoner of War game to know that
she was telling the truth. It was repugnant to me to have
a mother doing such a menial job. I listened to her story,
which is the same they all have, monotonous yet terrible—
the pains in the stomach from not enough to eat, the worry
over her small children, that complete loneliness since she
hadn't seen her husband in four years. Multiply her case
by thousands. She made her choice between going on the
sidewalks or shining shoes, and chose the latter. Povera
Italia, as they say! I wonder if they'll ever be able to pull
themselves together again. There isn't a day but that I don't
see something that makes me wonder whether there's any
bottom to human wretchedness. But as you've told me many
times, watching what has happened to others is the most
marvelous way of taking one out of himself.*

Had Burns been interested, sex for hire was easily within reach,
and not just for straight men. "For those of the opposite taste,"
he told Holger Hagen, "it is more than easy to maintain a young
carabiniere or *reduce** who has nothing but North Italian looks
and manners and the clothes on his back."

Burns waived the points he'd accumulated—which would
have moved him up in the line of soldiers returning home—and
contemplated a tour of France, Germany, and England. He mused
about a sabbatical for his mother in Florence, and how he'd rent
her a prime apartment on the corner of Via Tornabuoni and the
Lungarno. Exile still had its appeal; "because I suffer from ma-
turities and illnesses and virtues more European than American
in our present stage of development, I can be happy wherever

---

* A "survivor" of a battle or some other ordeal.

there is enough to eat, enough hooch, enough music, and enough people to prey on," he told Hagen. But shortly before his twenty-ninth birthday, he had another medical setback. This time it was hepatitis.

Once more he landed in the hospital, though not behind barbed wire. Far from it: he was on his own Magic Mountain, a former tuberculosis sanatorium in the Tuscan hills; the double doors in his room led out to a *terrazza* from which, when the mists lifted, he could see Florence's gargantuan cathedral, the Duomo, in the distance. But his gaze was on other, closer things. "I keep looking at my toes, 72 inches away from me under a GI hospital blanket," he wrote Hagen. "They're Theophile Gautier* saffron; in fact, every part of me is yellow." With this disease, unlike the last, Burns's own culpability wasn't clear. "Perhaps I drank some Arno water," he theorized. "Perhaps I dallied amorously with an Italian in whose liver the virus was already wriggling. But anyway, here I am on my back without any of the concomitant pleasures." All novel-writing stopped. Meanwhile, letters from home, the arrival of carpetbagging Americans, and the "cretinous fluff" from the American radio programs he was forced to listen to while convalescing had fortified his resolve to stay in Europe. "At my bedside the American radio station drools out our brand of civilization—half hour after half hour of screaming comedians with tittering studio audience, 'vocalists' with no perceptible variety or style, the same dozen tunes every program," he complained. "All calculated to numb the sheep. Sometimes it seems that our 'mass level' is merely an inane totalitarianism from a spiritual Ford Plant."

Continually on his back—"lying still and supine for four weeks has the effect of coloring one's thoughts with the tint of the dust under which we must all lie some day," he wrote his mother—he

---

* The French poet, writer, critic, and painter (1811–1872) who wrote extensively on color.

contemplated more trips, to Berlin, Munich, Vienna, or Marseilles. He read twelve hours a day, enough to finish three Armed Services Editions novels ("the only good thing to have come out of the war"). Some books came as pleasant surprises to him, like works by E. B. White and the early Maugham. After dark, he heard civilization returning to Europe via broadcasts from the cities of the late Third Reich; Mahler and Mendelssohn were back on German radio. He sent his mother Italian lessons, like the phrase for "poor, dirty baby." A former student from Florence had sent him the Sunday *New York Times* for September 9, 1945, even though, as he put it, "I did nothing in class to give her the impression that I might be so conservative as to be titillated by Mr. Sulzberger's rag." Again docked for his hospital time—suggesting, perhaps, that the army had come to its own conclusion about how Burns had contracted the disease—his finances grew so perilous that he had to ask his mother to send back fifty of the precious dollars he had sent *her*. When a woman in the hospital asked him if he'd found some love in Italy, he did not tell her that that was what may have brought him to the hospital in the first place.

His time there meant he had missed the start of the Florentine concert and opera seasons. Then, with the Americans leaving town, he moved with his hospital to Livorno. For him, it was storied territory: Shelley had drowned just off the coast of the city. After thirty-nine days on the wagon, his liver had rebounded, even though he faced another six months of abstinence. "The alternative is a relapse, convulsions, and *der Tod, das ist die kühle Nacht*,"* he noted. He read a biography of Justice Oliver Wendell Holmes, Jr., and *The Grapes of Wrath*, and reread Proust and *Anna Karenina*. Within a few weeks he was

---

* The title of a Heine poem—in English, "Death, That Is the Cool Night"—that Brahms, among others, set to music.

able to endure three foreign service tests, though the examination room was freezing and the questions rough. "I very much doubt whether Cordell Hull* himself would have showed up anything else but an imbecile on them," Burns told his mother. He was back in Florence for Thanksgiving, then ordered up to Milan, which, with its many languages and elegant stores, marked his first visit to a cosmopolitan city in several years; its women could have walked out of the windows at Lord & Taylor. "I was at first a little lost, and given to standing in the Piazza del Duomo with my mouth open, looking for the lions of the Public Library," he wrote Hagen. All that was missing was American cigarettes; to Herbert Tareyton's great consternation, he had switched to Lucky Strikes, and asked his mother to send him a carton every week. Statelessness suited him. "The third Christmas away from home was so pleasant that I must rest convinced that I'm one of those rootless amoebae who are happiest independent of everything except life itself," he wrote Hagen.

His day job now consisted, as he put it, of investigating the claims of Italians knocked off their bicycles by American jeeps. He moved into the Hotel Continental, and awaited the reopening of the bombed-out La Scala in February, though he could still see two operas a day elsewhere in town. (Even in temporary quarters, the Milanese opera was the best he'd ever heard, marred only by Italian fans so ill-mannered that *he* lectured *them* about *gentilezza*. "I like them better in my arms than in a concert hall," he told Beulah Hagen.) It was in another gallery—the Galleria Vittorio Emmanuelle II, the prototype of the Galleria Umberto—that he encountered, in furs and a black Homburg, the elderly Umberto Giordano, the composer of *Andrea Chénier*, another of the operas Burns had seen repeatedly, and come to love, in Naples. "Together we wept over Italy for half an hour," he told Hagen. He

---

* Then the United States secretary of state.

also resumed his dipsomania. "My renovated liver seems to be taking its alcohol douches very nicely," he boasted. *The Gallery* remained stalled: two-thirds complete. "I wish I could soooffffer a little so I could write the last three chapters," he complained. Meantime, Burns had met the latest love of his life. This one was named Mario.

16

Burns felt sure he'd land a State Department post. "They'll take me for my snob value and eddication," he predicted. But it never happened. Did he fail on the merits? That seems improbable. More likely it was his homosexuality or his alcoholism, or his hospitalization at Camp Croft, or his bouts with syphilis and hepatitis, any one of which could have emerged during a background check. Whether Burns agonized over this turn of events, or tried to find some other way to stay in Europe, isn't clear. There's a gap in his correspondence between late December 1945 and February 1946, and when it resumes, he's suddenly back in the United States. Perhaps, he wrote Hagen a few months after his return, it was all just as well. "My only justification for leaving Italy is that I too must shortly have been under the care of a psychiatrist," he mused. "My only wisdom is that one American couldn't shed all the tears of forty million people and live." But returning after twenty-four tumultuous months was not easy.

What made it bearable was *The Gallery*, but that was iffy: for all his literary pretensions, he was utterly unknown.

He'd landed back in New York in February 1946. Not quite ready to deal with the place, he quickly retreated to far more manageable Boston. More manageable, maybe, but unpalatable: instantly, he was turned off by American-style hucksterism, escapism, materialism, optimism, hedonism. Burns the rampant dreadful had suddenly grown almost puritanical. "When I came back to America from Italy, I was shocked at what you call the American schizophrenia," he wrote a former student named Henry Breul. "To be sure, everybody was fucking everybody else, both naturally and unnaturally. But they did it without the generousness one expects in love. In other words, the experience of predatory and indiscriminate sex had narrowed them and made them meaner. They have all kinds of psychic blocks against real frankness. They pretend to be so nicey-nice." Having inexplicably alerted neither of them beforehand, in mid-February he sprang on both MacMackin and Beulah Hagen that he was back. He promised MacMackin he would come down to New York soon. In the meantime, he invited him "alla Sodoma di Bostone," but noted that with all of his servicemen brothers newly returned, the family's apartment was too crowded for putting him up. "And you'll guess the situation with the hotels in this strange little city," he went on, in Italian. "There isn't even a room available for the strangest and most ephemeral of weddings, much less so for the dear, sad one of the (pair of) lovers!" Burns's mistakes made his message, already ambiguous, even more cryptic.

"All I do is rest and finish up *The Gallery*, dedicated to you and Moe," he wrote Beulah. "I've got to make something of my life, said he seriously." He told her his novel was "one of *the* manuscripts of the twentieth century." He told MacMackin that the book was "like nothing since *King Lear*." He even showed it to strangers. A man in Boston later recalled that when he'd picked

Burns up one night at Phil's Punch Bowl, a gay bar on Piedmont Street near the Statler Hotel, he had been carrying the manuscript; when they retired to the man's apartment, Burns read him a bit.

Not one morsel of Burns's newfound humanity extended to his countrymen, or his country. It was just as he had feared: "Most of the Americans are numb and even more lacking in dignity than they ever were," he told Hagen. "The only worries are butter and Nylons. The returning service men are either utterly brutalized and surprised that they can't have every twelve year old girl they see, or in a fuckedup daze because they can't or won't find jobs. Most have learned nothing but to love excitement for its own sake. Many would gladly return overseas—but only to exploit people who have already suffered enough from our loving hands." He decried American provincialism, xenophobia, and bellicosity, particularly against the Soviet Union. "Other than the fact that Russia has a dictatorship as vicious as Italy's and Germany's were, I have great admiration for her," he wrote. Americans had never attempted to understand Soviet Russia; "most of them have no idea of what Communism is other than some red bogey flung at them by William Randolph Hearst and their boss, who naturally is interested in flinging mud at a social system which is directly opposed to his own interests." But whether they liked it or not, the war and its role in winning it entitled Russia to become one of the world's two great powers. "It behooves us therefore to understand her rather than to snipe at her," he urged. "Or if we snipe, be sure that the Land of the Free isn't also snipeable-at." But a few unidentified people he had encountered in unspecified places, idealists without illusions, gave Burns hope that all was not lost. "All I have to do now is establish myself for what I Think I Am," he wrote Holger Hagen. "And I think I can."

What he needed was a perch, and with all its faults good old Loomis fit the bill, at least for now. As soon as he'd heard Burns was back, Mr. B made him what Burns called a "juicy" offer to come back to the Island and finish out the school year. Burns quickly agreed. "I figured the dough and the occupation were better than hanging around bars, which I do anyway," he told Hagen. To Batchelder, he mustered a bit more enthusiasm. "Naturally, I want very much to return to Loomis," he wrote him. "Sometime next month when I am completely rested and sane, I will be down to the dear Island to visit everybody." By early April, he was back in Windsor, and back to all the old routines—sort of. Aunt Olive had even returned his music. As he wrote Beulah Hagen in late April 1946:

> *I'm in a double-breasted suit and a bow tie. They tell me with condescension that I've made a nice adjustment to civilian life. This is because they don't see me in my spells of depression . . . So here I am back pushing around the souls of adolescents. I'm well paid, but I'm not too happy at it as I've always considered a New England prep school as unnatural and unholy. But it's one of the things I know how to do. After what I've seen and know of the world, the people here and what they worry about strike me as just silly. The only compensation other than the financial one is my phonograph and a thousand records—if I may talk of music as an opiate.*

Predictably, the new Burns and the old Loomis were a combustible combination. The pre–Pearl Harbor ground rules were increasingly hard for him to abide. It was just as his alter ego would put it in *Lucifer with a Book:* "Did he know too much of the world to be a bright-eyed scoutmaster for shrieking kids of twelve and thirteen?" Douglas McKee had stayed in France, and was aghast at Burns's decision. "I couldn't imagine why anyone would want to go back to Loomis, which was worse than the army," he later wrote. Burns's other faculty friends, the Eatons, had also moved on. The school had hired a "bleating old fool" (Burns's words) as its new chaplain, part of what Burns, who'd have to endure his sermons from the organist's bench, viewed as a more general decline. There were all the usual minutiae. "I'm still as busy as ever about nothing, and Henry Adams' remark that the Teacher affects Eternity doesn't console me," he wrote Beulah Hagen.

Perhaps worst of all, the new chairman of the English department—that is, Burns's boss—was Norrie Orchard. And the war had only fortified Burns's old prejudices against him: by serving in the military while the chairman hadn't—like Frank Sinatra, he had had something wrong with his eardrum—Burns was now even more of a man than Orchard. It didn't matter that in his letters to MacMackin, Burns was far more "swish" than Orchard ever was. Orchard was the sort of conspicuously effeminate man Burns had disdained in his unit, the old lady type more masculine gay soldiers resented for confirming the straight stereotype of the homosexual. Burns may have distanced himself from Orchard because, on some level, he feared he was so much the same. "To serve in a department headed by his chief abomination must have ignited his war-induced smoldering ire and unconcealed scorn," Sidney Eaton later wrote. "He returned, then, to a seeming alien community in a bitter mood."

Burns let himself run amok, at least by decorous prep school standards. "We're making a shambles of the Institute," he wrote MacMackin, who had, since Burns's departure from Loomis, gone on to Harvard, dropped out, and moved to New York, where he moved into a building on West Sixty-seventh Street designed for musicians and took on musical odd jobs. "There's simply a landslide of brwaugh and dreadfulness here now. Well, this weekend we entertained a Louer* in our apartments, and tonight we have another who hasn't forgotten us since Naples. We drink

---

* Probably a male prostitute.

THE
LOOMIS BULLETIN

NORRIS ELY ORCHARD 1911 - 1957

VOLUME XXV   JULY, 1957   NUMBER 3

Burns's nemesis

sherry in my room at teatime then barge into the dining room and hold a salon at our table." In a parody issue, the *Log* took note of his return.

When it was first known that Mr. Burns had decided to stay on at Loomis, we put on our Florentine shawl and bustled over to Mason Second* for an exclusive interview. There in his salon we found Mr. John Horne Burns clad in a night chemise sitting on the mauve ottoman. He was by his record player (the one with the twin speakers) listening to Signora Pataleoni as Desdemona in Verdi's Othello [sic]. "Shh," he hissed, "she's just finished Piangea cantando, the Willow Song. Emilia has retired and now—(At this point the two speakers sobbed Ave Maria plena de'grazia) she retires to her couch, Othello steals in, dagger in hand—(Here we were frightened by somber contra basse) and . . . now . . . he smothers her, then—oh –"

At this point he swooned away in sympathy and we had to ply him with sal volatile and gillyflower water. When he arose he brought out a hoarded supply of Bruciate Briachi and zabiaone (toasted chestnuts and egg punch) and passed it to us . . .

In a more serious vein, the *Log* reported that "Mr. Burns has the distinction of being the only Loomis Master ever to have written a full-length novel." In fact, it noted, he was working on the last chapter. In fact, he was soon writing *the last words* of the last chapter.

Burns had been unusually antisocial that spring, passing brusquely by students on his corridor, then closing his door to drink (they surmised) and type (they could hear). "I felt the man

---

* His dormitory suite.

had a huge chip on his shoulder," recalled one student who, having heard about the legendary Burns, had eagerly anticipated his return. "I don't remember ever seeing him smile. I sensed anger. He wasn't the same man that had been described to me by other people." And finally, sitting at his desk one night in late April, the rows of elms blossoming outside his window, Burns somehow conjured up the building, and the city, four thousand miles away, that had moved him so deeply. "Outside the Galleria Umberto is the city of Naples," he wrote. "And Naples is on the bay, in the Tyrrhenian Sea, on the Mediterranean. This sea is a center of human life and thought. Wonderful and sad things have come out of Italy. And they came back there in August 1944. For they were dots in a circle that never stops." At the bottom of the page he marked the remarkably short life span of so ambitious a project: 18 June 1945–23 April 1946. Then he listed the book's long and unlikely itinerary: Naples; Caserta; Florence; Leghorn; Milan; Boston; Windsor, Connecticut. And then he was done, and on Shakespeare's birthday at that. "I fell across my Underwood and wept my heart out," he wrote Hagen. "*The Gallery*, I fear, is one of the masterpieces of the twentieth century." "My God!" his sister Cathleen exclaimed when she read it. His mother wept all night when *she* did. But from Burns's perspective, the most satisfying appraisal came from another soldier: "Unarty." "He said, 'Jeez, I tought I was reading just anudder war novel, and pretty soon an atomic bomb dropped on me,'" Burns told Hagen. *The Gallery*, he wrote Beulah Hagen, was the first truly good thing he had produced. The problem now was getting it noticed. He would get it published, and that year, he told Holger Hagen, "if I have to give a facejob to every publisher and agent in New York City."

17

There's an arcade in Naples that they call the Galleria Umberto Primo. It's a cross between a railroad station and a church. You think you're in a museum till you see the bars and the shops. Once this Galleria had a dome of glass, but the bombings of Naples shattered this skylight, the tinkling glass fell like cruel snow to the pavement. But life went on in the Galleria. In August 1944 it was the unofficial heart of Naples. It was a living and subdividing cell of vermouth, Allied soldiery, and the Italian people . . . Everybody in Naples came to the Galleria Umberto.

The Gallery was divided into nine portraits—primarily of American soldiers but also of two Italian women—and eight "promenades": personal reflections of an anonymous narrator as he wanders from one image, and one place, to another. Its closest counterpart isn't in literature but in music: Mussorgsky's Pictures

at an Exhibition, a piece Burns knew well: it was one of the recordings he had left in Aunt Olive's care. "You're quite right in
guessing that it defies description," Burns wrote Hagen. "It's not
arty, clever, or even recondite. But I fear (and in how many senses
this may be taken!) that there's nothing like it in literature. It has
a form all its own, a unity all its own." It wasn't really a novel.
Burns himself didn't know what to call it; "A Mediterranean
Sketchbook," it was originally subtitled.

The promenades retrace his path through North Africa and
into Italy. But only when Burns reaches Naples, and the Galleria,
does he seem fully engaged. At one point or another, everyone
profiled in Naples finds himself or herself under the Galleria's
shattered canopy. There's Michael Patrick, the lonely, homesick
Irish-American soldier—named, if not necessarily modeled, after
the GI who cried on Burns's shoulder at the opera—who's temporarily been spared another trip to the front by a case of trench
foot. And Luella, the officious, self-satisfied, proudly provincial
Red Cross volunteer. There's Major Motes (devilishly named
after one of Burns's Camp Croft lovers, from Biloxi, Mississippi),
the onetime petroleum engineer turned censorship czar, a martinet, faker, and empire builder who, having had the time of his life
abroad, dreads returning to his arid marriage back in Roanoke.
And Father Donovan and Chaplain Bascom, clerics on opposite
ends of the Christian spectrum engaged in a friendly theological
rivalry as they serve the troops. And Giulia, a nineteen-year-old
Italian girl determined, despite all odds and pressures and the
poor example of her peers, to protect her virtue from the American occupiers. And the nameless soldier who, in a searing chapter
called "Queen Penicillin," recounts Burns's own nightmarish encounter at "Mussolini's fairground."

Only that chapter of the book can compete with what is clearly
its most remarkable portrait: of Momma, the proprietress of the
Galleria's gay bar. After the evasiveness and subterfuge in Burns's

own life, it is a ringing proclamation of his homosexuality, bursting out astonishingly, unexpectedly, unambiguously from the pages of the book, even though nothing in it is ever quite explicit. Writing it was an act of enormous and almost inexplicable courage: it is hard to see from what part of his soul Burns had suddenly summoned it, and how, having written it, he could have ever expected to return to the closet afterward—except, that is, if he somehow knew that anything having to do with homosexuality was so taboo that "Momma" would simply never be acknowledged—as, indeed, it almost never was.

Theatrical and vain, Momma isn't actually Neapolitan at all: she hails from Milan, and has a typical Northern Italian's contempt for Italians from the Mezzogiorno. But she'd married a local and she and Poppa, who are childless, had lived sumptuously in Piazza Garibaldi until the bombs fell, forcing them to move into a dreary suite on the Galleria's third floor. What she'd lost in elegance, though, she'd gained in convenience. For, beginning right after the Allies liberated Naples in October 1943, and running every night but Sunday from 1630 hours to 1930, gay soldiers from every branch of the Grand Alliance—Americans, Brits, Canadians, Australians, South Africans, French—have gathered at her bar downstairs, in the heart of the Galleria. Some come by themselves, some as couples, some in groups; some come to look, some for action, some just to show up. They run the gamut from macho to effeminate; some sport wedding rings. Racially, too, they're varied, to a degree unusual in what was still a segregated American military; a black second lieutenant who frequents the place likes to sing "Strange Fruit."*

For all their geographic and stylistic diversity, there is a homogeneity to these men, and, with an exception or two, men is what they all are. They are bound together by their wisdom,

---

* The 1939 anti-lynching song popularized by Billie Holiday.

refinement, brilliance, joie de vivre. Burns's portrait is tolerant, indulgent, affectionate: there is none of the hostility he displayed toward his gay colleagues at Loomis or in the army. In his trailblazing study *The Homosexual in America*, Edward Sagarin (writing under the pen name Donald Webster Cory) disclosed a few years later how he, as a gay man, "alternately felt myself trapped by a human tragedy to which I could never adjust, or blessed as one of the elite of the world." In "Momma," Burns placed himself squarely into Sagarin's second group. Whether he was celebrating himself or simply trying to convince himself he was really all right, any ambivalence or self-hatred had at least temporarily been shelved.

> *They had an air of being tremendously wise, older than the human race. They understood one another, as though from France and New Zealand and America they all had membership cards in some occult freemasonry. And they had a refinement of manner, an intuitive appreciation of [Momma] as a woman. Their conversation was flashing, bitter, and lucid. More than other men they laughed much together, laughing at life itself perhaps. Momma'd never seen anything like her boys. Some were extraordinarily handsome. They had an acuteness in their eyes and a predatory richness of the mouth as though they'd bitten into a pomegranate. Momma dreamed that she was queen of some gay exclusive club.*

Momma's boys know that they have been born alone and are "sequestered by some deep difference from other men." Momma herself knows of the Four Freedoms the Allies are forever preaching, one of which is surely to be left alone. But not *stay* alone, at least if they, and she, can help it. Everyone in there has Burns's own darting eyes.

When Momma's bar was full, it was like a peacock's tail because she could see nothing but eyes through the cigarette smoke. Restless and unsocketed eyes that wheeled all around, wholly taken up in the business of looking and calculating. Eyes of every color. Momma's bar when crowded was a goldfish bowl swimming with retinas and irises in motion.

On familiar ground in "Momma," Burns is at his most sincere, and comfortable, and wise, and empathetic, and effective. And edifying: through a conversation between two comrades who today would be described as "good girlfriends"—British sergeants calling themselves "Esther" and "Magda"—he attempts to illuminate a world that most people would have preferred not even to acknowledge, let alone understand. He explains the ties, beyond the purely sexual, that bind gay men together: "Since the desire to live, in its truest sense of reproducing, isn't in them, they live for the moment more passionately than most." For all they share, though, he offers a taxonomy of gay types, suggesting the great pain and turbulence that comes with being a homosexual. As he saw it, there were three, all neatly represented among Momma's clientele: "Some hold back in their minds and distrust what they're doing. In them are the seeds of schizophrenia and destruction. Others give themselves wholly up to their impulses with a dizziness and a comic sense that are revolting to the more serious ones. Lastly there's a group which sees that they can profit by everything in this world. These are the sane." And this is where Burns would have placed himself. And once having sated their appetites, their reactions, too, diverge: some feel defiled; others crave more; still others will try for something, or someone, different the next night.

Summing up the chapter, Burns expresses the hope that out of the war, and the species of horror either invented or refined during it, will come a new code, one permitting this repressed but irrepressible portion of humanity to surface and prosper without any adverse judgments attached. "How can we speak of sin when thousands are cremated in German furnaces?" he writes, in one of *The Gallery*'s few references to Nazi atrocities, or to Germans at all. "These people are expressing a desire disapproved of by society. But in relation to the world of 1944, this is just a bunch of gay people letting down their back hair."*

One crucial question looms over "Momma," one that appears never to have been raised, either when it first appeared or ever since: whether any of it is true. Everyone had a reason not to ask this question. Straight people, particularly in the American military, may have been too embarrassed at the very existence of such a place, or else too indifferent to it. Gay people of that era, especially anyone who may have frequented Momma's, may have been too sheepish or fearful to have acknowledged it. And, simply as a point of pride, gay people later on may simply have assumed it had really been. By the time anyone thought to question the genuineness of Momma's bar, everyone who would have remembered it was dead. That includes Burns himself, who appears never to have elaborated on the topic, probably because he, too, was never asked. For decades, "Momma" has sat there, unexamined.

It seems astonishing that Burns could have invented a place so vivid, richly detailed, and persuasive. Back home, gay bars sprang up in every major city where American soldiers congregated, and one could have appeared in wartime Naples, too. While, even in the book, military police threaten to close the place—"You're getting away with murder in this joint," a major with a porky hand tells Momma. "Either you get rid of most of the people who come

---

* Though it's startling to see the word "gay" appear (twice) in something written in 1947, it had already been in use for a decade or more. And with thousands of gay soldiers circulating it during the war it became, as Sagarin put it, "a magic byword in practically every corner of the United States where homosexuals might gather."

here, or we'll put you off limits"—they may well have just have been going through the motions. The sexual enlightenment World War II provided went both ways; for many straight men, too, it marked an education in sexual culture—their first prolonged encounter with homosexuals; three years into the fighting, they had presumably grown used to them and, whatever were the rules, content to live and let live, which was why Momma's, if it really existed, wasn't shut down.

What's mystifying, and disconcerting, is that no one besides Burns—whether journalist, memoirist, or Neapolitan—ever described Momma's, before or since. This, despite its extreme conspicuousness—a bar catering exclusively to men (American gay bars often had mixed clienteles) in the very heart of the very heart of a homophobic Catholic city, and one under the control of a military administration in which homosexuality was officially proscribed. Additionally puzzling is that as minutely as they chronicled dreadful Naples, Burns's letters to MacMackin never mentioned Momma's. Even vanished institutions leave remnants, and no one in contemporary Naples seems to have heard even rumors of such a place.

It seems more likely than not, then, that Burns made the whole thing up, creating an elaborate fantasy of openness and tolerance to challenge his storytelling skills, proclaim who he was, defend his culture and his friends, and plea for greater understanding and acceptance. "It was his very own cathartic cantina where his projections and fantasies played out nightly . . . in his mind," Larry Ray, a journalist and longtime resident of Naples, has written. At best, he speculates, Momma's was "a huge exaggeration of what might have been some casual meeting place in the Galleria for 'cruising' by some homosexuals," not a bar per se but "some dark seedy area like the archway and *cortile.*" But whether it is a work of reportage or wishful thinking and magic realism or something in between—indeed, in part *because of* that very uncertainly—"Momma" is astonishing, one of those artistic miracles that is almost impossible to explain. As Mark Bassett has pointed out, even taken by itself it would have guaranteed Burns's place in gay literary history, and in gay history generally. But "Momma" doesn't stand alone. There are ample other gay or gay-style characters in *The Gallery*, both likable and loathsome.

The portrait of Hal, an unhappy GI who suffers a nervous breakdown, features a variety of what the gay historian Roger Austen called "bobby-pin clues" about his homosexuality, like calling himself "dear" and hanging out at Pennsylvania Station at five in the morning. The captain who returns from the dead in Sicily to speak to him had been a chorus boy on Broadway. One of the fussbudget flunkies around Major Motes twitches his mustache "daintily," mops his face with a scented handkerchief, and wears a flowered kimono before bedtime; another carries around Fowler's *Modern English Usage*, organizes a glee club, and teaches his French students the poems of François Villon. (Clearly, Burns was not above mocking himself. The man even had thinning blond hair.) A "gentian-eyed" former dancer who befriends the anonymous patient at the VD clinic actually rails against gays. "I'm so fed up with the arty boys," he complains. "I'm so bored with sitting around in cliques and drinking and talking poetry and scandal." In depicting various alter egos, Burns makes further stabs at heterosexuality, but once again, they're not very convincing. When the virginal Michael Patrick finally gets around to kissing a woman, for instance, he doesn't seem to know where on her to do it. Quite apart from *Momma*, the very profusion of gay characters underlies what a breakthrough *The Gallery* was: unlike prior gay novels, in which the few homosexual characters are tormented, exotic, or dangerous, and invariably effeminate, here they are everywhere and, while they have their quirks, they are, collectively at least, *normal*. And, certainly for the first time, most of them are in uniform.

Very nearly as startling about *The Gallery* is its pervasive anti-Americanism, which neatly tracks Burns's letters to family and friends. America, he writes in it, is "a country just like any other, except that she had more material wealth and more advanced plumbing." And Americans are "very poor spiritually," with "bankrupt souls." And American soldiers are worst of all.

Burns's disillusionment with them begins on the troop ship to Europe, when he sees GIs stealing from one another. It picks up in the second sentence of the opening portrait: Michael Patrick keeps "saying *scusate* because he wanted to make amends for the way the other doughfeet yelled at the Neapolitans and called them *paesan*." Almost without exception, whatever their rank or station, American soldiers are coarse, bigoted, exploitative, inarticulate, provincial, predatory, dishonest. Around Naples, honest Americans are nearly as scarce as former Fascists. They flood Naples with their Palmolive soap, clothes, cigarettes, gum, pens, and K-rations, lining the pockets of their khakis on the American taxpayers' dime. They are heartless pigs, gorging themselves in their mess halls, then throwing away mounds of uneaten grub while starving Italians look on. Their very posture—the way they loiter and lean and loll about—is surly, insolent. They are (hetero)-sexually insatiable, turning the city into a giant bordello and the Galleria into a sexual bourse. "A soldier who gave food to a hungry girl for love," he writes, "was outside the human race."

In fact, Burns's GIs aren't human at all; they are Fauvist monsters. They are fat and animal-like, with double chins, pot-bellies, and jowls. "Under his helmet she saw his yellowish face, pitted with the craters of his adolescence," he writes of one. "His eyes were like oranges in blood. His mouth was a line of purple." American officers ostentatiously squire around mistresses while their wives wait ignorantly back home. Soldiers push old ladies off sidewalks and hit draymen with clubs. That the Italians had been enemies "was taken as a license for Americans to defecate all over them." In contrast to the GIs, the Italian POWs, especially the officers, are dignified and worldly. Italian whores are far more simpatico than the most upright WACs. Burns's Italians actually look back at their Nazi occupiers with nostalgia; of the Americans' abuses, he writes, "I don't think the Germans could have done any better in their concentration camps." Burns is actually angrier at the Americans than the Neapolitans ever were. His loathing seems to tap into something far broader than what was happening in Naples—into a more general revulsion for mainstream American, and American straight culture, the culture of his ostensible betters. *The Gallery's* few sympathetic heterosexuals are misfits, or at least atypical. One, the Brooklyn cabdriver Moe Schulman—he even gets to wear Burns's most endearing sobriquet—is a Jew. A second and third are the two clergymen. A fourth, Giulia's American fiancé, is so ugly that he almost *has* to be nice.

Nearly all of the most sympathetic figures in *The Gallery* share one trait: they sound like Burns. "I annihilated my own personality completely in producing it," Burns told Holger Hagen. That's not right. In fact, he cloned it. *The Gallery* is a gallery of Burns doppelgängers who, though varying in rank, appearance, erudition, nationality, religion, and even sex, are all empathetic, alluring, aloof, and wise.

Burns is the narrator in the promenades, who must go abroad to learn empathy. He's also Michael Patrick, the lonely, sensitive young man who's going bald at twenty-seven and likes even the street urchins who steal from him. He's Hal, the antisocial but charismatic second lieutenant, who finds people boring but inexplicably drawn to him. He's the mysterious parachute captain in Oran, gorgeous but effete, who believes the war is America's fault. He's Father Donovan, wondering how Americans can teach seven-year-old Italians how to pimp. He's the Yalie second lieutenant in Algiers who laments how "the queer, the beautiful, the gentle and the wondering" are losing out to "a race of healthy baboons with football letters on their sweaters." He's the bespectacled Jewish

PFC, regularly interjecting wise observations about everything. He's the American captain who'd sooner return to the front than hang around decadent American officers in Naples. He's Giulia, who finds the faces of American officers "angry or soiled or lined or predatory." He's Moe Schulman, who importunes the beggar girl in the Galleria not to tell her grandchildren one day that *tutti gli Americani errono horribile.* (Moe, too, considers Americans worse than the Germans, because they already have everything they need. Amazingly, he, too, declares that "it doesn't matter what the war means or who wins it," even though this particular Burns is a Jew.) And even though (for obvious reasons) Burns distances himself from him—making him straight and semiliterate (he prefers to read comic books)—Burns is the poor soldier with syphilis, compelling enough for that "gentian-eyed" sergeant to invite him to the ballet once he's completed his cure.

One final trait ties together many of Burns's characters, including those who aren't Burns himself. Whether they are men or women, gay or straight, sympathetic or monstrous, alone or with others, happy or despairing, virtually all of them drink all the time. Louella the officious Red Cross volunteer is prototypical: in an average day (after she has woken up with a hangover) she has seven glasses of vermouth. Even Chaplain Bascom, a teetotaler, is prevailed upon to imbibe. The reflexive ease with which everyone turns to drink is but one more respect, also unremarked upon at the time, in which *The Gallery* is autobiographical, though alcohol works slowly, and characters in a set of short stories aren't around long enough to self-destruct.

18

G reat war novels inevitably follow great wars, and in literary circles everyone was wondering what would succeed *A
Farewell to Arms* and *All Quiet on the Western Front*—and who
would write it. But perhaps because of its unusual format, perhaps because it lacked blood and guts, perhaps because the war
was barely over and the author completely unknown, *The Gallery*
proved a hard sell.

In early May 1946 Burns sent the manuscript—507 pages
in a pair of bound books, wrapped lovingly in brown paper that
made it look like two pounds of smuggled butter, insured to the
hilt—to Robert Linscott, an editor at Random House. Three
weeks later, Burns complained to MacMackin that it remained
stuck on Linscott's desk. In fact, it had already been cleared away.
The sketches "are rather well done but (I would say) completely
unsaleable at the present time," Linscott wrote, without elabo-
rating, in his internal evaluation. The editors were more polite,

telling Burns it would work only as a traditional novel, which to Burns was not an option. They also asked to see his next book, tentatively titled *Chain Reaction*, though it would not be done for another year. "At present I'm quite writ out in the best Vermont Yankee sense and quite depressed," he told Beulah Hagen. The *Log* reported, on Burns's say-so, that Random House rejected the book because it was "not entirely pro-American." It would have to be shopped around.

In late May, Burns was finally ready to face New York. Or, as he told Hagen, "after four months I decided that I was sufficiently calmed down to venture a visit, with none of the Tintern Abbey overtones of five years afterward."* With surprising tentativeness—as if realizing he'd made of their relationship something it had never been or could ever be—he broached reuniting with Beulah Hagen. (With equally revealing unease, he'd asked MacMackin if he could crash on his couch. It was as if they were the only two people he knew.) Back came a telegram from Beulah, inviting him to dinner. So, on the first of June, 1946, carrying a bouquet of tulips and ferns through a downpour, Burns made his way to 38 Sutton Place South, and to "Frau Moe." "When she opened the door to 4-A my emotion was so overpowering that all I could do was thrust the flahrs at her, burbling something," he wrote Holger Hagen, who'd yet to return home. Even at Frau Moe's, war had brought its dislocations: the Bechstein was now on the other side of the room. Before long, the tulips were in a blue pot and a martini in Burns's hand.

His evening there was truncated—he had a "date," presumably with MacMackin, on Times Square at nine-thirty—with almost no time for music making. But the next afternoon, "a drowned rat in the peltingest rain since Father Noah," Burns

---

* A reference to "Lines Written a Few Miles Above Tintern Abbey" (1798), William Wordsworth's rumination on nature and the passage of time.

showed up again, and this time he planted himself at the piano as Beulah Hagen stood over him, and they had at it for two and a half hours, taking time out only for beer, crackers, and cheese. They did Schubert, Strauss, Mozart, and a "tender Gaelic job about the barren woman who hears the pigeons crying at night." They concluded, naturally, with *Frauenliebe und -leben*, "almost as good as on 9 August 1943." Once the music stopped, though, Burns found that the two of them had precious little to say. So detached did Beulah seem to him, Burns later wrote her husband, that he felt like an intruder. "Sitting and talking to her makes me feel queerly gauche, as though she really weren't there at all, or a coolly smiling ghost," he wrote. All that intimacy was easier to sustain with an ocean between them. Their correspondence continued, but soon "Frau Moe" became simply "Beulah," and "Moe" just "John," and not just because a bubble had been popped: the Hagens' marriage proved another casualty of the war.

Burns returned to Loomis and taught summer school, which brought in a bit of extra money, and then, after wangling a trip there aboard an army plane, spent a month in Italy. According to the *Log*, the visit was "to see his fiancée and other acquaintances and to testify at the War Crimes Trial"; Burns wasn't pressed on the former and refused to discuss the latter: too sensitive, he declared. It was all probably a ruse to see Mario without upsetting Batchelder. Though he'd just come back, it was good to get away. "The United States is a suffocating place to be right now," he wrote Holger Hagen that August. "When they are not worrying about a new '46 car, everyone is dedicated to a frenzied optimism." He saw the Jazz Age redux, with crazes and speculation and hucksterism, with another Great Crash waiting in the wings. "There should follow one boom after another, Harding scandals, sex crimes," he predicted. "1929 should arrive in five years." He was feeling Italy's familiar tug. "Often after three beers (only three!) I reach the melodramatic conclusion that I would rather die among people I loved in Italy, many of whom had nothing and still were great and noble, tha[n] to swelter among imbeciles who have everything including a swollen Windsor tie (that's the latest) at their Adam's Apple," he wrote.

Burns had by now moved into a larger second-floor apartment in Taylor Hall, just down the Quadrangle from his cramped old quarters. It came with a balcony, and whenever he opened his French doors, the sound of Brahms and Beethoven filled the air. One early morning in mid-August 1946, he fell asleep with a lit cigarette, and nearly incinerated himself. Spotting smoke billowing out of his apartment, the custodian sounded the alarm, then dragged Burns out while a French teacher, Francis Grubbs, carried a fire extinguisher into the room and doused the blaze. A faculty wife recalled Burns strolling nonchalantly on his porch—probably enjoying another smoke—while the fire was brought under control. (Burns later blamed the blaze on the mentally disabled three-year-old son of the teacher who lived upstairs, who for some reason he regarded as the devil's spawn, and from whom he fled whenever he approached on his tricycle. He also believed the boy had poured talcum powder into his record jackets.)

Somewhere between a dozen and a dozen and a half publishers ultimately rejected *The Gallery*; for all that was new and true about it, Burns lamented, only former GIs seemed to get it. That September, editors at Vanguard Press plied him with steak and whiskey at Longchamps, "then settled down to taking me and *The Gallery* apart." (They considered the promenades pointless and wanted to cut them, something he again refused to do.) Even Helen Strauss, the hard-boiled New York literary agent Burns had hired in late September, couldn't pull off a sale. Burns had had an in all along: Beulah Hagen worked at Harper and Brothers, as an assistant to its president, Cass Canfield. She knew Harpers was worried that the public appetite for war literature had already been sated, but rather than let Burns go to another house, she mentioned the book to Canfield's right-hand man, Frank Mac-Gregor. He, too, was aware that war novels were a hard sell. "I said I've got this problem," he recalled telling Canfield and another of his top editors, Edward Aswell. "I said I had this book that was quite fascinating, but it was about war and war conditions. And I described the manuscript, I guess enthusiastically, and I said, 'Well, what do I do with it, Cass?' And he said, 'You publish it, of course.'" Within two weeks, Harpers had accepted it. Three publishers—Vanguard, Viking, and Harpers—eventually vied for the book. Harpers won out, partly because, convinced it had a major new talent on its hands, it promised to buy Burns's next two novels as well. Just what he got for *The Gallery* is unclear, but one could probably extrapolate from what he would collect for the two books to follow: two thousand dollars.

From there, things proceeded quickly. By November, Burns had had his author's picture taken. "They are dramatic in the worst sense of commercial photography—the stagy lights, the cigarette, The Look," he complained. "I resemble a Greenwich Village poetaster sitting for the effigy of his tomb. My general expression is of rapt horror, possibly as though I were considering the implications of my manuscript." At the publisher's request, he also drafted that promotional mini-memoir. "For the next few pages I'll give you all the Dirt about me—all that I own up to in my conscious moments and all that won't make your eyebrows twitch for the ceiling," he wrote. He wasn't kidding about the caveats: large swaths of his biography were omitted. It was, he fibbed, the first time he'd ever talked about himself, ostensibly because he found such self-regard embarrassing.

Over several pages Burns reviewed his first thirty years. With considerable poignancy, insight, and candor (except in sexual matters: though he was writing for history, he must have assumed that some things—like public attitudes toward homosexuality—were so fixed that he would never be found out) he concluded:

"The Look"

*I am enthusiastic over very little. I spend most of my
time alone. I have few friends: whether my mind works
very much faster or very much slower than most people's
I've never discovered. I like to make and listen to music,
to take long walks, and to drink beer. I prefer European
women to American ones: they are really more complex and
aware of their purpose in life. I live in a peculiar removal
from life which makes me watch people as though they
were swimming in an aquarium. I cannot bear cruelty—
since I know that I too am cruel, I prefer to keep it within
myself, for I know that socially it will always redound to
me like a boomerang. I specialize in needling people for the
same affectations that I once owned myself. I cannot bear
fussing of any sort, particularly over details or material
possessions. I find myself removed spiritually from anyone
who hasn't experienced the war; therefore what friends I
have are among veterans. I love flowers and fear crowds.
And something within me drives on to a perfection of quiet
madness. When I find it, I shall be dead. The only point I
can offer in defense of myself is that I can be as nasty with
myself as I can be with others. In other words, I have hopes
for myself and for almost everybody in the world. I should
like to live a little longer just to see what will happen.*

In December, Burns sent MacGregor a revised text. The book
was not to appear for several months, but already there was buzz.
"John Horne Burns, whose first novel, *The Gallery,* is scheduled
next fall by Harpers, is apparently a major discovery. Those who
have read the manuscript are already speaking of Mr. Burns as a
new Dos Passos," the *Washington Post* reported in November. In
December, another prominent publisher came a-courting. "Unfortunately for Little Brown & Co I find myself in the position of a
literary Sacred Cow or Untouchable," Burns told them, noting that

he was under contract with Harpers for his first three books. He then rubbed it in a bit. "The first, *The Gallery,* will be published by them in a couple of months," he wrote. "It is a long job on the war in Italy, and is, I fear, at least as good as *War and Peace.* I have a little bet on with myself that I'll make every American writer up till now look sick. Do forgive my megalomaniacal exuberance, but these days I seem to be living in rooms filled with helium."

Throughout the fall and into the winter, the book bounced back and forth between Windsor and New York. Burns took pride in grammatical precision, so all those marked-up pages were both humbling and pleasurable to him. "In my simplicity I imagined that the manuscript was in fair shape for publication, but I soon began to love the anonymous copy editors who whipped the massive monsker [*sic*] into shape," he told MacGregor. "Many times I felt as though I'd had my wrists slapped by Mister Noah Webster and Mister Fowler—justly, I believe." Ditto for what he'd considered his impeccable French and Italian, though after the corrections all his Neapolitans were speaking perfect Florentine. On three consecutive mornings in January 1947, Burns received chunks of the newly typeset copy, and on three consecutive afternoons he sent back his changes.

Harpers' lawyers from Greenbaum, Wolff, and Ernst—the New York firm that had helped lift the ban on *Ulysses*—now got into the act as well. Burns was oblivious to libel concerns—for instance, using the real name of the army officer in charge of his censorship squad. Burns fixed that, but there were lots of other concerns to allay. No, the secretary to Fedhala's only doctor wasn't a whore; in fact, Fedhala didn't have a doctor. No, the Red Cross director in Naples wasn't really "the sort of thwarted old maid who sublimates all her repressed love urges into a passion for organization"; in fact, the director had been a man. Yes, the cork magnate's wife who'd slept with a GI did resemble Dolores del Rio, but there were lots of magnates with Spanish-looking wives. And yes, he need not specify that another sexually promiscuous woman worked at Lord & Taylor. "I know of no such person, but remove if it will make everybody happy," he wrote.

Sexually explicit literature still faced charges of obscenity— the highest court in Massachusetts had just held Lillian Smith's *Strange Fruit* obscene—and the lawyers asked Burns to kindly clean up his language. "The danger arises from the frequent use of the word 'fucking' and variations thereof," the attorney assigned to the project, Mrs. Theodora Zavin, wrote solemnly. "The word is used in some cases as a swear word, e.g. 'shut ya fuckin' mouth' (Galley 180A) and in other cases to describe the act of sexual intercourse, e.g. 'I fucked up just like the rest of them.' (Galley 106)." Before assuming the risk of litigation, she went on, "you might wish to review Galleys 39, 47, 65, 65A, 96, 106, 120, and 120A." Burns reluctantly complied. "In all cases I bowed to Missus Grundy,"* he explained to MacGregor. But someone, he suggested, really ought to tell Mrs. Zavin that "I fucked up" was not to be taken literally.

One thing that did not seem to concern Mrs. Zavin and the other lawyers was the book's gay undertone, and its apotheosis in "Momma." They might simply have been oblivious to it: people unaware of what "fucked up" meant could easily overlook a book's homosexual tint, even when it slapped them in the face. Perhaps homosexuality, however uncomfortable or unfamiliar, had no legal implications. Or perhaps its literal foreignness in *The Gallery* made it unobjectionable. "Not coincidentally (at least as far as the editors at Harpers were concerned) the gay bar is not in America," John Loughery writes in *The Other Side of Silence*, a history of twentieth-century gay culture. "In certain ways, 'over there' was still a nice idea."

Judging from those receiving galleys, Harpers had high hopes for the book: Erich Maria Remarque (author of *All Quiet on the*

---

* The priggish, censorious character, originally appearing in Thomas Morton's 1798 play *Speed the Plough*, who came to symbolize standards of conservative propriety.

Western Front), Laurence Stallings (coauthor of the World War
I play *What Price Glory*), James T. Farrell, and John Steinbeck,
among others. Harpers got back glowing reviews. "It makes me
feel like a clumsy artisan when I see how he handles words and
makes people come alive," the sports novelist John Tunis wrote
Harpers executive Simon Michael Bessie. "He makes a mon-
key out of the Chinese saying that a picture is worth a thousand
words. Not a thousand of these words. You're damn lucky to have
the boy in your stable." Thomas Heggen—whose own war novel,
Mr. Roberts, had already appeared—weighed in with a blurb that
suggested how some blurbs are born.

> *Of necessity I had to read it very hurriedly, and because
> I did I'm not quite sure just how good it is. I think it is very
> good, however, and if it's of any value you're welcome to
> this as a jacket quote: "This is a book to be compared to
> Alfred Hayes' ALL THY CONQUESTS; which means
> that it is in the same company with the very best novel of
> the second World War."*

But undoubtedly Burns's greatest coup was praise from John
Dos Passos, an old friend of Robert Hillyer's who, as the author
of one of the great novels of World War I, *Three Soldiers*, was
uniquely suited to bless a novel about World War II. It came on
a badly typed and much-edited note from Provincetown, Massachusetts, which, when cleaned up, would look excellent on a book
jacket. "So far as my very limited reading goes, with the exception
of [Godfrey] Blunden's *[A] Room on the Route*, it's the first book of
real magnitude to come out of the last war," he wrote of *The Gallery*. "It is written with a reality of detail and a human breadth and
passion of understanding that is tonic, healthgiving. If Americans
can still write in this sort of exultation of pity and disgust of the foul
spots in the last few years of our history then perhaps there is still

hope that we can recover our manhood as a nation and our sense of purpose in the world."

In May, *Harper's* magazine printed an earlier version of one portion of the book, calling it "Promenade in Naples." Burns handed off one of his two free copies to Batchelder. "At lunch the Headmistress was in orgasm about my writing," Burns wrote MacGregor. But approbation around Loomis—"this hepped-up tutoring school for the upper middle classes"—was rare for him; from the moment he'd returned there, Burns had been at a low boil. True, he still loved teaching, and had been given a nicer apartment and a small raise. But, as he told his father, "drops of blood are being squeezed out in return": he was now teaching four classes, plus playing the organ during chapel services, plus directing the choir, plus supervising the literary magazine, plus shouldering various clerical and policing duties eating up fifteen hours a week, all of which sapped his creative energy and confined what he called "my wild centrifugal spirit." "New England prep schools are rooted in the tradition that the boys must never have a moment of leisure, for fear they might start thinking," he griped to Beulah Hagen. The same seemed to apply to its teachers.

Loomis's sister school, Chaffee—where he was spending still more of his time, deconstructing *La Bohème* for a music appreciation class—was, he wrote, a place "Jane Austen would have enjoyed." "These Little Women are bobbysoxers or virgins with nobility obsessions. They copy one another's papers, weep at low grades, and occasionally are smitten with me. But it is all rather Angora, with the claw showing under the fur. I really don't like sixty adolescent girls with their female teachers. The atmosphere is always charged and tittery, with dangerous undertones." He was also having trouble readjusting to the bleak New England winters. "January in Connecticut is the nadir of dreariness," he wrote Beulah Hagen. "At one moment we're freezing and our sinuses are stickily clogged; or we watch a dismal thaw in June weather under a leaden sky. More and more I can account for the accumulated poison of the Puritan Fathers: the shadow of some inhuman vulture constantly spreads his wings over the landscape here and blights all life below."

Only the temporariness of the situation made it tolerable. "Since I hope soon to be a fulltime writer, I suppose that eventually I'll have to pull out of Loomis," he wrote. "Though I was certainly wise in coming back here to ease the transition out of the army and into Something Else. I'm handled with kid gloves by everyone in the school, since they believe that shortly I'll be a celebrity." But even that wouldn't keep him on the campus. "As Bennie the Meatball* said before being rubbed out: 'I'm gettin' outa dis racket—but fast,'" he told Beulah Hagen. Meanwhile, he began acting more boldly, even recklessly, having friends from the Hartford Ballet up to his apartment, almost daring to be found out. He sang arias from *Tosca* in the chapel with a handsome doctor friend from Hartford Hospital whom Loomis people believed to be a lover. A young male teacher complained to a faculty wife that Burns had "been making overtures" to him and was "definitely a pervert."

Then, of course, there was alcohol. Not surprisingly, Burns became well acquainted with selected bars in Hartford. He had never learned to drive, but a friendly and loyal day student named Dave Brewer took him regularly into town, either to the bar at the Heublein Hotel or to a basement saloon on Asylum Street. Though he was underage, Brewer sometimes stayed for a drink and a chat. (Burns was very soft-spoken, but never did it occur to Brewer that Burns was "bent." Discolored, yes: while the rest of Burns was fair, his fingers were orange from nicotine.) When transportation wasn't available, and especially when he was writing, Burns surely drank

---

* Benny Gamson was a top deputy to the mob boss Benjamin "Bugsy" Siegel until his murder in 1946.

alone in his apartment. In either case, the results were hard to miss; some mornings he looked hungover, and you could smell booze on his breath. Sometimes, after a long weekend off campus, he'd miss his Monday classes. During a New York vacation, a student spotted him at the opera, obviously liquored up, obviously with an obviously gay man.

Still, once he got before a class, Burns did not cut corners. He continued to stimulate students—or at least the best and most receptive among them—with novel challenges and stratagems. Those who faked their written work would find drawings of manure piles with shovels stuck in them sketched into the margins of their papers. To spot kindred souls and, perhaps, to inspire curiosity in them, in one class he gave a wide-ranging culture quiz on the first day—containing, among other things, questions on Gilbert and Sullivan; a popular advertising slogan; and the name of Clark Gable's latest costar, properly spelled.* In another, he came in and wrote ten questions on the blackboard—including "What is a 'rune'?" "Who says '*Finalemente mia*'?" and "What is the plant that screams?"—and gave everyone three minutes to answer. "You won't be graded—this is just to show me if you're cultured," he told them.† He described the Renaissance as "a bunch of mungy little men in togas swarming over the Italian peninsula," forcing everyone to go out and learn what "mung" meant.

If the Island was an island, Burns provided a periscope, allowing anyone adventurous enough to peek in and peer out. "He had no attraction to the sub-morons whose fathers got them in by giving money to buy new uniforms for the football team," recalled Brewer. With papers, too, he tolerated no shoddiness. "John

---

* Deborah Kerr, in *The Hucksters*.

† A Finnish or Norse poem; Scarpia in *Tosca*; and the mandrake, e.g., "and shrieks like mandrakes torn out of the earth," from *Romeo and Juliet*.

Horne Burns was the best teacher I ever had anywhere, in anything," David Goodrich, later an editor and writer, wrote in his
memoirs. "He was constantly asking for our opinions and chal-
lenging us." (When Goodrich needed a thesaurus, Burns advised
him to buy one that was "buckram bound.") Richard Rifkind,
who went on to become a physician, remembered Burns as the
"only really *cultured* teacher we had . . . The others were Span-
ish teachers, history teachers. He was an *everything* teacher. He
knew the world, and he shared it with us. He was open to all ideas.
Nothing was wrong."

Jerome Kohn, later a philosophy professor and protégé of the
philosopher Hannah Arendt, was "fascinated" by him. "He had
a brilliant mind and he was terribly funny," he recalled. "He was
a louche character. And wicked. He was a wicked man, in the
best sense of the term." (There was his lesson, Kohn recalled, on
how to differentiate "major" from "minor" poets. "Now which
is Edna St. Vincent Millay?" he asked. Clearly "minor," several
students replied. "No, *of course not*, you fools!" he snapped back.
"Anyone with the name 'Edna St. Vincent Millay' is a *major* poet!
Obviously!") "What he did was kind of put down all the stereo-
types, all the traditional categories, the way people discriminated
between things. He had no use for that," Kohn recalled. He would
compliment a student on the "urbane ironies" of what he'd written, leaving him to ponder what "urbane" meant.

Burns became especially close to a student named Henry White.
White, too, was musical—he played the violin and organ—and
dabbled in painting; both his grandfather and father were noted
artists. Young Henry was also striking: dark, like his Italian-born
mother. With his lively and creative family, Burns could unwind,
talk art, speak Italian; he visited them periodically at their home
on Long Island Sound, in Waterford, Connecticut. But he continued to irk school administrators, especially Mr. B, with his provocative stunts, like devoting a chapel talk to the bawdy musical

Kiss Me, Kate, or assigning comparatively edgy books like *Studs Lonigan, What Makes Sammy Run?*, and Stephen Crane's *Maggie: A Girl of the Streets.* Boxes of paperbacks, at twenty-five cents a pop, would arrive in Burns's class, and by semester's end his students had put together their own semi-salacious libraries. Once, Batchelder sidled up to a student named John Stuart Cox, and asked him whether Mr. Burns was really doing his job. *"Doing his job?"* Cox replied. *"He's the best teacher I've ever had!"*

While some students assumed Burns was gay, he did not advertise it. He still tried to throw people off his trail; on display in his apartment, for instance, was a picture of his "fiancée," the daughter of a professor at the University of Florence. From time to time he'd briefly and ostentatiously "date" one of the young Chaffee teachers. "Your wife is warm, charming and clever, which is a rare trait in women," he wrote the editor of *Harper's* magazine. "Perhaps I too should look things over in Scotland." Some considered Burns a misogynist, but charmed by his wit, a coterie of faculty wives formed around him.

One of them, though, wasn't so sympathetic. She'd been uncomfortable when Burns had come around for coffee, telling someone afterward she thought he had "homosexual tendencies." Word got back to Burns, who approached her one lunchtime in the dining hall. "I understand that you said you consider me a homosexual," he told her. "Yes, Jack, I did say that," she replied. Burns, she recalled, just turned around and walked away. Some people thought him downright subversive; another Loomis wife called him "the most dangerous man on the faculty." "She probably sensed my schizophrenic pattern, by which I lead an existence quite independent of the school," Burns wrote. "Sooner or later the two lives will cross, and then there'll be hell to pay."

In the spring of 1947, Burns's frustration began boiling over. He boasted of leaving the campus just to leave the campus. "I've taken a room at the Hotel Bond [in Hartford] in order not to be

cheated completely of my weekend, and tonight I shall drink myself into a genial stupor with members of the Inner Circle," he
wrote MacGregor. "I've decided not to return to Loomis, where
I've taken nothing but crap and sniping all year long." "This
must be the last year for me of this hermaphroditic sapping life
with other people's spoiled Philistine children," he wrote Beulah
Hagen. He pursued another State Department post and put out
feelers to the University of Oklahoma, of all places. But amid the
gloom, one bright prospect loomed: *The Gallery.* Publication was
set for June 4, 1947.

19

It was priced at three dollars. On the cover was a photograph taken inside the Galleria near the end of the war that Burns had been given by a merchant marine.* In what had to have been an act of pettiness on Burns's part, any reference to Loomis was omitted from the author's biography, both on the book jacket and inside, though he found a way to tout his alma mater. "After four years at Phillips Andover, he went to Harvard where he played squash and sang in the glee club," it stated. "Upon leaving Harvard, Mr. Burns taught English in a boys' preparatory school for several years," it went on, and "is now again teaching in a boys' school." It wasn't even clear that it was the same one.

On the night *The Gallery* came out, MacGregor threw a party for Burns in New York. Always nervous around strangers, some

---

* The photographer, a GI named Nat Knaster, originally went uncredited; he later demanded, and got, an acknowledgment. Only a few days before taking that picture, Knaster had photographed Mussolini and his mistress, Clara Petacci, hanging from their feet in Milan.

Jacket of The Gallery

of whom might be reviewers, and thrown by the recent disinte-gration of what had been for him the Hagens' idealized marriage, Burns did what Burns usually did: he drank, then drank, then drank some more. Then he vanished, and for several days no one knew where he'd gone. "They didn't know whether he'd left New York, whether he'd fallen under a truck," Beulah Hagen was to remember. "I feel perfectly horrible about my departure from your marvelous party the other night," he wrote MacGregor once he'd surfaced. "A tension had been building up in me for weeks, and I guess I simply blew my top after I'd gotten some alcohol in me. The last thing I remember at all is sitting down to a steak; then everything is a blank till I woke up when the train hit the South Station [in Boston]. The homing instinct of drunkards." The decompression went on a while. "Under doctor's orders I've spent a week in bed, an idyllic time of sleeping and changing my personality to fit my new notoriety," he wrote Beulah Hagen ten days or so later. "The publication jitters are almost gone now, and I shall shortly arise anew and recreated, like the phoenix."

Burns could have relaxed, even without the booze. The re-views were not only almost uniformly good, but ecstatic for a first novel. In the *New York Times*, Charles Poore praised Burns's "rancorously vivid portfolio of portraits," while in the *New York Times Book Review*, Richard Sullivan noted the book's sensuous, sympathetic tone, one that more than made up for its weaknesses: that Burns's "appreciation of the Italian people grows occasionally into something like sentimental idolatry," and that his "bitterness against American crudity comes close in places to a youthful in-tolerance." "John Horne Burns—you'll remember the name and you'll remember the book," Gerald Roscoe wrote in the *Boston Globe*. "Read *The Gallery*. It will introduce you to one of the finest writing talents in the country."

As remarkable to many reviewers as Burns's achievement was his potential. William McFee of the *New York Sun*, who invoked names such as Henry Adams and Kipling, was intrigued by this meteor suddenly lighting up the sky, and just where it was headed. "Whether [Burns] will use his definite talent to write more novels of this caliber is anybody's guess," he wrote. "He has been recklessly extravagant in squandering material in this book. The clever professional novelist would have made half a dozen novels out of it." While acknowledging Burns's excesses, Edmund Wilson, perhaps the era's most respected literary critic, was also struck by his promise. Burns, he wrote in the *New Yorker*, had "unmistakable talent"; "even the worst of these pages are the bad writing of a man who can write." "I feel pretty certain," he went on, "that Mr. John Horne Burns, when he has worked at his craft longer, will give us something both solider and more intense than this already remarkable book."

Also striking was the praise Burns won among his peers: men who'd also served in Europe. "It is astonishing that out of the corruption that was Italy in 1944, a book could come that is strong and beautiful," another army veteran, Hubert Saal, wrote in the *Yale Literary Magazine*. "John Horne Burns saw everything other American soldiers saw, but he remembered what the others forgot or had not discovered. He uncovers the squalor of Italy and finds below an aching purity. From the language he brings back not profanity but tenderness; from the country, not loot but the sound of her music; from her men and women, not just the anguish of starvation and prostitution, but the indomitable core of human dignity." The writer and essayist William Zinsser, who'd also served in North Africa and Italy, spoke for many of Burns's contemporaries. "It was 'my' book for 'my' war—the book that every returning veteran, if he's lucky, gets written just for him, distilling his own experience," he later observed. Like Burns, he, too, had been a sheltered Ivy Leaguer, blinking in the sunlight of some strange place he'd never heard of and knew next to nothing about before; in fact, they'd been to all the same spots. "I could hardly believe how many of the same streets we had walked—in

Algiers, in Oran, in Naples—and how many of the same gratitudes we shared," Zinsser wrote. "The novel validated where I had been and what I had felt and thought."

To another GI, an aspiring novelist who'd finished up his six-month hitch in Naples just as Burns had arrived, *The Gallery* rang equally true. This was William Weaver, an ambulance driver during the war and, later, the translator of Italo Calvino and Umberto Eco. Like Burns, Weaver was a gay American who experienced Naples at its rawest, watching drunk soldiers cavort with prostitutes in the boxes of the San Carlo because they had nowhere else to go. "In his pages I found all of the Naples I had come to know," he later wrote. "He had heard the same noises, had smelled the same odors." Praise also came from Harry Brown, whose own novel about the Italian campaign, *A Walk in the Sun*, had already been published. Brown had been at Harvard with Burns and had beaten him out for a poetry prize—"grounds," Burns wrote MacGregor, "for a lifelong enmity"; that Brown had gotten out a novel on Italy before Burns had—particularly since "the gossip said that Harry wrote it on furlough in Paris"—only irked the hypercompetitive Burns more. ("Pardon my pettiness and my proprietary sense," Burns explained. "If I weren't a prima donna, I couldn't goad myself into doing whatever I have done.") But the antagonism and competitiveness evidently went just one way. "Mr. Burns has a marvelous feeling for mood and style," Brown wrote. "Perhaps both occasionally run away with him, but at his best he has succeeded in recreating that sense of utter sadness and loss that everyone in the Army who found himself overseas, whatever his job, experienced then and everlastingly." People who served with Burns attested to the novel's veracity. "I like your book a great deal; it has a nightmare quality which comes under the heading of exact description, and I am glad that it has been set down in print, even if there is no reason why anyone should believe it," Arthur Bullowa, later an influential art collector in New York, wrote him.

There were dissenters. Some reviewers complained of Burns's vulgar language, others of sensory—and particularly olfactory—overload. "Mr. Burns may be said to have written part of his book with his nose," huffed Harrison Smith in the *Saturday Review*. In *Commentary*, Raymond Rosenthal called *The Gallery* "mediocre, confused, and most often, downright maudlin," filled with "flabby caricatures of grossly misapprehended 'types.'" Because Burns had no ideas of his own, he charged, he had contented himself instead with "laying hands on all the stray, half-baked notions which happened to be around." In its own way, Burns's work was as superficial as Ernie Pyle's, but it read worse because it was a novel, in which "everything becomes strangely inflated under the influence of sentimental rhetoric." Rosenthal's criticism must have stung, for he, too, had spent many years in Italy. But such pans were rare.

So, too, were reviews that picked up the book's most unusual elements. Few noted, let alone faulted, the book's shrill anti-Americanism. The *New Republic* was one exception: Burns's "imaginative sympathy operates too exclusively to the benefit of the Neapolitans, and his final position is too angry, too desperate," it complained. Even American boorishness and immaturity could be the flip side of "certain substantial national virtues." No one seemed inclined to engage Burns on his criticisms. By 1947 Americans were sick of war, well acquainted with how it had disfigured its soldiers, saturated with a steady diet of wartime propaganda, and not inclined to wax indignant on the matter. Soldiers were too familiar and too ubiquitous—sixteen million of them had served in the war—to be sacrosanct. "Recruiting officers will not like some of the chapters and ideas in *The Gallery*, nor will professional glamorizers of America care for his pictures of the GIs in Italy," wrote William McFee in the *New York Sun*. "The high command will agree that this is nothing but the truth, however. We have to make armies out of the material available.

Kipling reported the dearth of plaster saints in the British Army long ago." Decades would pass before the revisionist deification of the "greatest generation" took hold, and the GIs became officially unassailable.

The Gallery's gayness was also almost entirely overlooked or, perhaps more accurately, ignored. *Time*, which considered itself hip, was bold enough to mention Burns's "first-rate" depiction of "an evening spent in a homosexuals' hangout." Few others touched the subject, at least at the time. ("You'll also remember for a long time 'Momma' who ran a café in Naples but her patrons had to have special qualifications in order to be welcomed," was what readers of the *Hartford Courant* were told, though only well after the book had appeared.) Discomfited or uninterested or oblivious or downright hostile, most straight reviewers either missed the topic or pretended it wasn't there. It was a familiar trope, one that affected gay writers like Walt Whitman and Oscar Wilde as well: the homosexual dimension of their work simply went unrecognized. (As the cultural historian Michael Henry Adams has noted, "being ignored is one of the bitterest forms of bigotry.") So *The Gallery* was just another war novel, and Burns, just another war novelist. Oddly enough, this conspiracy of silence insulated Burns from the hostility that greeted Gore Vidal's *The City and the Pillar*, which appeared the following year.* Its gayness was simply too explicit and conspicuous to be overlooked.

The silence extended to the gay community itself. Because there were no gay publications to speak of, there was no gay commentary on the book. There can be little doubt that *The Gallery* was widely read, and discussed, in literate gay circles, in part because there *were* literate gay circles: homosexual men were not nearly as isolated or disconnected as has generally been thought.

---

* To the *New Yorker*, Vidal's book was the terminal point in the ongoing decline of homosexual literature that had begun with *Death in Venice*. "A sick book about sick Americans," the *Herald Tribune* called it.

A gay grapevine did exist, and so unusual a book—one that portrayed gays humanely, came from an old and reputable publisher, and was highly literate—would have been well represented on it. But this culture was sub-rosa and poorly documented, leaving behind only anecdotal traces.

According to the diaries of Christopher Isherwood, for instance, the writer and connoisseur Lincoln Kirstein admired *The Gallery* "extravagantly." The first homosexual Baedeker, *The Gay Girl's Guide* of 1949, included "Momma" in its literature section, calling it "splendid," with "superb dialogue and portraits." The straight writer Frederic Morton read *The Gallery*—and remembered "Momma"—because he'd heard about it at Yaddo, a writers' colony which gays frequented (Truman Capote and Leonard Bernstein were there with him), making gay topics less taboo. "Gay men in the postwar years were desperate to read about themselves and to see representations of their experience in serious fiction," the gay historian John Loughery has noted. "It's highly implausible to think that gay men who read novels in the 1940s and kept up with current literature wouldn't have discussed this book and recommended it to their friends. A book that even Ernest Hemingway liked, and with a scene in a gay bar—that would have been talked about among bookish gay men."* The squeamishness of the *Philadelphia Inquirer*'s Abel Banov neatly captured Burns's daring: Banov danced around *both* "Queen Penicillin" ("an American sergeant . . . repents his sins while undergoing medical treatment") *and* "Momma" (he described the proprietress simply as "a highly respected Neapolitan dowager who runs a bar"). But by at least hinting at the subjects Burns had confronted, Banov was more courageous than most reviewers.

---

* When, sometime around 1970, a sympathetic English teacher named Ty Florie, himself a World War II veteran and closeted, encouraged Loughery to discover life beyond New Britain, Connecticut, it was *The Gallery*, along with books by Gide, Proust, and other gay writers, that he recommended.

Sales started slowly. But they soon picked up, and it became clear that the book might just buy Burns the financial and artistic freedom he craved. That provided him some solace when a second, "sumptuous" State Department post fell through; it was not surprising, for apart from Burns's checkered personal and medical history, as the Cold War heated up gays were increasingly being weeded, or kept, out of the military and diplomatic corps. "Fuck 'em," Burns wrote that July. "I'm making enough out of *The Gallery* and alien and domestic gratuities to be as independent as I like."

Burns himself did not do much for sales. When, in August 1947, he appeared on the immensely popular radio show hosted by Mary Margaret McBride, he was either late or drunk or both. "I was embarrassed and amused all during the terrible thing so that my tongue got in my cheek and stuck there," he wrote afterward. But by mid-September, bookstore orders topped ten thousand. "Myself, I hope it will maintain the principle of inertia in motion, and like a tank keep crawling for another year or so," Burns wrote. Most Loomis students cared little about his success, but his acolytes bought copies for him to inscribe. "To Richard Rifkind, the sharp analyst, the impeccable student, the sifter of world values from Palestine to Pisgah. Best wishes from the author, who is also his teecher [*sic*]," went one. "For Dave Brewer, who used to write me themes on *Mom* and *Pop*. Now he has to read *me!*" "For David Gyger—an earnest student and a driving journalist, with all best wishes from the author, who is also D's teacher—poor D." But at least one copy—to his mentor at Andover, Emory Basford—he inscribed with due reverence. It was he, Burns wrote, who "more than anyone else taught me to read and write, and to think with feeling for manners, style, and values."

Suddenly, Burns was not only a public intellectual, but a sexy one, undoubtedly the first author ever to be praised simultaneously in *Harper's* magazine and *Harper's Bazaar*. The second

Burns as a "Man of the Moment"

named Burns, along with Michael Redgrave, Stephen Spender, Robert Ryan, and David Lean, among others, one of its "Men of the Moment," and ran a romantic photograph of him taken on a gritty New York street. Praising him in the first was John Aldridge, poised to become another of America's most influential postwar critics. With writers like Norman Mailer, Irwin Shaw (*The Young Lions*), and James Jones (*From Here to Eternity*) still to weigh in, Aldridge pronounced Burns emblematic of the new crop of war writers—more worldly, resourceful, and resilient than their counterparts from the last war, less likely to retreat into European exile. "Burns sees truth with a ferocity of insight any age before ours would have found impossible to bear," he wrote.

By then Ernest Hemingway had, indeed, discovered Burns, and praised him to several people. "Read some damned good books. Latest *The Gallery*—wonderfully written," he wrote a friend in September 1947. Later, he urged the Italian writer and publisher Alberto Mondadori to include the book in a series Mondadori would sponsor and Hemingway curate. "Very controversial book. Will raise hell to publish it. But really good," Hemingway wrote him. Hemingway's former wife, the journalist and war correspondent Martha Gellhorn, sent her accolades directly to Burns.

> *I have never discovered how a reader should write to an author, yet it seems the least a reader can do when an author has given him, with what sweat and work, a whole extra set of lives to live. We found your book by chance in a store in Atlanta, that looked as bright and chromium as a Rexall's and miraculously stayed open at night. And thereafter I had one of the finest days and nights for a long time, going very slowly back to Italy. I think you write like an angel and see beautifully, and the book is a triumph and I thank you . . . I hope many, many people are reading it,*

*for though that is no test at all of a book, it is on the whole
more fun to be read than not. But whatever happens to the
book, you don't have to worry: you did it: and you've got
that to keep you warm.*

Burns was buoyed by the book's fortunes, which augured well
for the vaguely internationalist-pacifist worldview he'd been for-
mulating. "I came back from Italy convinced that there was no
hope anywhere," he wrote one fan. "Now I think that there is—a
little—but it must come from America and from people like you
and me who know the score and are not even yet so paralyzed as
to give up hope for a way out of the world's anguish. We are in
the minority, but we do exist; we are not yet dead." Even more
thrilling than the book's success and "my glossy new reputation
as one of The Young Men," he went on, "is the number of people
like yourself, mostly veterans, who have taken the trouble to sit
down and write to me. I often wonder how many of the majority,
whooping Americans who even now are screaming for an atomic
bomb on Russia have any idea of what I have tried to say."

"*The Gallery* Becomes Best-Seller; John Horne Burns Lauded
by Critics," blared the *Log* for October 31, 1947. The book, it
reported, was now in its seventh printing. It had brought Burns
many interesting letters, the story related, including both a death
threat and a marriage proposal. It also noted credulously that
Burns had turned down entreaties to go out to Hollywood to
write. "He says that he prefers Loomis life, and even the Loomis
climate, to that of California," it stated. Burns was being diplomatic, or else concealing his plans to flee. Burns's real feelings for
the place were no doubt better conveyed by the chapter of *The
Gallery* he chose to read aloud during a chapel talk: "Momma."

Only a few months after amassing rejection slips, Burns was
now in a position to advise aspiring novelists. "Practically everyone from whore to bishop imagines herself or himself producing

at least one novel," he wrote a man named Roul Tunley. "And they very well could. But the chief recipe is one which sounds almost nasty when it is put into basic English—you must get a typewriter and thousands of sheets of paper, and you must sit down to these tools each and every day for a certain period of hours, whether you feel like it or not. Greater novels have been buried with people than have ever come from the press. Don't let yours do the same." He also attracted interest internationally, including from the British publisher Fredric Warburg, to whom Edmund Wilson had recommended the book. (It was heady stuff: Warburg also published André Gide, Jean-Paul Sartre, George Orwell, and Thomas Mann.) Despite a postwar paper shortage, *The Gallery* went on to sell 11,000 copies in England in five years. Understandably, Warburg wanted to see more from "Horne Burns."

20

In July 1947 Jane and Paul Hazelton, a couple in their late twenties, lived in an apartment on Taylor Third, a flight up from Burns. They'd come to Loomis only three years earlier, and had never planned on staying very long; it was a convenient perch while Paul Hazelton finished his master's in education at Yale. Jane, meantime, raised their son—that little boy on the tricycle who so spooked Burns. In the largely friendless Loomis to which Burns had returned, Jane Hazelton became his closest confidante. Some mornings, after her husband had left to teach or headed for New Haven, Burns came upstairs to visit. With Jane, a nice Catholic girl from Maine, he could let down his guard, and stop performing. Perhaps because it was her nature, perhaps because her sight was starting to fail and she clung to what she could still see, she observed him closely and sympathetically. Burns elicited feelings from her, like curiosity and compassion, he rarely prompted from anyone unwilling to burrow beneath the brilliance and the cruelty.

Burns, she thought, had coveted, even cultivated, his alcohol-ism. It was clear from the childish way he boasted about drinking: he wanted to shock people, especially at staid old Loomis, to show what a big boy he was. It was part of a general pattern of reckless-ness, the same impulse that led him to invite young soldiers up to his apartment; through the walls, she could hear them giggling, at least until his guests left shortly before dawn. More than get him-self kicked out of Loomis, she believed, Burns wanted to destroy himself: that's what his drinking and smoking were all about. Burns hated himself—was *punishing* himself—for not being a real man, she thought. She, on the other hand, accepted him for what he was, which was why they got along.

Until he died, or left, or was thrown out, there was one sure way for Burns to be noticed around Loomis, and that was to write about it, which he began to do on July 27, 1947. Even be-fore the war, Burns had toyed with the idea. "Mr. Burney is writ-ing a novel about this school which, he claims, will cause him to be fired," Alfred Duhrssen, class of 1943, wrote in *Memoirs of an Aged Child*. But he'd waited until after the war to tackle it, and understandably, for how much riper for ridicule would the place look to him now? Anyone in the school brass who'd thought about it for very long should have surmised that Loomis had a time bomb on its hands. Added to the childishness, the irrever-ence, and the outrageousness was Burns's mounting irritation with Loomis and his disgust with himself for returning there. And joining all these things was his newly swollen noggin. "Of course he loved the good reviews," Beulah Hagen later remem-bered. "And got his feet on the ground. And began thinking how he could do more damage in the next novel." "The sudden liter-ary blaze of . . . *The Gallery* may have turned his head a bit and given [him] the 'what the hell' confidence to turn Swiftian in his caustic exaggerated portraiture," Sidney Eaton later theorized. There was now, as Eaton put it, "vitriol in his ink."

Around Loomis, people could sense him gathering material, as if he did not have enough already. Howard "Squirrel" Norris, a longtime Loomis science teacher who sometimes joined Burns and Orchard for impromptu opera recitals, later recalled a party in which he'd watched Burns watching everyone else, filing every-thing away and, before long, turning it into prose. During his morning visits, Burns began showing Jane Hazelton what he was writing. As with *The Gallery*, he needed an audience, but the ranks of potential confederates—people with little emotional connection to Loomis, who would not go off tattling to Mr. B—were few. He'd leave her with a few typewritten pages, ostensibly to see if they worked, but probably to shock her, too. And they did, especially as they moved beyond general descriptions of the school and toward portraits of particular, readily recognizable individuals, most notably and predictably Norrie Orchard. Ha-zelton liked Orchard, and urged Burns to desist, knowing well he never would. She did not tell Orchard what was happening, though her husband may have. But word probably reached him anyway: Burns was apparently blabbing about the book to his disciples, who did not keep the secret to themselves. So Orchard had to wonder what was about to hit him, and his own role in it: a story persisting for decades after is that Burns had done all his dirty deeds on a typewriter he had borrowed from Orchard.

The pressure on Burns would be great. Not only were second novels jinxed, but the second wave of World War II novels had begun to appear, threatening Burns's temporary hegemony. Gore Vidal later wrote that three novelists—Burns, Calder Willing-ham (*End as a Man*), and himself—made the "O.K. list of writers in 1947," but when *The Naked and the Dead* appeared the follow-ing year, Norman Mailer had eclipsed them all.

At first Burns tried following up on *The Gallery* the easy way: recycling something he'd already written. He'd long cherished hopes that his unpublished novels might one day appear; "the world should be ready for them in its postwar brwaugh," he'd once told MacMackin. So, shortly before *The Gallery* was born, he dusted off his copy of *Learn Valor, Child*, dating back to the summer of 1936, and pawned it off as something new. Whether either Helen Strauss or MacGregor was fooled isn't clear; in any case, both quickly concluded, as Douglas McKee already had, that Burns's juvenilia were unsalvageable. Strauss put it bluntly, in terms that would arise again. "That all of your characters are stinkers is besides the point," she wrote. "What I really think is basically wrong with the book is that it doesn't ring true. I suppose there are such people as you've written about, but somehow they emerged as caricatures." His next book was crucial, she warned, and this one certainly shouldn't be it; better to return to the brand-new novel he'd hoped to write that summer. MacGregor concurred. "John, this ain't the thing," he told him. Burns was calm, but curious, about the rejection. "What I want to know is, is it really a bad book, or is it just too nasty in its implications?" he asked MacGregor. MacGregor's response doesn't survive; his answer would probably have been "both." Burns never submitted another of his old novels again; *The Cynic Faun* and the rest remained safely salted away. So he returned to *Lucifer*.

In the late summer of 1947 he showed the first forty pages to MacMackin; by summer's end he was already on page 240. "There are too many dreadful distractions here for us to woo the Muse in that privacy we'd like," he wrote from Boston in early September. But a month later Burns informed MacMackin that his novel on "Miss Sophia"—the desiccated spinster who would stand in for all the real-life Loomises—was now on page 300, with "100 to go to her orgasm." By then he was back in his dormitory apartment, spending his evenings concocting new scenes and characters, interpolating tics or peccadilloes he'd spotted earlier that day in a faculty meeting or the dining room.

"I am nearly finished with a passionate affair with my *Lucifer with a Book*, which means that this new novel is very good indeed or else that I am already far gone in a senile and impotent passion," Burns wrote to John Fischer of Harpers on October 23. "It is like nothing else I know, and certainly not of a piece with *The Gallery.* A year ago I couldn't have written it. It's rather like Congreve* shot through with warmth. I hope you will like it and that my beat-up Muse will continue her frantic coition for a few weeks more." On December 11, he informed Fischer that *Lucifer* was still "three inches from completion." It must and would be wrapped up during the forthcoming Christmas vacation, he promised. But Mr. B wasn't helping. "I suffer under a headmaster who boasts of having a creative writer (spoken with a pious intake of breath) on his faculty," he griped. "What the senile old fellow omits to mention is that the creative writer gets precious little creating done when school is in session. Our headmaster is at that last stage of mental tabes dorsalis† in which he distrusts all his faculty and sides with the students. He piles more and more work on us, believing that we are in business to cheat him. To me it is exhausting and futile."

Batchelder never did see that rant. But the day Burns sent it off, a story about him—a local boy made good—appeared in the *Boston Globe.* Impressed that the normally reticent Dos Passos had endorsed Burns's book, the *Globe* reporter, Paul Kneeland, made his way to Waterford, Connecticut, where Burns had installed himself for a few days in the little fieldstone cottage belonging to the parents of Henry White, that favorite student of his. Though he played hard to get, Burns felt few inhibitions; Kneeland found him completely relaxed, sitting in a rocking chair, a half-smoked cigarette in one hand and an American highball in the other. With each, it was only the first of several. Kneeland later recalled Burns

---

* The British playwright William Congreve (1670–1729), author of several comedies of manners.

† A form of late, untreated syphilis producing, among other things, mental degeneration.

*"The Gallery" Is Ninth Novel He Has Written,
but Others—"Fortunately"—Weren't Published,*

"Born Snob," John Horne Burns
Turned Down Hollywood's Gold

By PAUL F. KNEELAND

WATERFORD, Conn.—Harvard graduate John Dos Passos, acclaimed for writing THE novel of World War I ("Three Soldiers") has acclaimed Harvard graduate John Horne Burns for writing THE novel of World War II ("The Gallery"), according to a press notice. All of which is really a signal honor in the book world—down there in Provincetown where bright-anxious yellowgreen grass-blades peak up through cracks in sidewalks in Summer time and shoreline houses are chalk-white, Quakerish, shy restrained Dos Passos has been keeping out of controversial critics' corners for years.

And all of which caused us to look up Dos Passos influenced, unmistably talented Burns in his little fieldstone cottage here on Long Island Sound. We found him to be completely relaxed in a living-room rocker with a half-smoked cigarette in one hand and an American highball in the other.

● ● ●

"I shall tell you quite frankly,"

JOHN HORNE BURNS—Five years in the Army gave him the background for "THE Novel of World War II."

"O! I'm strictly longhair," he warned, "and I suppose you might call my tastes rather chi-chi on occasion. In classical literature Dickens and Austen are my favorites. The contemporary English novelist? Well, I can remember reading one of Somerset Maugham's latest books while crossing the Mediterranean about three years ago and then throwing it over the rail and into the sea."

Protesting that no one could possibly be the least interested in what he likes to read, Burns nevertheless praised Betty Smith's "A Tree Grows In Brooklyn" for its "sincerity and warmth," but condemned Thomas Wolfe as vendor of "verbal diarrhea."

"I wouldn't last very long as a critic. My reviews would be quite scathing. It annoys me no end"—and Burns even looked annoyed when he said it—"that so many readers want formula-ridden stories. You know, loaded with the business of 'all eyes followed Laurie as she entered the room and her lips swept a slash of cat mine.' Just drivel, that's all drivel. And it's madness."

To many authors, it would have been even greater madness if they had turned down a $20,000 Hollywood contract as Burns did when "The Gallery" hit the bookstand

An article to ruin Mr. B's breakfast

striking effeminate poses against the mantelpiece, gestures that reminded him of Bette Davis, though he did not write that. But that much of what Burns *did* say and do that day would find its way into print and quickly reach Loomis either hadn't occurred to him or didn't perturb him in the slightest. Kneeland quickly concluded one thing about his subject: "You like or dislike him right away." Anyone writing such a thing usually doesn't have to specify into which camp he himself would fall.

"I shall tell you quite frankly that I detest being asked questions," Burns told Kneeland, in a Harvard accent and with "a smile which quickly developed into a constantly recurrent and particularly devilish grin." Burns was not above flattery, though

with some self-aggrandizement mixed in. "I am usually the one—
at least others tell me so—to prod and pry and try to discover exactly what is behind an individual personality," he went on. "But
you have turned the tables and cleverly employed a little psychology to get me talking, which is one of the most difficult things in
the world for anyone to do—especially a stranger. I suppose then,
that since I have started talking I may as well shock you by telling
a truth about myself—I'm a born snob."

Burns was "a good-looking blond," Kneeland wrote, with
"keen blue eyes, a rather casual manner, and strong white teeth
that flash when he smiles. It takes a few minutes by the way to
figure out whether he's laughing with you or at you." Having evidently answered that question for himself, too, Kneeland simply
resolved to let Burns speak for, and hang, himself. *The Gallery*,
Burns told him, "is being whispered about now at cocktail parties, and in one New York store I understand it's not being sold to
young girls because of a couple of 'grisly' chapters. I don't think it
would have stood up under Boston censorship either, unless my
editor blue-pencilled 29 of those four-letter words that apparently
make current best-sellers."

Burns mentioned all those youthful novels of his—eight of
them, he said—that "fortunately" had never been published. He
then described his postwar path back to Loomis and his "veg-
etative life" there. "I am now almost immune to the shrieks and
guerrilla warfare of nurse-maiding other people's children," he
said. It was a familiar refrain to his friends, but surely a shock
to any Loomis parents picking up the *Globe* that day. Burns proceeded to praise Dickens and Jane Austen, recall tossing Somerset Maugham overboard, and denounce the "verbal diarrhea" of
Thomas Wolfe. "I wouldn't last very long as a critic," he declared.
"My reviews would be quite scathing. It annoys me no end that
so many readers want formula-ridden stories. You know, loaded
with that business of 'all eyes followed Laurie as she entered the

room' and 'her lips were a slash of carmine.' Just drivel, that's all, drivel. And it's madness." He claimed that, wanting no part of the movie industry, he'd turned down $20,000 (worth more than ten times that in 2013 dollars) for film rights to *The Gallery*, and now hoped soon to finish "a highly clinical novel on America's higher institutions of learning." "Please don't be at all surprised if I characterize an occasional professor or two in it as *'Lucifer with a Book,'*" he told Kneeland. He did so, the reporter noted, with "a satanic leer."

Burns's family was horrified by the piece. But the real problem was Batchelder, who hauled Burns into his office a few days later, quite possibly just as Burns had anticipated, and maybe even had hoped. Only speculative fragments of their conversation have survived. Harsh words were evidently exchanged: "You've got to decide whether to be a schoolteacher or a celebrity," Mr. B supposedly told him. Burns subsequently called Batchelder's criticism "the meanest cut of my life." "You give me no alternative

Mr. B

but to leave," Burns supposedly declared. And maybe he did; the line has the theatricality and panache of something he could already have prepared. "So I walked out on the spot," Burns wrote afterward. With his royalties from *The Gallery* "getting fatter by the hour," he told MacMackin (only several weeks after the fact), he had "flounced out within the hour."

Once again, Burns had exaggerated: in fact, he hadn't "flounced" out anywhere, let alone so fast. But here, at least, he actually sold himself short. In fact he staged a more drawn-out and dramatic exit which, strictly from the standpoint of style, was far more impressive. He was going to have to leave the school soon—he certainly could not be there when *Lucifer* appeared—so why not exit in almost operatic fashion?

Yet another of Burns's many cursed chores at Loomis was conducting the combined Loomis and Chaffee choirs in the school's annual Christmas pageant: the "York Nativity." It was a big production, coming complete with angels and wise men, kings and messengers, frankincense and myrrh. (The show was under the overall direction of Norris Orchard, one of whose conceits was to have genuine Jewish students cast each year as Mary and Joseph.) As was also customary, there were to be four performances—one at four-thirty and one at seven-thirty on two consecutive days in mid-December. Burns participated uneventfully in the first three of them, with nary a hitch. But between performances on the second day, he didn't just hang around killing time. Instead, he completed something he'd been planning at least since his contretemps with Batchelder and probably well before.

When the last light over Bethlehem dimmed and the audience for the afternoon show filed out of the chapel, Burns, too, departed. He then walked out of Founders, crossed the Quadrangle, and walked beneath the colonnade to his dormitory, went up a flight of stairs to his apartment, and picked up two packed bags. Then, suitcases in hand, he walked back outside, took a left turn toward the dining hall, crossed the Quadrangle, and proceeded down the steps toward the infirmary. Slowly, he then made his way down Island Road into Windsor, where the Boston bus stopped to pick up passengers. Someone—the stories vary, but it was probably the curmudgeonly football coach, Ralph Erickson, a man as temperamentally different from Burns as two humans could ever be—happened to drive up behind him, and offered him a lift. The short ride to Windsor Avenue was undoubtedly the most time they'd ever spent together.

Probably while putting her young son to bed, Burns's upstairs neighbor and friend, Jane Hazelton, happened to look out her window as Burns took his leave. It was dusk, and, as he made his way off the campus, she saw him only from the rear. But with her failing eyesight she'd come to recognize people by how they held themselves and carried their shoulders, and even in the gloaming she identified Burns instantly by his gait—the way he swished a little as he walked. She was startled; he was supposed to be conducting the pageant, she knew, yet there he was, a lonely silhouette awkwardly balancing his valises—Burns had never been one for physical exertion of any kind—as he faded into the distance. Maybe he couldn't get a taxi at that hour, or maybe it was just more dramatic to stalk off. But proceeding resolutely, never turning around for a last look, Burns threaded his way between the baseball diamond and the football field. At the train tracks the road turns and dips, and Burns disappeared from view. She never saw him again, but the image of Burns leaving Loomis that night remained with her for the next sixty-five years.

Only as the Loomis chapel filled that night for the second performance of the pageant did anyone realize Burns was gone. Even the Three Wise Men must have been baffled. Suddenly, Henry White realized why Mr. Burns had asked him to familiarize himself with the score the week before. So it came to pass that on that cold December night, as his students reenacted Jesus's birth,

Burns was winging his way northward into Massachusetts and up to Boston, to begin a new life. "Such melodramatic gestures have pleased me since childhood," Burns wrote a few weeks later. He'd told no one, not even the students to whom he was closest, about his plans. Dave Brewer had driven him to his favorite Hartford bar only the night before; the next time he called Mr. Burns, there was no answer. It was the end of the semester, and most everyone else learned of Burns's disappearance only when they returned from their Christmas break. In what may have been the greatest tribute they could ever have paid him, the boys in one of his English classes refused to accept his replacement—another homosexual, who later committed suicide—and Paul Hazelton, Burns's upstairs neighbor, took over. The *Log* dutifully ignored the story, though by the time the *Loomiscellany* for 1948 appeared, the topic was no longer off-limits. "Mr. Burns makes his exit to the remorse of those who had benefited from his refreshing brilliance," reads the diary entry for December.

Not long before, at a convention of the New England Association of Teachers of English in Springfield, Massachusetts, Burns had delivered a paean to his profession. "We don't really believe that the world will be saved by us alone," he had said. "But out of defense of the sanctity of our life work, we do find, squinting timorously out of our theme-blind eyes, that a great deal of the old ideal of education has been landed plump in our laps. It is a dreadful weight, but secretly we love it—as a mother loves a wayward child." Now, though, he had taught his last class. "The war had made him nervous, or possibly the publication of his first novel . . . went to his head," he later wrote of himself to his Harvard classmates. "It was a considerable success, and he decided to come out of the cloister."

21

The *Gallery* never did make the *New York Times* best seller list. But it would eventually go through twelve printings in hardcover in the United States, and sell 20,500 copies, a highly respectable number. So flat-footed was Harpers by the demand that it ran out of the paper it needed to print more. In January 1948 the publisher took out a full-page advertisement in the *New York Times Book Review* solely to showcase its novelists, and Burns was Exhibit No. 1. "*THE GALLERY* did not catch fire right away," the ad stated. "But as more and more people read it, they recognized in it an exciting reading experience and an even more exciting promise. Readers and critics alike are looking forward to the next work of this brilliant new writer. Which is how *first* novelists become *famous* novelists." "Promise" was a word often associated with Burns. *The Gallery* was a fine book. But he had only just begun.

"Since I am blond, I am their white-haired boy and white-hope," Burns told a fan. "The odd thing about *The Gallery* is that seven months after its publication it *should* by all statistics be dead. But it continues to sell an average of 500 copies a week . . . a novel that all the brighties said would fall flat on its face has had a considerable success. It didn't do a Laura Z. Hobson,* but it is doing wonderfully. My royalty checks are fat; most foreign rights have been sold; Ben Hecht[†] is forming a new independent movie company and has paid me $50,000 for the rights to the book. I don't know what Hollywood will do to *The Gallery*; but I've got my fingers crossed. It will probably be in Technicolor: Abbott and Costello in *Spaghetti and Moonlight*." (Nothing in Hecht's papers verifies Burns's claim. Certainly $50,000 was an enormous sum for the time, one that, were it real, should have set him up for many years to come.)

The next month, Burns made the cover of the prestigious and influential *Saturday Review of Literature*, which had named him the best war novelist of 1947. In describing him, the magazine chose an image that was unwittingly apt. "John Horne Burns at thirty-one sounds like a man who has drunk a heady draught—not really intoxicated, but engagingly exhilarated," it said. As for *The Gallery*, it was not a book for little boys, "but for adults who recognize the truth and know good writing when they see it . . . The author's place in American war fiction seems certain . . . Compared with *The Gallery* . . . [Dos Passos's] *Three Soldiers*, the novel that started off the realistic fiction of the First World War, was a fragrant and tender lily." Burns's writing routine—three thousand words in three hours, seven days a week—was now important enough for him to detail. "I put myself in a chair and write," he related. "I don't wait for inspiration, or I might never get started." He spoke of his love of music—"I play all the time, strictly long hair, the longer hair the better"—and

---

* Author of the best-selling 1947 novel *Gentleman's Agreement*.

† The American screenwriter (*The Front Page*, *His Girl Friday*, *Notorious*), journalist, and activist (1894–1964).

NEWCOMERS IN AMERICAN FICTION

Saturday Review

of LITERATURE

VOL. XXXI No. 7   FEBRUARY 14, 1948   FIFTEEN CENTS

SRL's *Choice for Best 1947 War Novelist—John Horne Burns. (See page 6)*

Thirteen Adventurers

By HARRISON SMITH

Cover boy

said he still thought of Italy. While he'd emerged from the cloister, he remained in the closet. "There is a girl there, daughter of a
banker in Milan—I may go back and marry her yet," he said. In
the meantime, he worked on *Lucifer*, scheduled for the fall. "He
anticipates much fur will fly," the magazine declared.

Had he gone to fetch his fictitious bride, Burns would have
found himself still more appreciated in his old haunts. Even before
The Gallery was translated into Italian, it had been discovered in
Italy: in 1947 the Italian critic Emilio Cecchi, who'd written extensively on American literature, had read it in English. He instantly
distinguished it from other American novels of the Italian war like
John Hersey's *A Bell for Adano*, which he found insulting, even
patronizing: a number of American writers, he complained, had
come to Italy three or four years earlier "expecting to arrive in a
land of monkeys." *The Gallery* was "bizarre," he conceded—just
why he did not say—and Burns himself both immature and deriva-
tive, with a certain *eau de* Ernest Hemingway about him. "He likes
giving himself a certain boastful air. To indulge in risqué, bawdy
particulars," wrote Cecchi. But unlike other Americans, Burns had
approached the Italians with humility and intelligence. The title of
Cecchi's piece said it all: "Someone Who Understood." He called
for an Italian publisher to take up the book—a book by an American "who understood a lot, and who makes up for the many others
who understood little or nothing."

The Italian publisher Garzanti rose to Cecchi's challenge,
and in 1948 the book appeared in Italy. Critics praised it for being
brave, and just, and unprejudiced, and empathetic. Burns, they
wrote, had understood something about Italian dignity and re-
siliency. And in criticizing his own culture, he had given Italians
recovering from more than two decades of totalitarianism a lesson
in democracy. They, too, ignored "Momma": homosexuality was
even further off-limits in Italy. "Queen Penicillin" also went un-
mentioned. But *La Galleria* won for Burns in Italy a reservoir of

affection and tolerance far deeper than what *The Gallery* gave him in the United States. The gratitude of Italians only grew when the book was compared to the devastating portrait of wartime Naples in Curzio Malaparte's novel, *La Pelle (The Skin)*. Malaparte, after all, was one of their own.

The Gallery was eventually published in Spain, Sweden, England, France, and Germany as well. Harold Acton, the British aristocrat who spent much of his life in Florence and wrote extensively about Naples, captured Europe's enduring appreciation for the book, which he called "unforgettable." "It is crude and slap-dash and abounds in clichés," he later wrote, "but Burns has grasped the main point: that Naples is preeminently a city where life is intensely lived, where in the darkest alleys, so grim to those who lack imagination, so sordid to those without aesthetic values, life is considered the greatest good and death the greatest evil."

Burns had never been spare with his own literary opinions. They crept regularly into his wartime correspondence, often with scant regard for the age and educational level of the recipient. For instance, to his mother, who was not especially well read, he opined that *The Picture of Dorian Gray* was "a not completely successful welter of Oscar Wilde's guilt complexes, epigrams that now seem studied as artificial aspidistras, and a confusion of neo-paganism grafted upon the uneasy Christian naturalism of the late nineteenth century," and denounced the "spidery sterilities of Henry James." But the success of *The Gallery* further emboldened him. In the summer of 1948 Burns made the circuit of writers' conferences—"a racket if ever I smelled one"—delivering a talk entitled "The Creative Writer in the 20th Century." Utilitarian America, he maintained, caricatured creativity, including the creative writer, reducing poets and singers to "queerness and outlandishness . . . Pianists were expected not to cut their hair; and poets were supposed to walk down Piccadilly with a poppy or a lily in their medieval hand."* Still, anyone trying to fashion something "beautiful, durable, and true" has little choice but to create. "It is the most futile ' occupation in the world, this setting down of your very best on paper. Yet if you have to do it, you have to do it."

And working in the author's favor, he went on, was American individualism, which meant freedom from critical orthodoxies, including the orthodoxies of past writers who, as Goethe had so succinctly put it, have "nothing more to teach us," particularly now that the world had almost been blown to smithereens. The war, Burns insisted, had made daintiness and gamesmanship obsolete. Perhaps he was "a mouse taking potshots at elephants who annoy him with their stamping," but he proceeded to name names. There was (again) Henry James ("this wonderful artist in cobwebs"); James Joyce (reading him was like "watching an advanced case of dementia praecox"); Thomas Mann ("has written nothing worth reading" since fleeing Hitler); T. S. Eliot (like "a Parisian abbot tasting marmalade just before the French Revolution"); and Franz Kafka ("Were he alive today, he would be teaching at Sarah Lawrence and lecturing at writers' conferences"). Even Oscar Wilde came in for it: renewed interest in him had "more to do with the Kinsey Report" than with the worth of anything he had written. Burns had little use for Ezra Pound ("a literary vulture") but assailed how, along with various figures from the musical world (the singer Kirsten Flagstad, the pianist Walter Gieseking, the composer Richard Strauss), he'd been excommunicated for taking the wrong side in the recent war. When it came to toeing party lines, he saw little difference between victors and vanquished. "In this respect we are no better than the

---

* The line is from Gilbert and Sullivan's *Patience*; it comes from a character named Bunthorne, thought to have been modeled after Oscar Wilde.

Nazis and the Soviets, who insist that art has a political bias," he complained.

Burns assailed writers who were in it strictly for the money, doing pieces for women's magazines or the "fat historical novel"— the kind of thing "with large chunks of copulation in the West Indies in 1745" and "a picture of a bosom on the dust jacket." They might do well, these people, but "in their hearts they feel themselves like hucksters who have somehow evaded the Pure Food and Drug Laws." The alternative—writing something for which there is no discernible demand—posed terrible dangers to the courageous few willing to risk it. "If they fail, they disappear into an emptiness far deeper than that reserved for beaten generals or vanquished Miss Americas. Their whole life and its aspirations are less than the Biblical chaff before the wind. In spite of sentimental Thomas Gray, there are *no* mute inglorious Miltons. They were either Miltons or they were nobodies."

But those who try and succeed, he went on, are "the happiest men on the planet." And their odds had improved, both because the country had "outgrown its diapers and the jam on its face" and because of what it had just endured. "Only one good thing comes out of wars," he said. "They arouse people from their lethargy." Newly enlightened publishers now welcomed writers with peculiar or personal things to say. With the breakdown of puritanical provincialism and hypocrisy and the pioneering work of some American novelists, "we live in a most promising period for American writers with courage, talent, insight and invention." And this time, because of the high prices in Europe and the sheer scale of destruction there, they would stay at home: "The torch has finally and irrevocably been flung across the Atlantic." This generation of writers was harder and "less inclined to feel sorry for themselves."

Burns was also now in demand for book endorsements, though given his temperament and extreme competitiveness—he admitted he rarely read books others recommended, out of shame that he had not discovered them for himself—this could be chancy. "We pan the shit out of them all. No more use of our name in blurbs except for some new Dante," he told MacMackin. Further exacerbating his mean streak was pressure from his publisher; presumably because it feared cannibalizing his own market, Harpers had gotten on Burns for praising a book by another war veteran, Merle Miller's *That Winter.*

The publicity director at Knopf discovered all this firsthand in January 1948, when he naively asked Burns to endorse *The Train from Pittsburgh,* a novel about a tortured ad man by one Julian Farren. Any sympathy Burns had voiced on the lecture circuit for writers quietly plying their craft evidently didn't apply to poor Mr. Farren, as Knopf learned upon receiving Burns's report.

Only in a snafu year like 1948 could such a worthless piece of trash be invested with significance and relevance. Has the house of Knopf no shame? The novel reminds me of a little boy masturbating in a closet and calling out his reactions in bad blank verse. The design and purpose, so far as I can see, are pointless. What makes it so meretricious is that The Train *is written in a style that to many Americans is good writing (to be said unctuously). A good writer could, I suppose, take the story and make something out of it. But not Mr. Farren. Into it he has poured all the ingredients of arty fiction of the past five years: 1) the degenerating alcoholic (for whom in this case one feels not the slightest concern or pity) 2) raw chunks of prep school sex whenever the going gets dull 3) dreary, mechanical use of the flashback 4) Freudian jargon—mother fixations etc 5) appropriate anthology quotations from the poets to give the piece an air of Kultchah and literary worth. It's quite a commentary of our times that a reputable house (indeed, one with a flossy reputation)*

*would publish such a piece as Serious fiction. I'm sorry. Not
since my last stag party have I seen a cheaper performance.*

He signed the letter "Cordially."

Undiscouraged, Knopf came back to Burns the following year
with the Irish novelist Elizabeth Bowen's *The Heat of the Day.* In
a letter to the boss's wife, Blanche Knopf, Burns was more gracious but no more laudatory, even though he'd admired Bowen's
previous work. As if slamming her was not enough, he took a
couple of other writers down with her.

*My exasperation began early in the work and mounted to
the preposterous conclusion. The story itself is incredibly
silly, and Miss Bowen's style has become so overwrought
that it emphasizes the feebleness of her plot—as in the
later works of Henry James. I couldn't imagine how anyone
could possibly have attenuated into nothingness a story of
wartime London. But Miss Bowen has succeeded. The war
seems to have shattered her sensibilities, as it did the late
Virginia Woolf's. And whereas the earlier Elizabeth Bowen
moved in a world of light and poetic validity, she has
now landed herself squarely in the grotesque camp of Ivy
Compton-Burnett.* Tsk, tsk.*

Burns knew he could be disagreeable. "I don't think you
would care for me as a person; and I prefer to be known from the
printed page," he confessed to a reader. One might have thought
Christopher Isherwood, also gay but twelve years Burns's senior
and already well established and respected, would be spared
Burns's bile, though in his diary Isherwood wrote that "a faint
darkish cloud" hung over his encounter with him, during which

---

* The English novelist (1884–1969).

the younger man "got drunk and became hostile and tiresome." (Still, he said, he wished he'd gotten to know him better.) Burns's antipathy to other homosexuals far outweighed any feelings of solidarity or common purpose. He quickly read, and trashed, Truman Capote's much-publicized 1948 novel *Other Voices, Other Rooms*. "Ten years ago it would have been good," he told MacMackin. "But the Decline of the West is progressing too fast for people to bother with such precious nonsense as Jesus Fever." Random House's infamous publicity photograph of Capote— "the fingernail polish, the waistcoat, the hairdo of a Mongolian idiot"—would finish him, he predicted.

Burns appeared to know Capote only from afar. But he had several encounters with Gore Vidal, leading to a highly charged rivalry that seemed to fascinate, and haunt, Vidal (who was nine years younger than Burns) for decades afterward. The two competed over everything, including which of them was more competitive. As gay veterans who'd written novels about the war right after the war—Vidal's was his first book, *Williwaw* (1946)—each was, as Vidal later wrote, "properly wary of the other." Had he known how Burns felt about his third novel—*The City and the Pillar*, which centered on the relationship between two men and was published in early 1948—the younger man would have been warier still. "Two weeks ago in a bar on 8th Avenue we came across *The City and the Pillar* (or is it arsy-versy)?" Burns wrote MacMackin. "We clutched it up eagerly, since we consider Mister Vidal our principal rival in the welterweight division. We hate to gloat, but we consider the novel a dismal failure."

By this point, Burns had moved to Boston, eventually settling into a one-bedroom apartment on Chambers Street Court in the city's marginal but somewhat artsy West End, whose small Italian presence would have made him feel somewhat more at home. (A schematic design of the place done by David MacMackin at the time of his housewarming included "plastic, cracked stiff yellow shower curtain along tubside," "jonquils—or daffodils—all over living room on all bearing surfaces," and "typewriter and writing table conspicuously absent.") But Burns still managed to make his way periodically to New York. "We are putting on our chasuble in two more weeks to descend on the pestiferous city, and will see you then," he wrote MacMackin in mid-January 1948, and, accompanied by a new boyfriend, he did. MacMackin threw a small party for him at the apartment of his friend (and, perhaps, lover), a dancer and choreographer named Paul Godkin.* Vidal, too, was there. Hanging out with the author of *The Gallery* was a moment of considerable consequence to Vidal, who pondered the man, and the experience, at considerable length in his journal over the next few days.

> . . . *then to Godkin's. This boy David was giving a salon for John Horne Burns his old prep school teacher. Burns, his boy, Donald Saddler, Johnny Paul and I made up the party.*[†] *Burns and David played on the two pianos Stravinsky etc. played beautifully . . . Then we all wrote one line of a poem (complete) without knowing what the others had written the results were funny—all I remember is my line 'on the final phallus now I fall' and Burns' which contained the name Oliant—the word smathema*[‡]—*foreskin [unintelligible]—When he and I talked a little about writing he made some pompous remarks about writers understanding + facing the "economic" situation—he talked about having roots +*

---

* Godkin did choreography for the film *Around the World in 80 Days*, as well as for *The Ed Sullivan Show*.

† Saddler is a prominent American dancer and choreographer; the identity of Johnny Paul isn't clear.

‡ The word was surely "smegma," which also appears in Burns's letter to Holger Hagen of March 4, 1944 (see page 104).

said the preceding generation (Wescott's) ran away, had
no roots and that whole generation failed. I said I couldn't
think of writers in generations and I said, too, [illegible]
and rather pompously that great writing was merely an
illustration of vision. There was mild antagonism in the
air. He is very odd, quite ugly; tall plump and fair a long
broken nose, flop ears and a high forehead; he's losing his
hair—his speaking voice is pleasant—he talks jerkily,
[unintelligible] to cover an obvious lack of ease—he says
unpleasant things about most writers, especially Truman
[Capote]. He hates precocity but I hear from David his
new book is very precious "flossy" is the word he uses—his
smile is charming.*

A few days later Vidal met Burns again, apparently at a party
in Beulah Hagen's apartment, to which both he and Burns had
been invited by Glenway Wescott. "It was a gloomy affair," Vidal
wrote in 1952.[†] "*The City and the Pillar* was just out and everyone
was attacking it. Burns was riding high on *The Gallery* and he
tended to be rather patronizing, saying polite things about *Williwaw*. All I can remember is Janet Flanner[‡] taking him aside to tell
him in her gruff bellow that he had written one of the finest, etc.
etc. No one, alas, praised me. I grew irritable. Glenway praised
and praised. Burns pouted and mumbled alternately, offending, I
was told later, everyone."

---

* Glenway Wescott, American novelist and brother of Beulah Hagen.

† In this journal entry Vidal recalled that the party was held in January 1947, but his chronology is clearly off. He also wrote that it marked his introduction to Burns, but his contemporaneous journal suggests otherwise.

‡ The *New Yorker's* longtime European correspondent, who wrote as "Genêt." Educated
Romans offered six reasons for their city's sudden popularity among American tourists, she
wrote in 1949. Reason No. 4: "John Hersey's having written 'A Bell for Adano' and John
Burns' having written 'The Gallery.'" Oddly, neither book had anything at all to do with
Rome.

In his contemporaneous journal entry, Vidal offered more details about that second encounter with Burns.

> *Met John Horne Burns, already described, he was tight and not really at ease—his phone wasn't working and he had to call his "roommate"—a word he used to the company a dozen times. I had to call Hal* so Burns and I went to a drug store together. He told me he was much in love with this boy, that he was tired because they had had, that evening, sex in the shower, that they wanted to mop up the streets with Truman Capote, that he'd [unintelligible] my first two books. Then we bought a valentine for Glenway but decided to give it to Beulah—said Burns, "this is the campiest thing I've done in a long time." Then the roommate joined us. He is plain, a better looking version of Burns.*

Beulah Hagen later recalled Vidal leaving that night in a huff.

In a masochistic stroke a few days later, Vidal, about to leave by boat for Italy, began reading *The Gallery*. Initially he found it "interesting" but "so easy to write." By the next day he'd read it all. "Finished Burns book I was much moved—astonished, however, at the similarity to my writing," he wrote. A week later, having arrived in Naples, he, too, went straight to the Galleria, which, apart from the repaired skylight, he found to be much as Burns had described it. (He quickly returned there twice more—to pick up young men.) In a fraternal gesture, he wrote Burns to introduce him to a rich Englishman hoping to film *The Gallery*. His letter did not survive, but in it he apparently touched on their similarities, and talked about his encounters with Italian "mice"—as Vidal later explained, code

---

* Probably the dancer Harold Lang, who later appeared as the title character in the 1952 revival of *Pal Joey*.

for the young Americans who had stayed in Italy, living off "the remaining crumbs of the GI Bill of Rights." Burns answered "Distintissimo Vidal" in March from Boston. "Many thanks for your note," he wrote. "I'm happy to know that you're picking up mice in Italy. Italian mice are most agreeable, and are known as *topolini*. As for your and my tending in the same direction as writers—that's a matter for Ph.D's in 2000 to write their dissertations on." Burns informed Vidal that a script for *The Gallery* had already been written, with shooting about to begin. "Your rich friend has come too late; though I'd prefer to have it made by an Italian company and Vittorio de Sica,"* he wrote. (About the things they shared, Burns had misunderstood him, Vidal later said. "I simply meant that we were each going to have the same hard time from the virulent fagbashers that dominated, then as now, book-chat land in the USA.")

Reminders of Burns's greater fame, and ability, stalked Vidal. Even his groupies seemed to relish taunting him with Burns's talent. "Have you had the very great pleasure of reading, *The Gallery*, by Burns [?]" a fan from Los Angeles wrote Vidal in June 1948. "Definitely a superior work, which should be required reading. Frankly, I think he even goes deeper into human nature than you did, although it's all there in your book, for those who care to see beyond the narrative. But Burns hits you right in the face with it, making it impossible to read his book for narrative alone. For this reason, a lot of people won't like his work, and yours should sell better." A few days earlier, a young advertising man from Westchester told Vidal that "*The Gallery* is THE great novel of World War Two." Following Vidal's evidently querulous response, the ad man hastily backpedaled. "I may have been a little premature in regards to John Horne Burns," he conceded. "There's only one writer I am consistently satisfied with, and you know who he is." But Vidal had to admit they were right. Burns, he wrote a few years later, "has extraordinary intuition and

---

* Italian film director (1902–1974) who made *The Bicycle Thief*.

brains," and *The Gallery* displayed a "compassion which has been unequaled by his dry, careful contemporaries who commit as little possible both emotionally and artistically."

That Burns (and Capote) had done so well with their books "reacts on me like a thunderstorm on a barometer," Vidal wrote in his journal in 1949. "There are passages in Truman that make me writhe they are so good . . . and the dignity of *The Gallery* is like a blow . . . if they were unsuccessful I suppose I could survive their excellence but the fact there are people who put one or the other or both ahead of me is too much." Vidal *did* have one thing over both men: he wasn't destroying himself. "But all the time I say this I know I shall outlast them all: longevity and production are worth more than all the spoils of genius that ever glittered to the delight of the New York Queens, the arbiters of the instant." That prophesy clearly consoled Vidal long before it came to pass. He kept tabs on Burns and seemed never to have gotten over him, bringing him up repeatedly over the years, unspooling provocative (and perhaps dubious) new details about their few encounters. "Burns was a difficult man who drank too much, loved music, detested all other writers, wanted to be great," he wrote many years later. "He was also certain that to be a good writer it was necessary to be homosexual. When I disagreed, he named a half-dozen celebrated contemporaries. 'A Pleiad,' he roared delightedly, 'of pederasts!' But what about Faulkner? I asked, and Hemingway? He was disdainful. Who said *they* were any good?"*

Competitiveness pure and simple, rather than competitiveness with another ambitious and erudite gay writer, explains Burns's most rancorous, if outlandish, literary rivalry: with James Michener. Michener's *Tales of the South Pacific*, like *The Gallery*, appeared in 1947. "Rivalry" is really the wrong word to describe their relationship; Michener readily acknowledged Burns was the better writer. He praised *The Gallery* publicly; the book "was so

---

* Among those he might have mentioned, besides himself and Vidal: Wescott, Merle Miller, Capote, Paul Bowles, and Thornton Wilder.

very good as to excite envy in most writers," he told a professor
in Virginia. ("I have not met him personally but know him by
reputation to be an excellent person," Michener added.) When
discussing Burns he took care to steer clear of his homosexuality,
for fear it would put off readers who would otherwise enjoy the
book. Michener predicted that Burns—who had what he called "a
handsome, somewhat feisty-looking face . . . with the half-sneer
of the detached and amused observer"—would one day attain the
stature of E. M. Forster (author of *A Passage to India*) and Gide.

At one point, Burns wrote Michener to thank him for his praise.
But such gratitude evaporated in the spring of 1948, when Michener won the Pulitzer Prize for fiction. Michener hadn't expected
to win it—collections of short stories never had—but Burns most
certainly did. In fact, he had thought himself a lock and, Michener
later wrote, was "savagely disappointed" when he wasn't. Even
Michener conceded that Burns had been robbed. At that moment,
Michener later recalled, Burns conceived a blazing hatred for him.
Early in 1949, *Life* magazine assembled five of the most successful World War II novelists—Michener, Burns, Thomas Heggen,
Irwin Shaw, and Alfred Hayes (*All Thy Conquests*)—for a group
photograph, to be taken by one of its first women photographers,
Nina Leen. When a *Life* editor tried introducing Michener to
Burns, Burns refused to shake his hand, then walked away. In the
picture itself, Michener remains in the background, looking as out
of place as he probably felt, while Burns looms in front, holding
his ubiquitous cigarette and glowering. Outside afterward, Michener was standing on the sidewalk with a *Life* editor when the
topic turned to Burns. "He's quite a faggot, you know," the editor
remarked. "When we turned [Burns] was standing less than a foot
behind us, his face an ashen gray," Michener wrote in his memoirs.

Burns's chance for revenge came in February 1949, when,
oblivious to the tensions between the two, the *Saturday Review*
blithely asked him to review Michener's second novel, *The Fires*

When Life *assembled its top war novelists, it placed Burns up front, with (L to R) Alfred Hayes, Thomas Heggen, Irwin Shaw, and James Michener behind him.*

of Spring. Burns should have declined the assignment: there was no way he could be fair. Instead, he seized it, and launched into an attack on both of Michener's books—the old *and* the new. "Unlike many recent war novels, which aim to effect a nuclear fission in the reader's consciousness, this delightful work concerned itself with the trivia of war," was how he described *Tales of the South Pacific*. "Mr. Michener was avowedly reporting; he made no pretense at that analysis and characterization which distinguish the novelist from the journalist. His *Tales* will probably remain a minor classic." "*Probably remain a minor classic*": you can't get much more dismissive per word than that. As for *The Fires of Spring*, it was "brilliant high school stuff," filled with "soggy prose" and "embarrassing dialogue." Its first fifty pages "are quite touching," Burns declared. "After that, it explodes into what may charitably be called a phony." The magazine had planned a cover story on Michener, but after so devastating a review, it changed its mind.

Burns's review shocked the writer Irving Stone, who told Michener it was "the lowest thing I have seen in our American literary life in the last twenty years . . . But then," he went on, "I taught with Burns at the University of Indiana Writers' Conference last summer, and if you could only know the man! If we can meet in New York I should like to tell you something about him." Here Michener's Quakerism came in handy. "The pale young man is a friend of mine, deeply resentful that his book of great merit did not win the Pulitzer Prize," he wrote a bookstore owner in Massachusetts. "I have no brief against him and shall probably continue to consider him my friend."

And he did. Michener went on to watch two other successful first-time novelists, Ross Lockridge (*Raintree County*) and Heggen, kill themselves when they couldn't repeat their success. But Burns meant more to him than they, and was, to his mind, the most talented of the three. He would continue to follow Burns's fate closely and, despite Burns's cruelty to him, sympathetically. And sympathy, as hard as it might be to summon, was what Burns would soon need.

22

On February 27, 1948, Burns completed *Lucifer with a Book.* This time, he did not put his head down on his typewriter and cry, as he had with *The Gallery;* it wasn't that kind of book, and writing it hadn't provided that kind of catharsis. And with no one in particular to whom to dedicate it, he spread his thanks around, to those determined to do . . . well, that wasn't quite clear. "To thousands of men and women in America whose heads are bloody but unbowed," the dedication declared.*

Even before Burns had completed *Lucifer,* his publishers were talking it up. "Incidentally, John Horne Burns is just finishing another novel, which he thinks is a good deal more mature than *The Gallery,*" John Fischer of Harpers wrote Charles Poore, the book critic for the *New York Times.* "We haven't seen the manuscript yet, but we have lively hopes." As indeed they would have

---

* The line is from "Invictus," a poem written in 1875 by W. E. Henley.

had, for anticipation of Burns's book was enormous. When he finally finished it the next month, Helen Strauss told him it was better than *The Gallery*. In mid-February she gave Harpers the first 469 pages, and on March 1 she sent along the rest. It had been a relatively easy birth.

All told, there were 581 pages to go through. But it would take the folks at the publishing house only a few paragraphs to realize that Burns's latest offering was very different from the last. Driving *The Gallery* had been a mixture of compassion, sympathy, and indignation, along with a fair measure of reportage on matters of great moment. The ridicule was confined to a couple of comical characters. But from the opening pages of *Lucifer*, ridicule was pretty much all there was.

The novel is set at a prep school established by a venerable New England family and located along a river where the original homestead still stood; "the Academy," as it is called, sure sounded like Loomis. There were other superficial parallels: tobacco barns nearby; the faux-Georgian architecture; the location of the headmaster's house near the founding family's manse. In real life, Loomis's most coveted graduation honor was the Nathaniel Horton Batchelder Prize for Industry, Loyalty, and Manliness; in *Lucifer*, it's the Sophia Abercrombie Medal for Valor, Application, and Dignity. But there were also plenty of distinctions. Instead of five founding siblings, for instance, there is only Miss Sophia. Her money, unlike the Loomises', has come from the "sweat of whores and the blood of black slaves," whose bodily fluids can still be detected in the metallic taste of the water drawn from the local well.

Miss Sophia is strictly a concoction. But the Academy's headmaster, Pilkey (he is never given the dignity of a first name), is clearly a send-up of Batchelder: he, too, has been its first and only leader, there most of his adult life. Pilkey is a tyrant, windbag, fool, and bigot. Negroes are supposedly welcome at his school, but few ever seem to come; a smattering of Jews is all right, so long as they don't become too prominent, prone as they are to "subterfuge and duplicity," "decadence and subversiveness," "free love and Communism." Pilkey is also homophobic—or, as Burns puts it, "suspicious of the masculinity and loyalties" of the single men who comprise much of his faculty, particularly the more gifted ones. He finds "something covert and cloying" about the boys' devotion to these men. He's generally wary of too much brilliance: it complicates things. Pilkey's wife, like Batchelder's, is an artist, but while Evelyn Longman Batchelder was a distinguished sculptor—a disciple of the great Daniel Chester French, who did Lincoln in the Lincoln Memorial, her *Genius of Electricity* long sat atop AT&T's corporate headquarters in Manhattan and appeared on Bell Telephone directories everywhere—Mrs. Pilkey decorates Wedgwood, and "her brain was glazed from licking the tips of little brushes with which she stippled eagles and gryphons onto old china."

Teachers at the Academy are almost uniformly odious—jealous, sycophantic, opportunistic, lecherous—and correspondingly unattractive: obese, venous, pimply, greasy, decrepit. The men have breasts, the women mustaches. The French teacher is "a fat little man with bald spots like tundra" and "pearly blue false teeth"; his eyes are rheumy and his breath reeks of drink. The comptroller's wife "has the face of a tart bursting with meringue." Pilkey's secretary is epileptic, ensuring "her lifelong virginity." Another faculty wife, a childless woman who gets off plying athletic boys with hot chocolate, has a pimply face and hair "like French fried potatoes before the grease is drained." A young English teacher is "hyperthyroid," a young mathematician "liverish." The fellow in charge of alumni and testing, one Dell Holly, is "a tall thin earnest man, pockmarked and platitudinous," while his wife, Lisa, is glamorous but cold, her laughter "a little spray of needles."

But most egregious of all is an English teacher named Philbrick Grimes.* Grimes is Pilkey's confidant, informant, and henchman. He is unmarried, nosy, jittery, fluttery, and sissified, a congenital busybody "only happy when he has a finger in every pie." Generally, Burns flits from target to target, never dwelling for very long on any. But he is obsessed with Grimes, and especially with his sexuality, variously describing him as "a male virgin with a horror of sex and its dishevelments," a "eunuch," and an "emasculated Machiavelli." His penis is "underdeveloped," and his libido so repressed that, though only thirty-seven, he awakens without an erection. Grimes was deemed too psychotic—"Old Biddy Type," his draft board decreed—to serve in the war. Instead, he "followed the headlines and read Housman[†] to his classes." Some of Burns's characters, while clearly wild caricatures, were quickly recognizable to the Loomis community; Minerva Mears and her daughter, Midgie—depicted, respectively, as a silly martinet and a slut—were supposed to be the headmistress of Chaffee and her daughter; Dell Holly was Francis Grubbs, the French teacher who'd helped put out the fire in Burns's apartment, identifiable in part by his complexion as well as by his marriage to a woman considered far more beautiful than he deserved. These were cheap shots, but chip shots, against minor players. It was Grimes to whom Burns kept returning, again and again, ladling on additional helpings of contempt. And there was no mistaking who *he* was. He was Norrie Orchard. He is the least sympathetic of an utterly unsympathetic bunch.

In *The Gallery*, everyone heroic has a bit of Burns in him. In *Lucifer*, only one character does: a newly hired history teacher,

---

* As Mark Bassett was the first to note, in the British novelist Evelyn Waugh's *Decline and Fall*, "Philbrick" is an ex-criminal turned butler, while "Grimes" is an incompetent teacher, pederast, and bigamist.

† A. E. Housman (1859–1936), British poet, author of *A Shropshire Lad*.

recently returned from the war, named Guy Hudson. With some cosmetic alterations—he went to Amherst rather than Harvard and is "Titian-haired" rather than blond—Guy Hudson *is* Burns: clever, arrogant, contemptuous of those around him, politically progressive—the type who reads the *Nation*, the *New Republic*, the *New Masses*,* and *PM*.† But he's been retrofitted and enhanced into everything Burns could never be. Guy Hudson (for some reason, he is always called "Guy Hudson" rather than "Guy" or "Hudson") is a guy's guy, tough and macho. Guy Hudson isn't some softy who stayed behind the lines, but an ex–infantry lieutenant who saw combat; instead of reading POW letters and taking in operas, Guy Hudson once strangled a German parachutist. Rather than suffering only anomie, Guy Hudson was maimed by an exploding shell during the Battle of the Bulge. That won him a Purple Heart, but it also rendered the left side of his mouth frozen in a permanent yet peculiarly appropriate sneer. Guy Hudson is athletic and hairy and buff, the sort awestruck boys gape at and discuss: "Musta taken a course with Charles Atlas," one remarks after seeing him in the shower. Guy Hudson wasn't exactly John Horne Burns, but he may have been Burns's way of asserting the manhood which, he believed, military service had conferred on him. While the army had thrust Burns, as it had tens of thousands of other homosexuals, into a larger and more variegated gay world than he had ever known, it had also been the first fraternity to which he had ever been admitted—the Harvard Glee Club really didn't count—and he wanted everyone to know it.

War has made certain workaday indignities more tolerable for Guy Hudson: anyone who has subsisted on C-rations won't bitch about prep school food. But knowing now what really

---

* A prominent American Marxist publication.

† An innovative and progressive New York newspaper.

matters—and only *he* really knows—Guy Hudson quickly and predictably hates the Academy and most everything about it, along with nearly everyone in it, especially the malingerers— like Grimes—who stayed behind: "Wasn't *his* reality after combat in France and Germany a stronger and truer one than these people who chattered as though life was an intellectual garden party and themselves sophisticated marionettes?" Guy Hudson finds his colleagues uniformly contemptible, though oddly enough, it is the gay teachers he seems to loathe most, because they are either too flagrant or too repressed. When not fleeing into town to get "stinking drunk"—he is an accomplished drinker—Guy Hudson struts around campus feeling superior and subversive. But at least he has a proper excuse: this is his first tour of duty at the school. Guy Hudson would have known better than to return.

Naturally, Guy Hudson is an inspiring teacher—where mediocrity reigns, excellence is another form of rebellion and revenge—though the Academy's students are invariably unworthy of him—stupid, boorish, cruel, muscle-bound, spoiled, unappreciative. They talk almost exclusively about sports, sex, and cars, all in the same mindless way. Guy Hudson is less cultured and hospitable than Burns—not given to playing "Das Lied von der Erde" for students in his apartment—but a bit more insightful; "it seemed to him more than a little incestuous for a man to surround himself with a circle of doting boys half his own age." Not that he shortchanges his students: in class he gives them "the hypodermic of his own personality," and gradually pries open at least a few of their "lacquered hardened little minds."

Guy Hudson *does* take a shine to a small cohort of students, each well out of the mainstream. There's Tad McKinley, one of the school's few blacks. And Ben Gordon, a Jew who, much to Pilkey's discomfiture, is president of the student council. (Gordon considers Guy Hudson both the greatest *and* the nicest teacher

in the school.) And there's Ralph Du Bouchet,* an artsy scholarship student who is sensitive, handsome, brilliant, and musically
gifted, and whose artistic parents have a home on the water.
There are clearly gay boys at the Academy—"young men of
decadent tendencies," Burns calls them. They hate the athletic
regimen at the place; all that "armor" they put on every afternoon makes them look and feel ridiculous. They write cinquains,
play medieval music or Shostakovich, read Rimbaud. Burns
calls them "an exotic little club" of "Pariahs" and "Untouch-
ables," "Dreeps," "Fruits," and "Awfuls" (though, oddly, never
"Dreadfuls"). While the "Normals" amuse themselves firing
water pistols or smashing furniture, these more precious boys
gather nightly for soirees and circle jerks. One of them is known
as "the Abbot"; his roommate—surname: McWaters—is "the
Abbess"; he wears his hair in a wave, and his fingernails glisten.
Together, in a room reeking of incense, its windows framed to resemble a Gothic cathedral, they hang out with assorted "monks"
and "nuns," all dressed for the part.

Burns devotes a chapter to these boys and their escapades,
but more to shock than to endorse; MacMackin notwithstanding,
they were not his types, nor Guy Hudson's. Guy Hudson keeps
his distance from them, though Guy Hudson is an enlightened
fellow, and to him their very presence reflects progress of a sort:
"America had made strides! Fifty years ago these arty children
would have been done to death at such an Academy as this. Now,
he supposed, they were uneasily tolerated, so long as they made
the gesture of masculinity." The better-mannered, less mannered
Du Bouchet is more Guy Hudson's style. And, again, the feeling
is mutual. On the first day of school Ralph spots Guy Hudson in
the Quadrangle, and, to use one of Burns's favorite images, it is

---

* The French poet André du Bouchet had been a student at Loomis shortly before World
War II; Burns may have known him, or maybe he just liked the name.

like Dante beholding Beatrice: "He knew that he'd have no peace until he spoke with this piercing person." The magnetism continues: "Feeling the secret and ambiguous waves that were forever traversing the interstellar space between them, Ralph would sometimes at midnight twist on his cot." Meantime, in class, all Guy Hudson's other, lesser students evaporate. "The boy lay open to him like a maiden," Burns writes. "He had the reflexes of a lover in bed." Soon, strictly as a matter of propriety, Guy Hudson has to steer clear of Ralph: "The resilient and wonderful boy . . . had stirred him as no other male ever had." Nothing untoward ever happens. But after they bid one another goodbye for the summer, Guy Hudson returns to his room "feeling in every fiber a drained sweetness such as he'd never known from having sex with anybody." Their semi-erotic reveries are the closest feelings in *Lucifer*—or in any of Burns's books—to love.

The pornographic etching Guy Hudson filched from Berchtesgaden is not the only thing kept in the closet. Guy Hudson rarely sleeps alone for very long, but never is it specified with whom or what he sleeps. Though he has eyes only for Du Bouchet, that's not his reputation around campus: indeed, "he knew that bets must already have been laid that he was committing adultery with some faculty lady." And sure enough, Guy Hudson soon falls for Betty Blanchard, a teacher at the girls' school affiliated with the Academy. Somehow, she feels very familiar. She, too, is handsome. She, too, is a veteran—a WAC who served in, of all places, Algiers and Naples. She, too, disliked the people with whom she worked: her women, too, were also crass and promiscuous, while her GIs also "expected from her the same violent evenings they'd had from hungry Italian and French girls." She, too, can't stand her faculty colleagues—she, too, finds Philbrick Grimes singularly repellent—or her students; they, too, are physically repulsive: fat and coarse and gabby and stupid and pimply beneath their calamine lotion. But she, too, can outsmart them all, and maybe even inspire a couple of them. She, too, is sexually ambiguous, world-weary, always dying for a smoke.

"But there was one male teacher who haunted her horribly," we are told. Guess who? In falling for one another, she and Guy Hudson are really falling for themselves. Their initial lovemaking—her first time, but most assuredly not his—could seem narcissistic, or incestuous, or masturbatory, were it surely not among the most brutal and unpersuasive (and least romantic) scenes in all literature. "It's necessary," he says in her ear. "Necessary for both of us, my dearest girl . . ." Until that moment, she was "not *quite* a woman." But Guy Hudson will fix that.

> *He became an executioner, an avenging ice pick against virgin ice. Crying aloud murderous and ravaging things, he reduced her beneath his hands and his lunging body to what she essentially was, to what she had come into the world to be. He drew her on like a glove. He took out on her whimpering shell all the little meannesses with which she had piqued him. This first time, he knew, he couldn't be tender or solicitous. At another time he'd have loathed himself and called himself a butcher. But now the need of penetrating her was too strong; he was rampant and boiling, and the ferocity of this first time annihilated whatever gentleness and wooing would come later. She screamed aloud in her agony:*
>
> *Won't you even kiss me, you devil? Kiss me, for the love of God! . . . No, no, not there! Dear God! Kiss me on the mouth!*
>
> *He shouted her down in fierceness and hate:*
>
> *No, not this time, you whore! Later, Betty, later! But not now! . . .*
>
> *And in the moment when everything was sucked out of his bowels, he gave one bellowing shout and crashed forward on his elbows:*

This is me! Me, you whore! . . . O, Jesus!

She gave a final scream, which broke off into a long low sobbing. He knelt up and looked at her in the moonlight. She was broken, slaughtered, as she lay on the white sheet that was smeared with her blood. And he too began to cry, the hard rending sobs of a grown man:

Betty . . . Betty . . .

At last she spoke, far away from him:

I . . . have never felt such pain. And it's you who caused it . . .

Don't ever forget that, he blubbered. It was my way of killing you. And now, Betty, you'll live . . .

Loomis boys (and Chaffee girls) must have gravitated to this passage—one can easily imagine the corners of these pages folded over in many of the locally owned copies of *Lucifer*—which would have titillated them far more than the machinations of Norrie Orchard. But in what has to be the only anthology in which anything from *Lucifer* appears—a collection of sex literature—the above scene appears under "Sadism."

Having essentially made love with himself, Burns, or Betty, is pregnant. At book's end, Guy Hudson and Betty Blanchard spurn the Academy and go off with their future issue to some place more deserving of them.

The war, Burns writes, had taught Guy Hudson pity, just as he'd maintained so often in his letters that it had humanized him. *Lucifer* makes clear, though, that this wasn't so, at least for very long, and that what the war really gave to Burns was yet another reason to look down on other people. As had *The Gallery*: rather than underline for him that he was at his best when he surmounted his own prejudices, its success emboldened him to view his usual pet peeves and petty grudges as high art or, at least, as effective satire. *Lucifer's* undisputed brilliance—the rich vocabulary, the elegant turns of phrase, all its wonderful metaphors—make it more awful, directed as it is at such Lilliputian targets. A prep school is a rich subject for satire. It is filled with eccentrics, observable at close quarters. But Burns was too furious to be subtle.

Sidney Eaton had been among Burns's few friends at Loomis before the war. But as Eaton later wrote, *Lucifer* was "an (in parts) brilliant display of an embittered sick man's revenge upon a community with which he was totally out of sympathy . . . professing to be told from the view of a clear-eyed and liberated man, it comes off as the angry and scoffing distortions of a mentally deranged man." It represented, he concluded, "a high talent devoted to sordid ends." "Jack may have believed that he'd matured, but in this later stage he had disintegrated in judgment and control of himself and his book . . . one feels the arrogance of 'What a bright boy am I.'"

In some ways, *Lucifer* represented a step forward aesthetically: a well-constructed, unified piece of work rather than a loose confederation of vignettes. But personally and professionally, it was regressive. It made *The Gallery*, with its tenderness and empathy, seem aberrant. Burns had fallen into the very traps to which, he'd lectured MacMackin, gay artists were vulnerable: *Lucifer* was loaded with "ugliness, negation, and nonessentials." It was just asking to be loathed, and all of Burns's recent strutting and pontificating would make him an even more tempting target. (The book's gay patina would not help, either.) And it could have been even worse: because, at Harpers' request, Burns had *cut* 50,000 words, readers were spared Pilkey's decision to rename certain buildings after advertising slogans; also cut was a scene in which Philbrick Grimes enviously ogles the black student Tad McKinley in the shower. ("Mr. Grimes tried to keep his eyes off the glories of the boy's onyx body. From some atavistic sense he guessed that the boy was flaunting it at him, implying that what was concealed by Mr. Grimes's tweeds and saddle shoes was wispy and inferior to his own.")

"John was a very intolerant character, very sarcastic and very bitter," MacGregor later recalled. "I was very fond of him because I got to know him well, but outwardly he was frequently snarling, at the world, sort of." MacGregor was clearly a very gentle man. The book "was not so good as I wished it had been," was how he assessed *Lucifer*, but he knew there was only so much fixing he could do. He tried, for instance, to have Burns mask his characters better. Why, for instance, did *his* headmaster's wife, like the real one, have to do something arty, like paint china? "You can have her do something else," MacGregor pleaded. "She can be running a gift shop or something." But asking Burns to change anything was futile. "He wouldn't say 'no,' but he would never do it," MacGregor recalled.

Burns always insisted his second novel had a larger message. "A ruthless exhumation of the plight of the teacher in America" was how he described it to a fan. "I think it much subtler and more relevant to the times than *The Gallery*," he went on. "It is certainly a much finer novel, as novels go. I hope I am saying what a hundred thousand teachers would like to say." But success had warped Burns's judgment. There was nothing remotely subtle about it. "More relevant to the times" than a war novel right after a war? And how, moreover, could teachers anywhere relate to so eccentric an institution and so Dickensian a cast of characters? How could Burns not have seen this? "We read the second novel of a promising writer with a peculiar sportsmanlike relish: Will he or will he not clear that second hurdle?" he had asked while reviewing Michener. He was about to learn.

23

"I am now as free-lance as the Pilgrim Fathers."
That was how Burns described his new life in the updated autobiography he put together for his publisher. He reported living in Boston in a "5-room apartment"—unless he counted bathrooms and closets, he'd renovated and enlarged the place in his mind—"done in gay colors," where people could quaff his special Manhattans, eat lobster, and "listen to a very powerful phonograph which is a source of complaint from my neighbors." He rarely went to bed before dawn, he noted, and hated rising before noon. He was writing constantly, gathering material for a third novel, brooding over some short stories, and working on a play called *Vessel of Honor* "which I pray will put me in Tennessee Williams's league." (It was a drama, he told the *New York Star*, "written in prose, not poetry or pseudo-poetry, and about a mother." And it was taking longer to write than either of his novels.) Burns was a contented man, much happier than he'd been

three years earlier. "I love to analyze the grime of Boston which silts up my windowpanes, and to savor the gentle and rather hilarious tempo of her society," he wrote. "And though it might sound pretentious, I'm aiming at a synthesis of naturalism and anthropomorphic ethics in the American novel. I will if I can, and I think I can."

He had another reason to be pleased. Cashing in on his celebrity, he'd signed on to do a series of pieces for *Holiday*, the lavishly illustrated and literate travel magazine, which had asked him to retrace his wartime itinerary—and, as he put it, to "catch nuances that escaped you when you were a resentful foetus kicking in the womb of that Great Mother, the United States Army." The space was ample and the money was good, helping to tide him over as the royalties from *The Gallery* tapered off and before those from *Lucifer* kicked in.

Burns's first stop was Casablanca, and his article from there set the tone for the pieces to come: erudite, sensitive, lyrical, contemplative. And, because he was not writing about people, kind. Freed from the need to be clever or the impulse to settle scores, Burns painted exquisite word pictures and told his truth. (About everything but himself, that is: when *Holiday* advertised that it had hired the "sandy-haired, rugged, six-footer," Burns claimed that he had destroyed all of his unpublished novels—written "just for practice," he maintained—and revised some private particulars. "I am still unmarried and hope to remain exempt until I'm 35—the deadline for men in my family," he told *Holiday* readers. If anyone, including *Holiday*'s editors, thought this a peculiar detail coming from Burns, it wasn't apparent.

From Casablanca he went on to write stories in Algiers and Tunis. But it was only when he reached Naples that he appeared fully engaged. What struck Burns immediately was how dramatically, despite scattered remnants of the fighting, Naples had rebounded in the nearly four years since he'd left. Only one vessel remained submerged in the harbor, and the piers had all been rebuilt. The streets seemed not just cleaner but wider, and for one simple reason: no longer were they clogged with soldiers. The Hotel Excelsior, which American bombs had flattened, had been rebuilt just as before, and become the biggest clip joint in Southern Italy. A new layer of stucco covered the Hotel Terminus, where he'd once lived. Still, Burns felt violated: people had tampered with the world he had known and described. Life there had gone on without him. It was silly, this proprietary sense of his, but he couldn't help it. "You're condescendingly pleased that the Neapolitans have done quite a piece of work in your absence," he wrote. "In the spring of 1949 the hoyden, sluttish city is probably as immaculate as she's ever been through her history . . . is it possible that you were once a soldier in this town? The vitality and the gusto are still here, but it's as though G.I.'s had never staggered on Via Roma, yelling for home or for *vino*."

Unavoidably, even a bit apprehensively, he made his way to the Galleria. As he had noted, the aftermath of war follows its own peculiarly compressed chronology: "five years was five centuries." He had to know that whatever he found there could never be as poignant or powerful to him as what had once been. Compounding the strangeness of his return was venturing into a place that he had himself immortalized. Single-handedly, he had made the Galleria Umberto a literary destination; his readers wanted to pay him homage and follow in his footsteps. These included Robert Loomis, another veteran who later edited the novels of William Styron,* and a Tennessee man named Kenneth Marconi, who wrote of feeling "the whispers of untold tales" there, and the poet Edmund Keeney, though so mythical had Burns made the place

---

* Styron himself had been inspired by *The Gallery*, which he called "beautifully crafted."

for him that the real thing couldn't possibly measure up, just as it never could have for Burns himself.*

So, "with a pang," Burns walked in. Not a soldier was in sight. Loudspeakers spouted advertising slogans, some of them, he noted without comment, for doctors treating venereal diseases. Half a dozen movie theaters and antique stores had joined the bars he remembered. "Yet even these aren't raffish any more," he lamented. "The liquor is better, but nearly everyone prefers *caffe espresso*—made today with real coffee—or tangy Neapolitan sherbets." What was now where Momma's had once been, if it had ever really been at all, he did not say, nor did he mark the spot on the wall against which his syphilitic double, the GI just sprung from "Mussolini's Fairgrounds," had hurled his souvenir vial of penicillin. As he watched the people sitting and reading their newspapers, Burns felt the inescapable, deadening hand of America, luring the locals to abandon their ways, robbing indigenous Italy of its vitality. America, he suggested, was quite literally poisoning the culture: "Is perhaps this new apathy connected with the fine white bread, made from American flour, that turns up in the restaurants?" he asked. "Once Neapolitan bread was dark and coarse."

Looking skyward, he realized that thanks to Italian corruption and lethargy, it had taken five years for the last pane of shattered glass to be replaced. But as far as he was concerned, the premises

---

* For another poet, Richard Hugo, it was a return trip: he, too, had been a GI in Italy. He marked his second visit in "Galleria Umberto I":

> I remember it a little more forlorn.
> Not just roof glass gone, but harsh arrays
> of junk on tables and pathetic faces
> broken by the war, and faces warped
> by cruelty they'd learned, and faces gone.
> It was here that John Horne Burns
> saw war summed up, the cracked life
> going on, taking what it would in gesture
> and a beggar's bitter hand.

had been transformed from one kind of shell to another. "The Galleria is no longer the shattered swarming place you remember," he wrote. "It's just another arcade, like the ones in Rome and Milan. And its brown walls are dingier than they seemed under the stimulus of a sadder time. Gone are the barter, the fever, the trickles of rain and vermouth on the pavement. And since this isn't the Naples you knew, you feel a little hurt, like a man attempting to relive his childhood."

Night fell, and Burns quickly realized that daytime Naples's newfound civility was "specious." The old pity and ruthlessness returned; hungry little children and procurers could still smell Americans (especially Americans who, like Burns, went about in seersucker suits) and descended upon them like carrion birds. And now, with inflation rather than war driving them to desperation, they seemed to Burns less sympathetic, enough almost to make him wish he'd not come back at all. "Today in postwar Naples your privacy and your compassion will be invaded five times per city block," he wrote. "And you will end your Neapolitan holiday taut and angry . . . A sole American in Naples today will find the city hard to take. The human need and the cancer of unplanned population begin to weigh upon him. Five years ago the parasitism and the finagling were spread over the entire Army. Now as a tourist you'll feel the need to slip away from the fever." Naples no longer made Burns feel good, or good about himself. He fled to one of the islands off the coast, where the city was now prettiest to him: from a distance.

The *Holiday* assignments—there were eventually nine of them—would also include earlier stops on Burns's journey, like Andover. In October 1948 he wrote to introduce himself to the man who had succeeded Claude Fuess as headmaster, John Kemper, explaining the article he hoped to write. He approached him with uncharacteristic modesty—"Perhaps you have heard of my war novel *The Gallery*, published last year," he noted. And mindful, maybe, of what he was about to unleash on Loomis, or simply more sentimental about the place, he all but promised a puff piece, filled with gauzy memories of childhood and school days. Whatever ailed higher education was something from which Andover, for some reason, was strangely exempt: with it, unlike with almost anything or anyone else, Burns was suddenly, inexplicably toothless. "I think you will agree that such a piece by an Andover alumnus will constitute a great deal of reputable publicity for the Academy," he gushed, noting that *Holiday* sold 800,000 copies a month. "Naturally I can't omit a portrait of the school's new headmaster, whom I have never had the pleasure of meeting," he took care to add; might Mr. Kemper have a few minutes for him? Having no notion of the vivisection Burns had just performed on a sister school, Kemper responded eagerly—the next day—and took Burns at his word. "The prospects of your Andover article in *Holiday* sounds [*sic*] good, and we will look forward to cooperating with you in any way that we can," Kemper assured him. The school's public relations man, Joseph Staples, seconded that.

For some reason, stopping by his own school reassured him that he'd gotten things right in *Lucifer*. "VISITED ANDOVER TODAY FOR HOLIDAY MAGAZINE DISCOVER THAT MY NEW NOVEL IS AS TRUE AS TRUE CAN BE," he wired MacGregor. In November 1948 he told the *New York Star* that the new book was his chance to sound off on American education. "I may have to leave the country when it comes out," he declared cheerfully. Rather than attack the teaching profession per se, Burns said, the novel would describe "the conversion of a veteran's mind from negation into constructive American democratic thinking." Stylistically, he explained, it was "very cool and a little like Jane Austen on a binge"—nothing at all like *The Gallery*.

With apologies for fouling up his Christmas, on December 15 Harpers informed Burns that he would soon receive the galleys of the new book, and would have less than two weeks to go through them. No problem, Burns assured them: "My mother always told me to respect manufacturing departments." In England, Fredric Warburg said there were few new books he anticipated more eagerly. Once galleys had been readied, copies went to selected readers. One, apparently presented as part of a grant application to the American Academy of Arts and Letters, reached Glenway Wescott, a longtime member of the academy. Burns was competing against several literary luminaries—other applicants that year included Delmore Schwartz, Joseph Campbell, and James Agee—but, as Wescott's journals indicate, that wasn't the only obstacle Burns faced.

> *Just at the last minute I got page proofs of John Horne Burns's forthcoming novel,* Lucifer with a Book *. . . Mark Van Doren* thinks* The Gallery *a no-account thing that anyone might have written; and my blessed dear Marianne [Moore] has just read it and she hates it, hates; a real tirade, but upon grounds of its coarseness, which I dislike yielding to. The new book is very different, just as shocking, but remarkably different from* The Gallery *in thought and style and construction. Miserable private lives of the faculty and terrible youngsters in a preparatory school—less like Thomas Wolfe, more like Dreiser—real satire, with moral indignation. It is not at all my kind of fiction; I have met him twice and not liked him, etc.—but I do believe that he is the most talented, the most promising of the youngsters since the war.*

Evidently only Wescott's final sentiment reached Burns. "I hear through the grapevine and from my much-admired Miss

---

* The poet, critic, and longtime professor of English at Columbia University.

Lillian Hellman* that you've been saying some very complimentary things about *Lucifer with a Book*," he wrote Wescott in late January 1949. "Naturally, my second novel is crucial to me; until it appears I have no real way of knowing whether it's as good as, or better than, *The Gallery*. Myself, I think it's an advance. And it's wonderfully reassuring to have some hint of what the reception will be from a critical sense as keen and as fair as your own. I know of no one whom I'd rather have trumpet my wares."

Meanwhile, the lawyers who'd cleaned up *The Gallery* were now having at *Lucifer*, and their hands this time were fuller. "As you are well aware, practically every character in the book is a libelous portrayal," Mrs. Theodora Zavin, back on the case, informed MacGregor. Her legal team had not tried to make the characters any *less* libelous; that, she conceded, would defeat the whole purpose of the book. Instead, they'd tried to ascertain whether particular characters were identifiable—a process that would hinge, initially, on whether the school itself could be. The chances of a lawsuit were slim, she noted: no fancy prep school would want to admit any possible connection to Burns's nightmarish place, as a lawsuit would necessarily do. And any such school would lean on any individual aggrieved by such a book to keep mum. The danger would come from persons who were no longer there.

A separate appendix listed those elements that could link Miss Sophia's Academy to Loomis. Was one faculty member really a cousin of U. S. Grant? Had the headmaster previously taught at the Friends School in Philadelphia? Was his wife really an artist who painted china? Did a river really separate the school from the village? Was one student really the daughter of the governor? Did a faculty wife really smoke a pipe and serve cocoa to the hockey team? Was one trustee really a delicatessen buyer for Macy's? Were there really students known as the "Abbot," the "Abbess,"

---

* American playwright, activist, and memoirist (1905–1984).

the "Body," and the "Bishop"? Next to each, Burns robotically wrote "no," even though it wasn't always true; he clearly found the whole exercise abhorrent, and couldn't be bothered with it. Only when he could no longer contain his annoyance did he go beyond monosyllables.

> Q: *The Christmas ceremonies . . . seem rather atypical, e.g. the Miracle Play, the Goose Dinner, the Pilgrimage to the Founders Grave.*
>
> A: *They're atypical because I invented them.*
>
> Q: *Is Mr. Pilkey's opposition to coffee, cigarettes and liquor characteristic of a particular principal?*
>
> A: *Aren't all American principals opposed to them?*
>
> Q: *Is Miss Pringle based on a real person? If so was she a former dean at a Western Womens [sic] College, a Greek Scholar and subject to epileptic fits?*
>
> A: *She died ten years ago.* *

Eager to fend off any possible litigation, Harpers weighed a series of precautionary steps: avoiding words like "shocking" in ads, for example, and stressing that Burns "had had wide experience with private schools." "It is suggested that factors pertaining to the school in *Lucifer* which differ from Loomis might be emphasized," went one memo. "For example: The Academy in *Lucifer* has a Negro student; has only one Jewish student; the girls' school and the boys' school are in close geographical proximity. None of the foregoing applies to Loomis." Further, it urged, "the regional angle *must not* be played up in advertising and promotion—no more pushing at Hartford or Boston etc. than anywhere else. In case of circulars or direct mail, lists of students or alumni of

---

* Burns and McKee once left up a toilet seat in the ladies' room used by the model for Miss Pringle, in an apparent attempt to induce an epileptic fit.

Loomis (or any other of Mr. Burns' schools) must not be used unless a considerable number of schools are circularized at the same
time and with the same promotion. Salesmen should not call attention to Burns's association with Loomis." This time Harpers,
and not just Burns, had a reason to omit Loomis from the author's
biography.

Still, there were alarming signs. In January 1949, someone
at the *Harvard Alumni Bulletin* who'd obtained galleys warned
Harpers that the book was libelous *and* obscene, "and that some
of the characters could definitely be identified with Loomis, especially since in book notes and gossip column [*sic*] during the
last year the interested reader has been told that Burns is a former
teacher at Loomis and that he was writing a book about private
schools," another internal Harpers memo related. "In the light of
new evidence of Loomis identification it seemed wise to thrash
the matter out with the author at the earliest possible moment so
that the lawyer could ask further and more leading questions."

So now the lawyers put together a list, one attempting to
link Burns's characters to their real-life counterparts. "Miss
Demerjian"—Syrian (or Armenian), unattractive, sex-starved,
with a mustache, teaching French and coaching dramatics, interested in Philbrick Grimes—was tied to a French teacher named
Zarifian, who had coached dramatics, was short and stocky and
had a mustache, and had had a rumored affair with an English
teacher. But she had been away from Loomis for some time, and
was now married with a child. Mrs. Batchelder was indeed an
artist. The Jewess who played Mary in the Christmas pageant,
described as the daughter of a "rich delicatessen mogul" (and
also as "the hottest snatch" in the school) *could* be the daughter
of a grocery store executive in Hartford. And "Philbrick Grimes"
sounded suspiciously like Francis Grubbs, the French teacher.
Had the lawyers deigned to show the book to someone actually at
the school, they'd have quickly known better, but lawyers being

lawyers—jealous of their prerogatives, more compulsive than strategic—this wasn't something they were about to do.

Burns quite rightly found the whole thing exasperating. "Mrs. Zavin must think I'm a complete fool," he complained to Mac-Gregor. "Or else she has no conception of what goes on in the brain of a writer. When I began *Lucifer* a year and a half ago, I was aware of what a juicy subject the whole business was for libel. Consequently I expended considerable ingenuity in changing anything that was like any person or place I'd ever known in my ten years of teaching. As in *The Gallery*, Mrs. Zavin is really paying tribute to the reality of my writing. She takes exception to things that seem to her *real*, when actually I myself invented nearly everything she takes umbrage at." The characters and the school were composites, Burns insisted; the Academy was based on a dozen schools he knew. Still, while copies of his first book contained a disclaimer that "All characters whose portraits hang in this gallery are fictitious," the new book did not. It would not have been true.

Harpers executives followed the lawyers' catechism closely. So when an associate of the British publisher Jonathan Cape asked Cass Canfield for a copy of *Lucifer*—Cape's son had gone to Loomis—Canfield enclosed the party line along with the requested book. "This novel is not about any particular school, but is meant to be a satire on the American private school system based upon the author's observations of a large number of schools over a period of many years," he dutifully wrote.

There was still the matter of obscenity. That Burns had suggested an unmarried couple like Guy Hudson and Betty Blanchard actually enjoyed sex (though the reference to the ice pick *did* make one wonder) was a concern, as was the idea that Blanchard's teaching improved postvirginity. "While there is nothing obscene in such a point of view as such," the lawyers cautioned, "it may enhance the risk of an attack based on the specific sexual incident of deflowering which is described in somewhat greater detail than appears in most books." They asked that one sexual tryst be moved out of the school chapel, and warned that the constant sexual references could make the book "lascivious" and "titillating." Burns agreed to delete the chapel incident but asked that the rest be left intact. *Lucifer* was "drenched with sensuality," he conceded, "but not nearly so pornographic as many novels pouring off the presses these days."

At some point Burns showed *Lucifer* to his younger brother, Tom, by then a lawyer in Boston. Tom Burns told him he should tear it up—that it was vitriolic, and bad for his career. But his big brother naturally laughed off his advice.

24

Casting all superstitions aside, Harpers set *Lucifer*'s publication for April Fool's Day 1949. Burns did not much like the cover—a red sheet with black streaks which reminded him of the much-despised Japanese flag—but could not manage to change it. Whoever wrote the flap copy had another challenge: how to say that *Lucifer* was like *The Gallery* when it wasn't, then make a virtue out of the differences. The solution? To say it was "written with the same fire, sincerity, skill and emotion," but that "with a postwar setting and theme, it demonstrates once again John Horne Burns's versatility and further entrenches him as one of the brightest stars on the United States literary horizon." *Lucifer*, it claimed, "lays bare the private aspects of a private school as surely as an earthquake tears off the front of a building, leaving the insides exposed floor by floor, room by room." It was "at once a savage exposé, a biting satire, and above all, a completely fascinating story of what does—or can—go on behind the ornate doors of a

Jacket of Lucifer with a Book

certain kind of private school." From the back flap, readers would be reminded that Burns had spent four years at Phillips Andover. But the "boys' preparatory school" in which he'd taught after that remained conspicuously unidentified.

In London, Fredric Warburg had made an offer for *Lucifer* in February 1949. The book was "brilliantly done," he wrote: Burns was becoming a modern Sinclair Lewis. But Warburg insisted on one cut: the entire gay scene in the Abbess's room, complete with circle jerk. He did so reluctantly, he said, but *his* lawyers warned that without such a deletion, the book could be banned and the company prosecuted for "criminal libel." Burns didn't resist. For all their scrutinizing, the New York lawyers seemed unconcerned by the gay material. As with *The Gallery*, there seemed an implicit agreement among all concerned to pretend it wasn't there, and a recognition that if no one—or no one of consequence—acknowledged it, it wasn't.

The same appeared true of the epigraph Burns selected for the book, from Canto XV of *The Inferno*.

In somma sappi che tutti fur cherci
E literati grandi e di gran fama,
D'un peccato medesmo al mono lerci.

As if enjoying a private joke, Burns did not supply a translation. Here's one:

In brief, note that all of them were clerks
And great men of letters and of great fame
In the world defiled by one [and the] same sin.

Neither in the book nor anywhere else did Burns explain his selection. They are, in fact, the words of Dante's teacher, Brunetto Latini, whom he encounters among the sodomites in the seventh circle of the Inferno. Dante has just asked Ser Brunetto to tell him what other famous figures resided there with him; they were too numerous to name, Latini replies, so he describes them generically instead. Dante clearly has mixed feelings about Latini: Dante the character thanks him profusely for his pedagogical gift—"in the world, hour after hour, you taught me how man makes himself eternal"—while Dante the author both outs him and consigns him to eternal damnation.* What matters most, though, is that according to Latini, the greatest writers, poets, and teachers of language and rhetoric are gay.

In selecting this passage Burns, who had translated it at Harvard but probably had to draw his own inferences from it—classroom discussions on sexual themes, let alone *gay* sexual themes, were rare in those days—clearly endorsed Latini's claim. (He also endorsed Latini, signing one of his letters to MacMackin with his name.) By invoking him at the outset of *Lucifer*, he could salute the gay mentors he had had, take pride in his own inspired (and deviant) teaching—he, too, had revealed to at least some of his own students how man makes himself eternal—praise the superior literacy of homosexuals, and protest the unfairness of their fate. (And undermine his own work, since he'd so blurred the sexual orientation of his hero in the story to follow.) Not that anyone but many Italians and a few Dante scholars would pick any of this up; most Americans, and all reviewers, would simply turn this page.

A month or so before *Lucifer*'s release, Burns took another nostalgic trip, this one not for *Holiday*: he returned to Loomis. And during his visit, he had an even more peculiar reunion, with Norris Orchard, in Orchard's apartment. Setting foot again on the Island, dodging Mr. B's disapproving glare, was gutsy, yet another of

* The gay scholar David Halperin has called this "the first and most literally damning student evaluation in European history." I am grateful to both him and Professor Gary Cestaro for their assistance here.

Burns's stunts. But visiting someone he had so clearly earmarked for humiliation—then availing himself of his hospitality—was positively cold-blooded. And it got worse. Spotting *The Gallery* on Orchard's bookshelf, Burns pulled it out and wrote what Tom Brush remembered to be "a pleasant, even flattering" inscription in it. (It's a pity that like everything in Orchard's library—and Burns's, too, for that matter—the book disappeared.) "He was, indeed, very pleasant to everyone that day, all the time knowing that in less than a month they and all the world would see what he really felt about them," Brush later recalled. "His sense of humor was warped; he liked to hurt people—being extremely sensitive to wounds himself—and as he drove the knife in he smiled."

Burns feigned a certain fatalism about *Lucifer*. "The reviewers will probably decide that it doesn't measure up to *The Gallery*, which is all right with me," he wrote. "It's not supposed to. It's an entirely different sort of book." He was right, and then some.

Rarely are book reviews truly brutal: the worst books never get reviewed—they are not worth the time it takes to trash them—and when they are, writers usually take fraternal pity on one another. But Burns was too prominent, and promising, and successful, and, when it came right down to it, obnoxious, to ignore or to coddle. In other words, he had asked for it. In his mini-autobiography, he acknowledged that his own cruelty could "redound to me like a boomerang," and so it now did, in ways that shocked even the most worldly literati. James Michener, for one, was aghast. "What Burns did to me seemed like a kindness compared to what the older and established critics did to *his* second novel," he wrote in his memoirs. "Never in my memory had they come so close to total annihilation of an author's work."

"Wretchedly bad," Orville Prescott called the new book in the *New York Times*. "There is all sorts of violence in these rancid pages, violence of material, of emotion and of speech," he wrote. "But there is no life . . . stiff and wooden characters respond jerkily to Mr. Burns's twitchings of their puppet strings." (Like virtually all other reviewers, he omitted any mention of Loomis, but he had an extra incentive: his publisher's son, Arthur O. "Punch" Sulzberger, had gone there.) In the *Herald Tribune*, Lewis Gannett declared that "the delicate pen-point with which Mr. Burns wrote *The Gallery* has turned into a scratchy stub." It was hard to believe that the same man had written both books. "Precisely those qualities which constituted the brilliant promise and achievement of the first novel are missing from the second," the *Christian Science Monitor* stated. "The sense of an immediate, tactile relationship to reality, the warmly human character invention, the exhilarating psychological honesty, the extension of a fine intuitive understanding to many kinds and conditions of men, and the compassionate humility in the face of humanity's perennial tragic-comedy; these are unhappily gone. In their place stands an angry lecturer with some very still stereopticon slides . . . *Lucifer* has sprung from the silt of malice rather than the soil of the creative imagination."

Besides Guy Hudson and Betty Blanchard, wrote Hiram Haydn in the *Herald Tribune*'s Sunday Book Review, *Lucifer* offered "the weirdest collection of freaks to have been brought together since Barnum." Prep schools, Haydn conceded, were ripe for humor. "But this book isn't actually satire. It is burlesque." Both Malcolm Cowley and the *New York Times Book Review* said *Lucifer* read like the result of a monumental grudge. Loomis's hometown paper, the *Hartford Courant*, said it was what a disgruntled office boy might stuff into a suggestion box. It was all just too relentless: "He seems to hold a list on which he is checking off, one by one, his many prep school gripes," it complained. "The fools, who are numerous, proclaim themselves fools every time they open their mouths." In the *New Yorker*, Richard Broderick called it "an amalgam of polemic, inept satire, and straight vituperation," and noted the asymmetry of the fight: Burns had directed his heaviest artillery at a "lightly defended" target. Its point, Broderick wrote, was that such a school prepared its students badly for life; another way of doing so, he observed, "would be to burn down a gymnasium." To *Life*, *Lucifer* was an act of "cannibalism."

Some of the more humane, and discerning, reviewers noted that the authors of *Lucifer* and *The Gallery* were clearly one and the same. In the *New Republic*, Burns's erstwhile champion, John Aldridge, stipulated that *Lucifer* was "a disappointing successor." "The style in many places is too feverishly brilliant; the metaphors often lose their potency for being used indiscriminately on commonplace material; and there are curious and unforgivable lapses into triteness," he wrote. "Yet despite Burns's rather startling technical failure, the power of indignation and protest which enhanced *The Gallery* is clearly present, and it is directed at a similar corruption of values." Others speculated charitably that Burns had only temporarily lost his way. "There are enough flashes of brilliance here to remind us that a first-rate talent is under wraps," was how William Du Bois put it in the *New York Times Book Review*.

"Sex is the garlic with which Mr. Burns garnishes everything he writes," Steele Lindsay declared in the *Boston Post*. That was too bad, given the "sheer beauty of imagery and incisive dissection of human character . . . [T]his is still a book that you don't want to miss, because Burns is an author you don't want to miss." In the *Daily Worker*, Robert Friedman praised Burns for lampooning a school for the rich, along with American materialism and militarization. But he quickly poked through the book's thin political veneer. "Chapter after chapter, in monotonous exaggeration, is devoted to the sexual irregularities, abnormalities and perversions to which seemingly practically everybody at The Academy is addicted," he complained. The widely syndicated columnist Walter Winchell skipped the political analysis and went right to the salaciousness. "The new book, *Lucifer with a Book*, is inviting censor trouble," he noted. "What he says kids do in finishing schools!"

Maybe the most sympathetic reviewer was Maxwell Geismar of the *Saturday Review*. He, too, found the sex scenes unconvincing. But he called Burns "the closest thing to Evelyn Waugh or the early Aldous Huxley that we have seen lately" and added that "there is in Mr. Burns's work a remarkably sophisticated sense of evil and malice." Burns also got an old-school boost from the *Harvard Crimson*. "With extraordinary dexterity, Burns has severed the suspenders of a certain unnamed New England private school, exposing its tattered foundation of tradition, clique, and petty prejudice," wrote E. Parker Hayden, Jr. "The parallel with this certain school seems all too accurate."* The few reviewers who noted the book's gay undertones did so with revulsion. "A gamier book I do not recall," wrote Victor Hass in the *Chicago Tribune*. The teachers in it were pinned to cards like insects, he charged. As for the students, they "range from blond, brainless, monied mastiffs popping bubble gum and winning the all-important football games to lushly effeminate numbers who make your skin crawl. In between there are a few misfits who came to The Academy to learn. They are, of course, Queers." "Mr. Burns has dipped his pen too deeply in gall," wrote the *Catholic World*. "Krafft-Ebing,† who is named only once, seems to have inspired the author frequently."

With *Lucifer*, as with *The Gallery*, it was hard to know how the gay community reacted, though it's very likely it did. Gore Vidal appears not to have weighed in, though Harpers sent him a copy.

---

* Hayden probably thought Burns had Andover in mind. It was close to St. Mark's, the prep school Hayden himself had attended.

† Richard von Krafft-Ebing (1840–1902), a German psychiatrist and pioneering student of human sexual behavior, including homosexuality.

Truman Capote wrote a friend from Italy to ask if he'd glanced at Burns's new book. In a letter to his friend Leo Adams, a New York department store executive who collected material on gay culture, a man named William Giles wrote to say that someone had just lent him a copy.

> *It's a finely written piece of work, tearing apart a boys' school—the sort of thing that has been done before, but I doubt if any author has used such finesse with characterization and so forth. I have been reassured that the school discussed really does exist, and that most of the characters are thinly veiled copies of their proto-types; must be some school! In many respects it reminds me of Princeton, or of what I see of Princeton—many of the same types are evident. Practically the whole student group in the music dept are fruity—most of them very unpleasantly so. But I do recommend the book—and will be eager to hear your reaction!*

"*Lucifer with a Book* by Burns was published about two years ago, it seems to me," Adams replied. "And I think it refers to the Kent school in the foothills of the Berkshires, but I am not positive. It has an awful bitch in it hasn't it? I mean a male one."

Anticipating heavy demand from Loomis students, parents, and teachers alike, Witkower's Book Store in downtown Hartford had a stack of *Lucifer*s at the ready. Not everyone could find copies—there were rumors that the Batchelders had bought them up in bulk—but those who did quickly retreated to their respective corners to read it. (Elizabeth Speirs, who taught mathematics at Chaffee, carried it around in a manila folder, but was found out anyway.) Some quibbled over particulars. "The circle jerk chapter is almost certainly drawn from Burns's Andover rather than his Loomis years," Tom Brush later insisted;

there were no places on campus where such things could have happened. "There was, in fact, no homosexual or proto-homosexual clique at all in Loomis in those days," Brush went on. "To be sure, there was no doubt the usual incidence of mutual masturbation, but I think there were no real gang bangs."

While Burns had thrown the lawyers off his trail, everyone quickly recognized who was who, or at least thought they did. They compiled and compared lists, often writing them on the inside covers of their copies, starting with Batchelder as Pilkey and Orchard as Grimes. Batchelder was an old man, nearing retirement, poised to leave the Island. But Orchard, like Philbrick Grimes, was only thirty-seven years old, had never worked anywhere but Loomis, and was unlikely to go anywhere. To wave after wave of Loomis students, *Lucifer with a Book* would now be as much a part of his résumé as his Yale degree.

As portraiture, Sidney Eaton later wrote, Grimes was a bit closer to the mark than some of Burns's other depictions, which made it all the more hurtful. "Orchard, though shrewdly sycophantic, was not so totally devoid of talent and decency as the jaundiced eye of Guy Hudson reports," Eaton wrote. Orchard had an equally loyal, and far larger, following than Burns, and many of his admirers were both heartbroken and furious. "Burns portrayed Orchard as a limp-wristed fag, which was totally unjustified," said John Stuart Cox, whose mother—who knew Burns from the Hartford Madrigal Society—tore up the book and threw it into the fireplace. And Orchard, unlike Burns, was beloved on the Loomis faculty. In taking him on, Burns had stabbed at the school's very heart, something he surely knew.

Publicly at least, Orchard remained stoic. "It's fiction," he was heard to remark. "He can say what he wants." Privately, though, he was said to have been crushed—and may have flirted with a nervous breakdown, and had to take some time away from the school. Later, he advised at least one student not to read the book. Forever

Miss Sophia Abercrombie - Loomis
Hookes, brother - Osbert Loomis
Pilkey - "Mr. B."
Twarkins - Jim Shaffer
Miss Pringle - Miss Hick
Miss Budlong -
Miss Hoskins -
Mrs. Budge -
Minerva Meakins - Florence Sellers
Betty Blanchard -
Whitneys - Morses
Rev. & Mrs. Smedley - Twitchells
Herman Pilkey - Ship Batchelder
Philbrick Grimes - NEO ✓
Guy Hudson - J. H. Barnes?
Dr. Sour - Sharpe
Midgie Mears - Jean Sellers
Amos James - Card
Hollys - FOG's
Dr. Hunter - O. Ross?
Miss Demejian - RAA
Lancelot Millers - Hendersons
Miss Hendrickson - RMA
Dr. Anderson
Mortimer Wesleys - HPM's
Mr. & Mrs. Mickewicz - Shinkens

Norrie Orchard
Frances Grubbs
Savages
Rose Adams
Avil Maynard

George Hickok's who's who for Lucifer

after, people knew better than to ask him about *Lucifer,* though in Orchard's case "forever" wasn't very long. Within a few years he developed a brain tumor; surgery left his head dented and his faculties, and especially his famous wit, crucially impaired. One afternoon in late March 1957, he left his parents' house on Cape Cod and did not return. A search party soon found him sitting in bloodied snow against a nearby scrub pine, dead of self-inflicted wounds to the throat and wrists. He was forty-five years old. Whether it was medically sound or not—he feared becoming a burden on his parents, the local paper reported—at least a few people blamed Burns for Orchard's early demise. "I gather that the Burns portrait was contributory to the illness and eventual suicide of the real Norris Orchard," Eaton later wrote. "Jack was not averse to hurting, but I don't believe that he intended to be lethal."

Even students who had liked and admired Burns found *Lucifer* appalling. One of them, James Munves, simply wrote it off as recycled prewar juvenilia; *Lucifer's* author, he concluded, was obviously half the mental age of the man who'd written *The Gallery.* Batchelder, who'd taken on more Jewish students as conditions worsened in Nazi Germany, and hired Burns when no other fancy prep school would, only to find that same man now depicting him as a bigot, said nothing publicly about *Lucifer.* He had never been much of a reader, at least of novels; he told a student once that he hadn't read one since *Robinson Crusoe.* But Burns's latest book he'd gone through within a week of publication, after which he sent a note to his soon-to-be-installed successor, William Speer.

I had resolved not to read Burns's book. I couldn't finish The Gallery *and I never meant to read anything else by the same author. Then, I came to feel that I was sure to be asked questions by alumni and parents, and couldn't answer them intelligently unless I read at least parts of the book. I skimmed it the other day, particularly*

looking for any sort of constructive ideas about education,
or even any intelligent destructive ones. I found nothing
but petulance, animosity and vulgarity. I can't see why a
reputable firm like Harpers publishes such a book. The
critics seem universally to have damned it. I am tempted
to say I am sorry that I even took Burns on to the faculty.
It has certainly proved to be a mistake. The fact was that
when he finished college, he felt he was discriminated
against because he was a Catholic. That made me boiling
mad. He had an excellent scholastic record and was a
talented musician. I thought he deserved a chance, which
we gave him. When he left for war, Mrs. Batchelder gave
him a splendid farewell dinner, with all the members of
the English Department and their wives. When he was
discharged, I felt I should offer him his place again, as I
had to all the other masters who had been in the service.
Incidentally, we had for him, as for others, paid the
entire retiring allowance, his share and ours, until he got
a commission, after which we continued our share. Some
of my associates would have been relieved if I had not
offered him his old position (at increased salary). I had
some uneasiness about him myself, but I wanted to be a
little more than just . . . Well, I can only say he has a
curious sense of gratitude. I don't think I can really be sorry
permanently for being generous and free from prejudice.

That much had been typed. Then he wrote out an addendum.

but I don't like to have my hand bitten.

According to one story, when Mr. B returned his borrowed
copy of *Lucifer* to Thomas Finley—a faculty member who
lived in the old Loomis Homestead across the street from the

headmaster's house—he'd carried it with a pair of fire tongs. And whenever the topic of *Lucifer* arose—say, around his table in the dining room—his face turned red. Later, Batchelder wrote McKee to say that Burns was no gentleman; were they ever to meet again, he would not shake his hand. "That's the thing about that wretched book and the unhappy man who wrote it: he portrayed the most viciously those who had been the nicest to him," Tom Brush later wrote.

"It wasn't horribly inaccurate," recalled Phillip Isenberg, the model for the Jewish student "Ben Gordon" in the book:

> *I thought he put his finger on all sorts of things that were true to some degree, but that it was written by someone who was very bitter and disappointed, who felt he was treated like an outsider, which he was and which he induced. It was negative, but it was also astute . . . there were so many small things which he picked up about people which were true. That's the tragedy. He hated himself and he spewed it all over the landscape on everyone else. His suffering was palpable, even when I was a fifteen or sixteen year old kid. His face was flush, his eyes darted around. He was just never comfortable with himself.*

25

B urns put on a defiant, even a flippant, face. He'd been "pre-pared for the screams of outraged virtue," he told one reader. "It was all very well for me to write about Italy, but when my target was closer to home, I knew that I'd be holding the mirror up to many," he wrote. "Perhaps eventually I shall be stoned like Saint Stephen. I haven't a martyr complex, but I will write what I see and feel. *Lucifer* isn't really about a school at all. It is a fable of the world today; I simply used for convenience a frame that I know well. As for a limited audience, so be it. I should rather write for a limited audience of a few thousand people like you than have Taylor Caldwell's* following. And arrogant as it may sound, I'd rather be John Horne Burns than Lloyd C. Douglas."[†]

---

* A prolific author of highly popular novels.

† An American minister and author whose popular novels, e.g., *The Robe*, were mainly on religious themes.

"They over-reached themselves in their righteous indignation," he told another reader. "They would have liked to oblit-
erate the book. Instead, they have caused many people who
otherwise wouldn't read it to buy it and discover what has made
the 'critics' so wild with anger. *Lucifer*, three weeks after publication, is 12th on the national best-seller list." He continued:
"Many bookstores refuse to stock it, and bad teachers all over the
land are up in arms. Just what I planned. America thinks now
only of new television sets and a war with Russia. What an obscene spectacle! And to assuage their consciences they read such
horrors as Lloyd C. Douglas and Winston Churchill. Christi-
anity was never closer to extinction." "I'm less embittered than I
was," he concluded. "The furor I am causing delights me to the
depths of whatever malice and virtue I possess . . . Regards to
who ever still approves of me."

At Harpers, Canfield reflected on the difficulty of promot-
ing *Lucifer*: if the ads included only the favorable reviews (such as
they were), people wouldn't believe them; if they quoted the unfa-
vorable ones, people wouldn't buy the book. He asked ostensibly
objective sorts, including his own daughter-in-law, for guidance:
was the book *really* all that bad? Meantime, the publishing house
tried turning the vitriol into a virtue. "'Brilliant, revealing satire'
or 'A savage and distorted picture'?" proclaimed a notice in the
Times. "Whether you turn the pages of *Lucifer with a Book* in
anger, or with delighted appreciation, you'll keep turning them."
Burns's reputation largely overcame the bad reviews: *Lucifer* had
three printings totaling 17,500 books, only 3,000 fewer than *The
Gallery*.

The shelves of Loomis's library would not be the only ones
without *Lucifer*. Where the published criticism didn't suffice, local
watchdogs stepped in. The newspaper in Lawrence, Massachusetts, just down the road, or across the tracks, from Andover, reported that the town censorship board was weighing banning the

book from the community library. Calling it "the filthiest mess of writing I have ever waded through" and warning that if such "perverted dirt . . . were to get into the hands of [a] child, adolescent, or even certain adults it might do irrevocable harm," Robert Barr of New Canaan, Connecticut, asked Orville Prescott, the New York Times book critic who'd just lambasted Lucifer and who doubled as chairman of the book committee of the local library, to ban it from the place. "It has not the excuse of story, point, or good writing," he declared. "Rabelais at least had all three." Canadian customs officials refused to let the book into the country.

Harpers also heard from some indignant readers. So much had a Vermont woman loved The Gallery that when Lucifer popped up in the window of her bookstore in Montpelier, she'd rushed in and bought it. But this time, she wrote, Burns was simply all wet. His language, she conceded, was brilliant—his figures of speech were "out of this world"—but the man was clearly having a nervous breakdown. "The biggest crime of all is that Mr. Burns['s] dementia and self-sorrow and unstable fanaticism has led him to write badly," she complained. And it was a shame he couldn't have found a job at a better school. A doctor from Albany claimed that by "arousing the flame of sex into irrationalism," Lucifer was the kind of book "that had led to murder and every form of crime." He then turned to Freudian analysis and two-dimensional phrenology to buttress his case. "My knowledge of psychology and photography of people make it possible for me to read character from a photograph," he wrote. And the author picture on Lucifer's jacket (actually, a rather friendly and innocuous image) convinced him Burns was "an egotist, satisfied with himself and whatever he does regardless of the offense or results."

No critic was more aroused, and more persistent, however, than Edward D. Toland, the former head of the history department at St. Paul's School in Concord, New Hampshire. Lucifer, he said in a letter to a friend written in June 1949 and copied to

Canfield, was "insignificant and despicable," and implausible to boot: "Such an orgy as he describes during twenty-five lascivious pages just doesn't and couldn't occur in any school!" he bellowed. The deflowering of Betty Blanchard was "clinically and psychologically inaccurate"; Burns was "probably recalling his own experiences in fourth class brothels!" "Anyone so obviously vain, insubordinate, and undisciplined, and with an absolutely psychopathic complex about sex (which topic is brought in upon every possible opportunity, and to the extent of a degenerate or drug addict) was a *rotten soldier!*" he fulminated. "What chiefly surprises me is that any reputable publishing house would publish such obscene tripe." Then again, much to Toland's chagrin, Norman Mailer was getting published, too.*

Nearly a year later, Toland was still incensed enough to write Canfield directly, posing a series of questions, including:

(1) *Have any favorable reviews of that book appeared?*
(2) *Is it thought to represent any school, to say nothing of all schools?*
(3) *Has the author ever been in a sanitarium, is he a drug addict, or a homosexual?*

"The book and author," he went on, "are held in utter contempt by everyone, without exception, that I've talked to or written about it—and that includes several of Burns's former associates, one of whom described him as 'a four flusher . . . never even saw combat . . . about three-quarters skunk and one-quarter rattlesnake.'"

It fell to MacGregor, who hadn't much liked the book himself, to answer Toland. Harpers knew it would shock some people, he conceded, but *Lucifer* was "a sincere book, written by an author of

---

* *Lucifer*, Toland griped, was "nearly as degenerate and foul as *The Naked and the Dead*, which recently evoked a front-page editorial in the *London Times*, urging that the book be banned from Great Britain. Its author is also young (25) and also seems like a sex degenerate."

undoubted talent . . . While some reviews and criticisms have attacked the book, there have been an equal or greater number that have commended it highly." Toland was, quite properly, unpersuaded. "One of your dealers recently summarized it to me as: 'It would seem rather difficult to find a school or community where nearly every woman is a whore, every man a heel, and every boy a homosexual,'" he declared. It still surprised him that, as he put it, "Burns wasn't classified as a psycho by the Army!"

Others had more specific complaints. *Lucifer* contained a character named Ginny Snelgrove, whom Burns described as the "town pump." It turned out that a real Ginny Snelgrove had attended Windsor High School; her two brothers had gone to Loomis and taken classes with Burns. Their mother asked Harpers to kindly rename the character. "I still think of [Burns] as a young educator of unusual brilliance and ability," she wrote. "I hope from now on that he uses that ability to better advantage." The publisher agreed to rechristen Ginny "Hallie Newcomb" in subsequent editions. But since there were to be no subsequent editions, Ginny Snelgrove the town pump lived on, even reappearing years later when the book was finally published in paperback.

Meantime, alarm bells went off at Burns's alma mater. There were those two references to Andover on *Lucifer*'s back flap, just as there had been on *The Gallery*, but suddenly they posed a problem: school officials feared readers, and parents, might think Andover, rather than Loomis, was the prototype of Miss Sophia's Academy. At least one Andover mother, Mrs. Leon K. Richards of Waco, Texas, did. She told Andover's admissions director, James "Spike" Adriance, that she was having second thoughts about having sent her son, David, to such a place. "What did Andover do to Mr. John Horne Burns?" she wrote. The book has "given me an abominable week," she went on, "tell myself as I will that it is a wild slashing out of an embittered, unbalanced person." Adriance admitted that he had yet to read the book, though he'd heard it discussed by several Andover teachers as well as a "prominent Harvard official." Burns's former teachers had assured him, Adriance replied, that it wasn't Andover he was describing, but the school—he, too, left it unnamed—where Burns had taught. "There are rumblings of libel suits in the offing although they will probably never materialize," he noted. But he didn't believe for a minute that that school, with which he was more than passingly familiar, was as Burns described it to be. "I have heard various reasons ascribed to his ever writing such a book, including postwar disillusionment and bitterness but I don't pretend to know the real answer," he admitted.

Andover evidently shared Mrs. Richards's letter with Burns, for in a bow to his old school, he eventually wrote her as well, and not one of those defensive screeds he'd sent to other readers, but something patient, almost paternalistic. He regretted that *Lucifer* had caused her such alarm, he said, "but everyone has been awfully literal-minded about it, I think." He'd set the story in a prep school because that was what he knew but, he reiterated, the book was really "a parable of the world in 1949." As a day student at Andover, he'd gotten an incomparable education; it was *boarding* schools he distrusted. "*Lucifer* is about as accurate [a] picture of a boarding school as *Candide* is of French Society at the time of Voltaire or *Gulliver's Travels* of the year 1727," he continued. "They are all satires, fierce misanthropic fairy tales; and you must learn to read between the lines of the exaggeration. It is unfair to assume that I wrote about a prep school that I taught at." He wished more people had understood the book, Burns lamented. "It's probably my fault. But I'm not sorry I wrote it."*

---

* Young David Richards did return to Waco High School long enough to graduate, and to meet Ann Willis, whom he later married, and who, as Ann Richards, went on to become the governor of Texas. But he returned to Andover for a postgraduate degree as well.

Spurred by Mrs. Richards and reviewers such as Victor Hass of the *Chicago Tribune*, who took care to note Burns's ties to the school, Andover attempted some quick damage control, dispatching its public relations man, Joseph Staples, to New York to meet with Cass Canfield. And he got quick results: a Harpers official decreed that the following changes be made on the book's cover:

In line 2 of Mr. Burns's biography drop the word Andover—*just say* grew up in Massachusetts.
In lines 7 and 8 of the biography delete After four years at Phillips Andover. *Start sentence* He went to Harvard.

Staples promptly sent Canfield his thanks. "I know that the Headmaster will appreciate your thoughtfulness," he said.*

Andover wasn't quite out of the woods, however: six months after Burns's visit there his piece on the place for *Holiday* still hadn't appeared, and school administrators had, quite understandably, suddenly grown apprehensive. They need not have worried. "Andover: Town and School"—which, according to Tom Burns (another Andover graduate), he and his brother "wrote one day when we were half stiff" at Patton's, a restaurant on Court Street in Boston—finally appeared in March 1950. It was a love letter to the school, or a picture postcard. Part of it was built around two roommates who suspiciously resembled Ralph Du Bouchet and his roommate in *Lucifer*: "Bill" was the boorish jock, whose half of the room was festooned with pennants, an empty champagne bottle from the Stork Club, pinup girls and comic books; while the half belonging to "Hugh" featured a Picasso print, several Modern Library editions, and sheaves of

---

* How Loomis handled its far greater public relations challenge is unclear: whether deliberately or carelessly, it saved virtually no *Lucifer*-related records.

sheet music. The article also contained a photograph of Burns's old mentor, Emory Basford, "elegant in tweed and in diction."

As relieved as the school brass must have been, the student newspaper, the *Phillipian*, was dubious. It complained of "several inconsistencies" and "a few cases of confused factual material," essentially accusing Burns of fabrication. "The day two students like Bill and Hugh room together has not yet dawned," the reviewers wrote. Burns's younger brother Donald, a Merrill Lynch broker who'd gone to Andover as well, later told Burns's first biographer, John Mitzel, that after the story appeared, Andover placed $4 million of its money with Donald's brokerage house, netting him a $15,000 commission. "Just a thank you," was how Donald Burns described the gesture. "They were so afraid." But like his oldest brother, he was a bit of a boaster, and it's not at all certain this ever really happened.

For all the bad reviews, John Horne Burns was not afraid to show his face. In early May he spoke at a luncheon sponsored by the *Philadelphia Inquirer* on what he called "The Art of Public Undressing." His talk concerned the peculiar madness of writers, and was entertaining enough for the head of Random House, Bennett Cerf, to pass it along to Norman Cousins at the *Saturday Review*, who asked Burns to adapt it for his magazine. This Burns never did, perhaps because he soon departed for England, where *Lucifer* was about to be launched. In early June, Warburg had a party for him. "He is quite a tough guy, with plenty to say for himself," Warburg wrote to one invitee. "What a charming fellow he is, and what vitality!" he told Helen Strauss. But to MacGregor, Warburg was a bit more candid. Burns was "still very young and rather in the stage of regarding the world as his oyster," he wrote him. In September, shortly before the bowdlerized British version of *Lucifer* appeared, Warburg's colleague, David Farrer, asked Burns for a better photograph than what Warburg had called "the rather thug-like" portrait from *The Gallery*. Burns complied, but it didn't help. "What with the pervading air of rather hysterical denunciation, the cheapness of the satire, and the jokes about false teeth, virginity and varicose veins, this is plainly an ill-considered and immature piece of work," wrote R. D. Charques of the *Spectator* in a representative review. (An exception was C. P. Snow, who wrote in the *Sunday Times* that while undisciplined, Burns was clearly gifted and promising.)

The drubbing Burns took on both sides of the Atlantic would place increasing pressure on him the next time around, on the last book covered by his Harpers contract. He now had to write the rubber novel.

26

On the afternoon of November 20, 1949, the Memorial Hall Library, an impressive brick building on the fringes of Main Street in Andover, prepared to mark National Book Week. Recent additions to its collection would be on display, refreshments would be served, and the featured speaker would be a native son made good: John Horne Burns, now thirty-three years old. His upcoming appearance was noted on the front page of the *Andover Townsman*, which reported that his topic would be "Italy: Yesterday, Today, and Tomorrow."

In the fall of 1949, Burns worked on a pair of *Holiday* stories. And, in an essay entitled "Drunk with Ink" in the *Saturday Review*, he reflected on his recent critical battering—the bane, he argued, of any novelist the second time around. "Perhaps you may sweat three times as much in the writing of the second as you did with your first," he explained. "It will avail you nothing. Second novels are doomed from their conception. Critics who liked your

Whether or not you can't go home again, in
November 1949, Burns didn't.

first will claw you to bits for not rewriting it with a different title.
Critics who hated your first will cite the second as further proof
of your aberration. You have two choices: either write a third,
or retire to a barred cell with a padded typewriter." In fact, he
claimed, there was another option, which was to write a third, and
a fourth, and a fifth, because, when it came right down to it, he
had no other choice. "I fear I shall go on writing novels until my
compassionate agent comes down with myopia, and my generous
publisher discovers that all my books are being remaindered to
39c counters," he declared.

Burns had repeatedly scorned the expatriate life. He remained
convinced that literary Europe was a spent force; in his *Saturday*

Review essay, he reiterated his belief that the most vital writing these days was coming from America, a point that forced him to be uncharacteristically kind to other American authors: Robert Penn Warren, Eudora Welty, Mailer, Shaw, and even—in minuscule doses—"little Truman C." He had more choice words for old-school writers on both shores like Henry James ("unreadable"), Graham Greene ("overrated"), T. S. Eliot ("desiccated"), and Kafka ("claustrophobic"). Only certain snobs—he placed them on an axis running "from Kenyon College to Cambridge, Massachusetts, with milk stops at the little magazines and the liberal weeklies"—still bowed toward the Continent. "Those who have talent will not become expatriates but must stay and fight it out here," he had written John Fischer at Harpers in 1947. "Of all the garrets in the world, only the American one offers any hope whatever." In the next few years, he predicted, America would become a "New Florence."

But in *Lucifer*'s wake, the old Florence came to seem increasingly alluring to him. He continued to love Italy, and Italy continued to respect him. One could live there more cheaply. And he still had that contract with *Holiday*. Meantime, his life in Boston had soured. Publicly he put on a brave face after his literary failure. Tom Burns didn't remember his brother displaying any great post-*Lucifer* anguish at all. But he did recall the sloppy figure Jack cut around town; for all his elegance in thought and speech, Burns had never cared much about fashion, and his favored wardrobe these days consisted of army fatigues and a red corduroy hat. He would embarrass his brother whenever he showed up at his law office.

Such encounters with his family were rare, though. Burns had a soft spot for the women in his family. He remained close to Cathleen; he'd given a thousand dollars of his royalties from *The Gallery* to his sister Anne to cover what she'd lent their brother Joe, who had fallen into schizophrenia. And he remained devoted to his mother, cooking her a birthday dinner once—beef, plus canned cream of cucumber soup from S.S. Pierce—in his Boston apartment. But with his brothers he was distant. He took no other role caring for Joe, whom he'd once called a "Philistine," nor for Donald, who'd become an alcoholic. Burns kept to himself, living with what Tom Burns called a "low dollar" man who worked in a record store. He continued to maintain his mask: when Warburg, visiting from London, had breakfast with him in Boston, Burns identified the "flat-chested girl" who had accompanied him and another young man that morning as his fiancée. "This was a surprise," Warburg later recalled, "as I had assumed until then that he was exclusively homosexual."

From time to time, Burns cruised. In the fall of 1949, Preston Claridge was a twenty-one-year-old Harvard junior talking to a friend at the Napoleon Club, an elegant, sport-jacket-and-tie gay bar, when Burns came up and introduced himself. Burns was too old for Claridge; among Boston's gays the "Nap" was known as "the Wrinkle Room" because of its mature clientele. But Claridge had just read and loved *Lucifer* (word of books with homosexual characters traveled quickly along Harvard's gay grapevine) and told Burns so. He had all kinds of questions for him: Did the boys at Loomis have sex? Did the masters have sex with the boys? Were many of the masters queer? Did *he* ever have sex with a boy? Burns, who struck Claridge as shy and insecure—perhaps from the critical shellacking he'd just received—replied that the boys *did* have sex with one another, not because they were queer, but because they were horny teenagers. With few exceptions, he went on, the teachers did not have sex with the boys, though many were closeted. He'd never had sex with a boy, he said. They talked for more than an hour, with Burns buying him a couple of drinks. Burns asked him, politely, whether he would like to go to his place for a nightcap, and Claridge just as politely declined. That was that.

Around the same time, three recent Loomis graduates—
Jerome Kohn, John Cox, and Jake Spoerl—dined with Burns at
a restaurant in Scollay Square. Burns had always seemed tightly
strung but was now even more on edge, Kohn later recalled: he
had, it seemed, decided to move back to Italy. To Cox, he appeared
buoyed by the prospect. (Later, Cox heard rumors—unfounded,
it seems—that Burns was "shacked up" with Tennessee Williams
in Rome.) When Burns told MacGregor of his plans, MacGregor
heartily concurred. Italy had already worked its magic on Burns
once, and maybe it could do it again. "For God's sake, get back
into the mood of your first book and recreate something of that
same situation and it will be better than what you've been doing,"
MacGregor urged.

But Burns informed no one in his family about his plans. That
included his brother Tom, who stood on the platform at the Andover train station on the afternoon of November 20, 1949, waiting to pick him up and take him to the Memorial Hall Library
to mark National Book Week. Burns continued to love dramatic
gestures, like leaving people in the lurch; it turned out he wasn't
thinking about the yesterday and today of Italy, but only about
the tomorrow. Tom Burns never did see his brother that day, nor
did he ever again. Burns had opted for exile.

Looking back a couple of years later, Vidal concluded that
Burns's move made perfect sense. "His manner is vain, pretentious, and nervous, but not wry," he wrote in his journal. "He
regards himself with the most appalling (if justified) reverence
after *The Gallery*, a pose which changed to petulance and grief
when the second book was kicked around by every reviewer in
the country. I am sure that he felt he was taking revenge on these
barbarians when he left for Italy."

27

By January 1950 Burns was settling into Milan—at that point, only for the winter. Apart from his magazine work, he labored away on his fiction: he reported to Warburg that his latest novel would be ready in a couple of weeks, "and as usual I think it's good." His tone had changed: the old bravado was gone. But in early February *Lucifero con un libro* would be published in Italy, with an impressive press run of ten thousand. It was another sign of his undiminished stature there, as was the largely favorable reaction it received. Italian reviewers were more inclined to see it, with its harsh view of humanity, as akin to *The Gallery*. They also read it as a political book, and liked its take on an amoral America run by speculators and crooks, and on an elite school grooming their successors. (The Communist press especially liked it.) Unlike American critics, they also found it sincere and funny. They even took credit for Burns's enlightenment: his Italian experience had opened his eyes. But they really liked the book because they really liked Burns: they figured the same sensitive soul who had lionized them in *The Gallery* had magically reappeared in *Lucifer*, only now he was named Guy Hudson. It didn't matter that Hudson was an ass; he presumably still loved them. Even in Italy, though, the book was too much for some. "Lucifero con un bazooka," one review was titled.

Italy itself had continued to change, and Burns's romance with the place and its people continued to wane. "Italians, so far as I can see, have no literary taste whatever," he told Warburg. "They burble of Dante, Leopardi, and Manzoni,* but nobody of the present generation has read these works. But it's all of a piece with the chaos here. Out of the Vatican and the Demo-Cristiani† should come a dictatorship far worse than Fascismo." Only five years after Mussolini and his mistress had been strung up there feetfirst, Burns found Milan awash in the vulgarity and materialism he felt he'd fled. Here, just as in Naples, there was no escaping America's pernicious reach: American aid had made the rich richer. "At La Scala one sees style and automobiles undreamed of in London, Paris, or New York," he wrote Warburg. "Except that it has all gone into the pockets of new-rich and their whores. Perhaps the hydrogen bomb is the logical answer to such a society. I refrain from underscoring this last. But I feel like vomiting half the day long."

The *Corriere della Sera* of Milan regularly ran a column by the prominent journalist and historian Indro Montanelli on his encounters with notables, and he now devoted one to Burns, whom he described, oddly, as resembling Spencer Tracy, and even more oddly, as a kind of macho man. "How old might he be—this author of *The Gallery*, one of the most discerning and penetrating American novels of Italian society?" he asked. "Not more than

---

* Alessandro Manzoni (1785–1873), whose novel *The Betrothed* is a milestone in Italian language and literature.

† The center-right political party that dominated postwar Italian politics.

33 or 34, I think, and I feel a bit of sympathy for him. His rosy complexion is still childlike; his blue eyes, immaculately pure and quick to wonder; the nose, somewhat crooked; and his sturdy shoulders declare a familiarity with such rough and courageous athletic events as are suited to a fresh, barbarian, and ingenuous race." Burns, forever railing against muscle-bound American culture, must have found that last point amusing.

But to Montanelli, Burns was still an atypical American, and not only because he spoke perfect Italian. He was neither puritanical nor materialistic nor boorish, a fact Montanelli attributed to his Irishness and his Catholicism. All this the newspaperman pondered as he watched Burns fondle his wine—some Barolo dating back to 1938. "He lifts his glass and does not gulp down its contents all in one breath, as his compatriots do with brandy or whiskey," Montanelli wrote. "Oh, no! He hardly wets his lips, tosses a few drops around between his tongue and palate, smells it, regards it against the transparency of the window in the background, returns to relish a short sip, gazes at it, scrutinizes it. Finally, he concludes with a calm and steady voice: 'You don't drink wine . . . you admire it, you smell it, you warm it up in your hand, you savor it. And then . . . and then you talk about it.'"

Burns was enjoying his usual routine: sleeping until noon, working until eight, then strolling the streets until dawn, when he'd return to his hotel downtown. But he still thought of returning to America, or at least said he did, because those very brutish American mores he'd thought he'd escaped—mores that had led his fellow GIs to deaden Neapolitan women with alcohol, then kiss, beat, and marry them—had spread to Italy, threatening to rob it of the dearness and spontaneity he had always cherished there. "I wonder whether you feel at least a little pity, you Italians, for us Americans, so desperately alone in our crowded skyscrapers, so persecuted by a God also incapable of *simpatia*," Burns asked Montanelli. "I want to settle down here," he went on. "What would you say: would I do

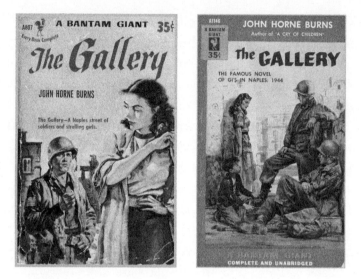

To appeal to the masses, The Gallery *suddenly went straight.*

well or badly to marry an Italian?" Very well, Montanelli assured him, but he wasn't taken in; he had not missed how, as they spoke, a "rather beautiful and elegant" woman had sat down at the next table, and Burns had paid her absolutely no mind.

That April Burns dropped by Florence, "vacationing from the book which he is writing in Milan," reported the Florentine newspaper *Il Mattino del'Italia Centrale,* which ran a small daily column (in English) chronicling the activities of the expatriate community there. Before long, Burns had come back there for good, and that made sense, for this was the city he loved. By May he'd taken up with a veterinarian six years younger than he from the small seaside town of Cecina, near Livorno, named Sandro Nencini. Soon, Burns's appearances around town, like being spotted walking along Via Tornabuoni in the afternoon heat, made *Il Mattino.* With some sheepishness, Burns had now officially changed his mind about the perils of exile, and decided he could tolerate Italy's creeping Americanization. Everything had fallen into place and, as he wrote Helen Strauss, he was happy.

This is probably the best year of my life so far. My nervous tension has melted away in the Italian sunlight, and I bask in the warmth of these people who on each inspection seem warmer, kinder, and more complicated. I shall probably never put my finger on what gets me about Italy; but as you well know it's the same school and training table for writers that Paris was after the last war. Perhaps it's the extraordinary variety and vitality here; squalor and beauty next door to each other, abysmal suffering and dizzy ecstasy of spiritual and physical love. At any rate I'll be a finer man and a finer writer some day. I hate to say it; yet you know it's true: there's something lacking in America for one who is trying to be an artist in some form or other. I've always had scorn for expatriates, and here I am pulling the same act for myself. But how else do you explain this influx, this escape to Europe? Everybody's doing it! as the old song says. In one month nearly everyone I know has passed through here.

That summer, Burns spent a month on the Italian resort island of Ischia, swimming and, as usual, getting sunburned.

Burns told Strauss, too, that he had begun his next novel, though he supplied few details. "I don't like either the title or much of the text . . . , but when I'm finally pleased, it will be way ahead of anything I've yet done," he promised. "Italy and a long period of contemplation and contact with real life will, of course, be to blame for this vast change. Can you blame me if I seek to get to the bottom of things in my own odd way?" In the meantime, his old work circulated in new guises, like the pulp paperback version of *The Gallery*. Its publishers tried to reposition it as a steamy novel of heterosexual sex, covers showing beautiful brunettes beckoning leering GIs. "The Gallery—A Naples street of soldiers and strolling girls," one of them declared.

28

If you walked a few blocks down the Arno from the Ponte Vecchio toward the American consulate and took a right at Piazza Ognisante, you'd find yourself in front of Florence's Hotel Excelsior. Then, if you continued into the lobby, went past the concierge, and took a couple of quick right turns, you would reach the famous Excelsior bar. And from the spring of 1950 forward, if you'd entered the place on any given evening from around six or seven until closing time and eyed the very end of the counter, the chances were pretty good that you'd have seen John Horne Burns. And that, maybe even more quickly, John Horne Burns would have seen you.

The Excelsior was on the Lungarno Vespuchi, a stone's throw from the river, directly across the piazza from another of the elite hotels in town, the Grand. Once tourists began returning to Florence in the late 1940s and early 1950s, the eponymous guide book author Temple Fielding ranked the Excelsior the top hotel

Burns knew the Excelsior inside and out.

in town. Florence had always been a sleepy place, but in the years following the war—when the damage the Germans had visited on the place was still visible, and the improvised GI-built Bailey bridge, replacing the one the Wehrmacht had blown up, still forded the river—it was even quieter. Some of the Americans and British in town were short-termers—the latest crop of Fulbright scholars; men from the nearby NATO air base; writers, artists, and musicians passing through. Others were businessmen, like representatives of the fashion houses. Then there were the long-termers, including a few who'd passed the war there. In a letter to George Santayana, the American poet Robert Lowell, who settled briefly in Florence in the fall of 1950, divided its English speakers into two classes: "very earnest, dissatisfied and bewildered" types, "usually women and 'Voice of America' officials"; and "the leisured—a little effeminate, cultured, good gossips, a bit pathetic and flotsamish—the best once had great talents or ambitions."

Lowell didn't mention Burns but could well have had him in mind; he lived just up the street from the Excelsior, which offered just about the only nightlife in town. Nor did Burns come up in a letter Lowell had written to the poet Elizabeth Bishop the following April, shortly before leaving town. But here, too, he might have. "What a lot of people (mostly Americans) we have seen going down the drain or crashing—for all sorts of almost unbelievably spectacular reasons," he noted.

The once-luxurious Excelsior could not yet afford to be expensive again, and, just as important during Florentine winters made even grimmer than usual by scarce fuel, it was warm. So, for the quarter or so it cost for an espresso or Negroni cocktail, you could sit in heated comfort all the evening long. Sometimes, celebrities came by: Libby Holman, Alan Ladd, Gregory Peck. There was also a fair assortment of Italian hangers-on, like Princess Doria of Italy, always with her small dog, and "Pussy" Ferroni, who fraternized with whoever happened to be running Florence, whether

German or American. And though it was a far cry from Momma's, Florence's gays also patronized the place. The Excelsior bar offered what was, for that city in that era, the closest approximation of elegance—with white-jacketed waiters buzzing back and forth—and conviviality.

Since he had been so famous so recently, Burns became a kind of literary landmark there, a highfalutin Florentine tourist attraction like the Strozzi Palace or Ghiberti's doors. "At the Excelsior bar, Florence fiddles while John Horne Burns!" was how *Il Mattino* put it. Burns, whom the paper called a "famous author and wit," could always be found in the same precise spot: at the near end of the bar, closest to the entrance. His niche was uncontested: regulars knew better than to fill it. Though stools were provided, Burns always stood, and not just in the same space but at the same acute angle, enabling him both to do his business with the bartenders, Enrico and Raffaello ("Henry" and "Ralph" to the English-speaking habitués), and to survey the scene, spotting patrons as they came and went. There was something territorial, almost defiant about his posture; though he rarely budged, he appeared to be strutting. Rarely did he speak to anyone, though he was quick with cutting remarks. His coign of vantage mattered enough to him that he grew upset—even staging what appears to have been a very short-lived boycott—when the bar was renovated. As well he might have, for the suspicion always was that he was not merely assaying things for entertainment's sake, but gathering material. "Since the redoing of the Excelsior bar there has been sadly noticed the absence of world famous author Mr. John Horne Burns from his nightly perch," *Il Mattino* noted in March 1952. "'Tis rumored that Mr. Burns does not approve of the wooden wings that have been added to each end of the bar, obstructing the view from his honored place, but Raffaello and Henri promised to build him a special private counter complete with a peep hole behind the loathed wing, so that he may continue to do research for his many short stories on Florence in peace and secrecy."

Winters, Burns wore turtlenecks; in warmer weather, he favored a coat and tie. Sometimes he wore a cape, or maybe it was the tippet he'd asked MacMackin to procure. There was nothing festive about his attire; after detailing the colorful costumes others had donned for Easter 1952—"A Dreamy Easter Parade"—*Il Mattino* noted that "Mr. John Horne Burns wore black." At his feet, even when it wasn't raining, there was always a furled umbrella, which doubled as a walking stick and all-purpose prop. His drink of choice was Bhuton cognac and soda—a cheap, ersatz substitute for real brandy, which in those days few could afford, poured from a pinched bottle suggesting synthetic elegance. Always, he'd be sucking on a piece of hard candy. He'd once scorned sweets—he'd trade his GI rations of them for cigarettes, or give them to the Italian POWs—but Sandro, his boyfriend, insisted they prevented hangovers, so the barkeeps kept a bag behind the counter for him. He favored them over the homemade potato chips and olives which were the bar's normal fare.

For all his love of the place and its people, Burns wasn't to be found in the coffee bars on the Piazza della Repubblica, where Florence's homegrown intellectuals hung out. Instead, he surrounded himself with the kinds of people he'd fled. But these folks would at least know him, and respect him, and maybe even fear him; the Excelsior was certainly the only remaining place on earth where this would still be true. It must have pleased him to see people looking his way and whispering, whatever catty things they might be saying. The Excelsior, as one veteran of the place put it, was "gemütlich": people there were friendly with one another. But Burns rarely participated in the conversation. Even those who had read and admired *The Gallery* knew to leave him alone: they somehow sensed that they would be intruding. "It was almost as if he had a 'do not disturb' notice around his neck,"

Brian Glanville, then a young British sportswriter, later recalled. "He was a sad and lonely-looking figure, a lonely boozer. He never talked to anybody else. Unless you're lonely you're not gonna spend the whole fucking evening standing in front of the bar talking to the bar man, especially a man with that sort of background and talent." Often Glanville would go with the American writer Patricia Highsmith to the Excelsior, where, as he later put it, the two "would see John Horne Burns drinking himself to death."

Berny Wolff, a U.S. Air Force corporal stationed in Florence at the time, recalled the winter when, perhaps for the first time after the war, vendors sold Christmas trees on the streets. Hundreds were assembled at the foot of the former Ponte Santa Trinita, a few blocks from the Excelsior. Wandering around there with his wife one cold and foggy night after the bar had closed, he was startled to see Burns sitting on the curb, staring ahead—and crying. Asked what was wrong, Burns admitted he was lost, and couldn't find his way home. In his visibly drunken state—unusual for Burns, who'd always held his liquor well—it appeared that the instant urban forest primeval had thrown him. Given his bearings, he got up and tottered away. To Wolff at least, Burns wasn't exactly pitiable; he was friendless by choice. To a kid from Burbank like himself, who had read and admired *The Gallery* at the suggestion of a beloved high school English teacher who knew she could never assign it in class, there was still something mysterious and romantic about Burns. He was like a foreign correspondent, or someone out of Eugene O'Neill.

Sometimes Sandro—whom one observer described as "English-speaking, unnaturally blond, and quite pleasant"—joined Burns at the bar. But since he lived out of town, Burns was usually alone, and would talk of going off to see *him*. "*Il Dottore*," he called him; amused bar mates who knew Sandro was a veterinarian figured that Burns, embarrassed to be dating someone beneath his station, had deliberately elevated him a few notches.

Sometimes, though, Burns's eyeballs strayed. Standing at the bar one day, he stared so continuously at a muscular airman from Brooklyn that the man threatened to deck him. On another occasion—the exact provocation is lost in time—a GI threw a drink at him.

In the fall of 1950, another American expatriate, a recent Harvard graduate named George Armstrong Leiper IV, also settled in Florence. Armstrong (he dropped his last name from his by-line as a tribute to Satchmo) had actually met Burns at a Boston bar a year or two earlier when, post-*Gallery* and pre-*Lucifer*, he was riding highest and acting haughtiest. Before long Armstrong, too, happened upon Burns at his customary spot. By that point, Burns had progressed to being "barely pleasant" with him. "I don't know whether anyone in Florence really knew John Horne Burns outside of the bar room of the Excelsior Hotel," Armstrong later wrote. "Except for a few chance encounters on the street, I never saw him anywhere else." Burns, he recalled, "would bow with mock-gallantry to acquaintances as they walked in but only rarely could he be coaxed to a table." He was cagey about where he lived—a series of local hotels, as it turned out. (For the book prepared for his fifteenth Harvard reunion in 1952, Burns listed his address as "USIS,* Via Tornabuoni 6, c/o Miss Ferguson, Florence, Italy.") Once Armstrong heard Burns play some arias on the Excelsior's piano, but generally still thought him standoffish, "sneering at we [*sic*] foolish kids." "I often found it hard to believe that the author of *The Gallery* could be so up-tight in ordinary social rapport," he later wrote. He wondered, too, why Burns lived in Florence rather than his beloved Naples, since he showed so little interest in the place. They'd finally bonded one night watching Maria Callas, in town for *La Traviata*. "He warmed up a bit when we both agreed that she was terrible,"

---

* United States Information Services.

Armstrong recalled. More than ever, it seemed, Burns relished other people's pratfalls.

Another of the Americans passing through Florence was William Weaver, then an aspiring novelist. Weaver had remained in Italy following his wartime service, doing graduate work in Rome. He already admired Burns's work, and Burns had admired his admiration, having read a favorable review of *The Gallery* that Weaver had written. Two young, literate, gay, opera-loving American Italophile veterans each savoring a land and a language they loved: not surprisingly, when they met in the spring of 1950, they'd hit it off instantly. Though Weaver was only seven years younger, Burns took an almost paternal interest in him, which was fine with Weaver. "Though he was often touchy and ill-tempered with others, with me John would relax, and I could appreciate the hidden warmth and the great humanity of his character (which was all there in *The Gallery*, where he exposes himself without that restraint that in life made him difficult and irritable)," Weaver later reminisced.

Though his visit to Florence was brief, Weaver quickly fell into what had become Burns's routine. First there'd be lunch, including Burns's customary liter of wine, at Ristorante Natale, a family-run tourist trap just up the street from the Excelsior. Then, in the fake stentorian tones of a radio announcer, Burns would call for them to head *"allo strumento"*—to the instrument, that is, to the small upright piano in the back, where they would pass the entire afternoon singing from their favorite operas, dividing the parts between them. Around five-thirty, they would head down to the Excelsior, where they would drink some more—Burns going through glasses of cognac, Weaver nursing a single glass of vermouth because he couldn't afford anything else and didn't want to sponge. Then it was back to Burns's hotel to pick up another operatic score—Puccini's *La Fanciulla del West* one day, Verdi's *Falstaff* the next—then back to the restaurant, where they'd eat some more, then sit around the piano again until nearly midnight. It was "marvelous," Weaver wrote in his journal the morning after his first such experience. "I don't know when I've found anyone so immediately winning and sympathetic. He has the same effect on me that his books had: immediate, honest and enjoyable."

Before long Weaver was calling Burns "a really fast friend." "It is amazing how closely eye to eye we see on everything," he wrote. "His example encourages me a great deal." A couple of days later they "managed to amuse themselves hugely" attending a mediocre recital by the pianist Rudolf Serkin. "When I think that we have known each other about two weeks, it seems incredible," Weaver wrote afterward. "We can take for granted our agreement on so many things, that our conversation remains always in the Empyrean. He asked last night to read my novel, and I was glad I had no copy of it with me, since I did not want to seem to presume on our friendship. I do want him to read it, however, and I would be enormously pleased if he liked it. Though, if he didn't, I don't believe I would like him any the less." Burns soon did read it, and recommended it to Warburg.

Weaver even postponed his trip back to Rome so that he could meet Sandro—"J.B.'s friend," he called him—who came to Florence only on weekends. It wasn't worth the wait. "S. is fairly interesting, and intelligent, with unmistakable signs of *la provincial*," Weaver wrote in his postmortem. "Not for me." Recalling Sandro years later, Weaver was more harsh, calling him "taciturn and grumpy." Sandro had grown annoyed when Burns and Weaver had spoken English. And he'd felt threatened, too, Weaver believed, though there was absolutely no need: the bond between Weaver and Burns was strictly artistic. Weaver could see Burns was difficult; he'd watched once when, drunk, he'd tangled with the biographer Francis Steegmuller. In September, the two attended the Venice Film Festival together. At an adjacent table was Emilio Cecchi, the literary critic who'd helped popularize *The Gallery* in Italy. Weaver offered to introduce the two, but cautioned Burns not to ask him about *America Amare*, a book Cecchi had written and published during the Fascist era that had been highly critical of the United States. "I understand that you've written a book about America," Burns promptly asked him. But having grown bored or fed up with Venice or the festival, Burns suddenly disappeared on Weaver. And for reasons that aren't clear, the infatuation between the two men quickly waned, then revived, though more tentatively, at least for Weaver. "John B. and I are in correspondence again, so that unfortunate disagreement is settled," he wrote a month later. "I'm really glad, since J. is someone whose virtues I can admire, without wanting to imitate."

Weaver would join the modest list of those with whom Burns had grown close, only to balk at anything more intimate or lasting. He lost touch completely with Holger Hagen after 1946, for instance.* And while they continued to correspond, he never saw Douglas McKee after 1943, even though McKee lived an easy train ride away in Paris. It is striking how rarely Burns pops up in the memoirs or papers of his most prominent gay contemporaries—a reminder of just how isolated he always was, even in his own community.

---

* Hagen became the German voice for such actors as Richard Burton, Burt Lancaster, Charlton Heston, and Frank Sinatra, and played some small film parts himself.

29

L ots of people came to Florence to write, but Burns was different: he was the real article. Around town they called him *"L'Autore,"* as if he were the only actual writer on hand; the elegant bookstores on Via Tornabuoni displayed his works in their windows in the same proprietary fashion that the Andover Bookstore would have. Among those visiting Florence and wishing to see him, word spread that Burns appeared like clockwork at the Excelsior every afternoon. It was a measure of his devotion to Burns, with whom he'd studied, that when Donald Cantor went to Europe with three Loomis classmates in the summer of 1950, he insisted they accompany him to only two places: the concentration camp at Dachau, and the Excelsior to see Burns. And at the appointed time, Burns sure enough showed up. Visiting writers stopped by the Excelsior to pay him homage and, with them at least, watch him hold court. One was Herbert Kubly, a former music critic for *Time* who spent eighteen months in Italy in 1950 and 1951 as a Fulbright scholar. His encounter with Burns so impressed him that he wrote about it twice, though—bowing to delicacy—only the second time did he identify Burns by name.

Before Burns had said anything to him, Kubly was struck by his appearance—"burly, virile, and handsome; an extraordinary specimen of a man"—and the power of his personality: you could feel his vitality. Kubly complimented Burns on his work, and told him he considered the reviews of *Lucifer* unduly harsh. "Those bastard critics!" Burns replied. "A writer can't write a line criticizing anything American. The critics won't stand for it. Italian critics adored the book. I think Italians are the greatest people on earth. They've got everything Americans haven't got. Italians are people of the heart; their country is the land of the soul. I love Italians. Italians love me. Italy is my home. You'll never see me leave it." In fact, his home was Florence; Rome, he said, he'd never been able to grasp. While surprised any place could be too large for someone so vibrant, Kubly thought he understood: "It was necessary for him to be in control of his environment and Rome was too overwhelming," he recalled. "He would have had to be Pope to be happy there."

Kubly looked on as a young Italian journalism student timidly approached Burns and asked whether reading *Time* was a good way to improve her English. She'd touched a trip wire. "The worst possible way," Burns replied, his fluent Italian resounding through the room. "You see, my dear girl, it's not written in English. Americans are a nation of illiterates. They can neither write nor read English." The frightened girl quickly fled. "She may have seen that he was drunk; perhaps she thought he was mad," Kubly wrote. A man at the bar—apparently Kubly himself—asked Burns what he was currently writing. "Right now I'm in a lazy period," he replied. "I'm too god-damned happy. I can't write when I'm happy, only when I'm unhappy. It's the damnedest thing. It's beginning to make me unhappy as hell that I'm too happy to write, so I may start a new book soon." And what might that book be about? Kubly asked. "He looked down on me—for he was a tall man and he had a hauteur that made him seem even taller—with withering scorn and replied, 'About love, of course. What else is there to write about?'" "He might have said loneliness," Kubly later reflected, "for Burns was a lonely man and he must have realized there is more loneliness in the world than love."

Though he never saw Burns again after 1948, Vidal kept apprised of his life, perhaps through Armstrong, perhaps through his friend and relative, Louis Auchincloss, who seems to have visited Burns in Florence once. He somehow knew all about the brandy and candy. And he knew better than to ask too many questions about him. "In those years one tried not to think of Burns," he later wrote. "It was too bitter. The best of us all had taken the worst way." No amount of that hard candy could counteract the two things always hanging over Burns: the state of his career and the fate of his next novel. Warburg, who had become his greatest cheerleader and prodder as well as a surrogate father of sorts, reminded him that given the split decision over the first two books, his third was crucial. Burns knew it, too. Gone were the days of dashing off a thousand words an hour three hours a day and then going out for drink and dreadfuls. "How right you are about the importance of my third novel!" he wrote Warburg in June 1950. He'd been mulling that over for almost a year, he said, writing and rewriting a supposedly completed book. Whether Italy was helping by picking up his spirits or hurting through constant distractions was unclear. "At home I was getting like an overtuned E-String; here I'm as relaxed as I've ever been; indeed, my natural laziness has taken precedence over my natural vitality," he wrote Warburg.

All that rewriting was worrisome. Someone—either Burns's agent, his American publisher, his British publisher, or all three—should see his manuscript, Warburg suggested; Burns had clearly lost his perspective. In early August, Warburg was still waiting, and prodding. Finally, Burns started to chafe. "It was your own hand that wrote me in January that this third novel was crucial, and now you're lamenting that I'm 'rewriting and rewriting it'!" he snapped. "Like you, I want it to be really good. So who can blame me if I try *my* hand at perfection? You and I both liked *Lucifer*, but nobody else seems to have. In Florence I've met many people who seem to remember me as the author of one very good book and one horrendous one. It galls me, you know."

Writing *The Gallery* had been almost a public event, with Burns indiscriminately handing out pages fresh out of his type-writer. Even the man who'd picked him up at Phil's Punch Bowl in Boston had heard a bit. But now, bruised and gun-shy, Burns kept his manuscript to himself. For better or worse, everyone would see it at once, and only when he was ready to show it. "I think it's going to be very good, with a sheen and tautness that even the best British writers might envy," he wrote. But October came, and Warburg was still waiting. Nothing had changed by the following March. With Harpers, too, Burns had all but disap-peared. "He . . . is a very bad correspondent, and we rarely hear from him," Simon Michael Bessie of Harpers told an editor in France.

Much to Helen Strauss's unhappiness, Burns was settling in. He'd taken an apartment in Corbignano, a hamlet in the hillside town of Settignano, just above Florence. It was a portion of a larger house known as Villa La Bicocca, *bicocca* being an endearing term meaning both charming and in disrepair. His landlord was the British composer Reginald Smith Brindle; the family of Brindle's Italian wife had owned the place for many years. The house, por-tions of which dated back to 1695, had numerous charms. Inside it was cozy, with a terra-cotta dining room stove. Out its windows were rolling hills and olive orchards and a panoramic view of Flor-ence including the church of Santa Croce and—if you craned your neck a bit—the Palazzo Vecchio. It was enough to inspire anyone; many other writers and scholars, Mark Twain among them, had sojourned nearby. For Burns, the setting was as timeless and tasteful as the United States was immature and tacky. It was even semi-snooty, only a fifteen-minute walk from I Tatti, the famous villa of the nonagenarian American art collector and scholar Bernard Berenson, whom Burns had once visited in the spring of 1950, and had found disgustingly pampered and pompous.

Burns must have relished having a villa, or at least a piece of one, in the same neighborhood. And the place was cheap, surely far cheaper than hotels in Florence, and costing only a fraction of what he would have had to pay to live in the States, even though it came with its own cook. But there were disadvantages, too. It was a long way from the Excelsior—officially, only fifteen or twenty minutes by bus, but that was once the bus came. It was a trek even to the closest bus stop, whether above the house in Settignano or below it, by Ponte a Mensola. The walk there was shorter and downhill, through a canopy of trees that made the ancient, narrow road feel like a sylvan tunnel. But without the narcotizing effects of the cognac to come, after hours in which those words that were once impossible to dam up just wouldn't flow, the walk down the hill in the dwindling light afforded him ample time to ponder his problems. And the way back was not just steep but bleak and, in the pitch black, a bit dangerous even when sober; Burns would have had to hug the ancient stone wall whenever a car sped by. And after all that, what awaited him at the end of the road was an empty, drafty flat with an expectant typewriter.

There would be no more trips back to the States; when his sister Anne married, Burns stayed put. A growing household immobilized him further. "Mr. John Horne Burns is now the proud owner of a lovely dog, a Siberian Wolf trained to bite only personal friends," *Il Mattino* reported. It was from his new quarters that he wrote Strauss in October 1951 to say that he really, truly, would deliver his new book soon. Now it even had a name: *A Cry of Children.* "I think it's a honey," he told her. "I assure you I haven't gone dry. It's just that this place is exciting and difficult to work in. The ideas keep pouring in, and besides, I feel the need to live, which I'm doing in an unhectic way—mostly meditating. After all, we children mature sometimes."

Strauss promptly forwarded the letter to Frank MacGregor. "He really is alive and there really seems to be a manuscript!" she marveled. Burns reiterated his good news to Warburg. The new book, he said, had "cost me much blood these last two years," but "it seems to have a depth and a sadness and a sweetness I never dreamed myself capable of." He felt compelled to defend his new life. "As the last of the romantics, I find everything in Tuscany— good cooking, a kitten, a collie, and the love that I need," Burns wrote. He was living "sumptuously" on forty-five dollars a week. Everyone in the village was a Communist, "and they treat me marvelously."

But Warburg, like Strauss, was dubious. "I should not dream of criticizing your stay in Tuscany," he assured him. "But you are a novelist and if living in Tuscany means that there are no novels, I am against it, not only because we would not have the pleasure, and I hope, the profit, of publishing them, but also because you would be frustrated and feel, sooner or later, that you had wasted your life, or a large section of it."

Even while failing to produce anything new, Burns took a critical hit from a onetime friend. In what became his most famous study, *After the Lost Generation,* John Aldridge reversed his verdict on the postwar writers: what had originally seemed like maturity and seasoning in them now struck him as stylistic conservatism. He still had kind words for *The Gallery,* "a fine book which almost everyone read," but *Lucifer* was pure technique: the subject matter wasn't worthy of it; few, if any, readers could share his bitterness. He then confronted the unmentionable: the gayness of the two books, which he considered undesirable. Like recent works by Vidal and Capote, he wrote, both *The Gallery* and *Lucifer* were "often obsessively concerned with homosexual types and situations." Worse, Burns dealt with them only obliquely—with "coy posturing and giggliness." Burns's women, while feminine enough, were "simply lust objects." Aldridge's book—the first sign that Burns had gotten caught up in the homophobic culture that Vidal had identified—was not the only belated hit that *Lucifer* took. Consigning it even further into oblivion was another prep school novel, this one by J. D. Salinger. *The Catcher in the Rye*'s Holden Caulfield proved infinitely more appealing, and enduring, than Guy poor Hudson.

In early December 1951, Burns finally placed the first 192 pages of *A Cry of Children* on a TWA flight from Milan to New York. But it took him nearly two months to send Strauss the rest, and understandably so. *A Cry of Children* is a poor novel, lacking the lyricism and warmth of *The Gallery*, the dynamism and wit of *Lucifer*, and the casual sophistication of the travel pieces. It is built around the implausible relationship between the latest Burns surrogate, an elegant and cultured concert pianist named David Murray, and Isobel Joy, his vulgar, cruel, slatternly girlfriend—a relationship of utter implausibility and little interest. It is to Isobel's brother that David is really attracted, but he is a brute and a bore. Surrounding them is a roving band of trivial ancillary characters, including a crudely portrayed Jewish-style landlord, complete with halitosis. Potentially adventurous topics, like Isobel's decision to abort her child by David, are lost because it's hard to care very much about either one of them. The book played to all of Burns's weaknesses: because he was never in love with a woman, he could not write about it; because he had few old friends, he could not describe friendship; because he did not much like people, he couldn't capture them; because he could not or would not write about what he knew and cared about most, except in occasional digressions, he had to write about what he didn't. (If Helen Strauss could urge another of her clients, James Baldwin, to burn *his* gay novel, *Giovanni's Room*, in 1954, would she have counseled Burns any differently several years earlier?) Burns's ability to shape characters, so evident in *The Gallery*, had evaporated on him, and the one character he could have written about persuasively—himself—he left unexamined.

The work is not only misanthropic but, surprisingly, poorly written; the opening passage is a moving description of a big city stirring at dawn, but once its characters appear it is all downhill, and on a steep grade. Only a few years earlier, Burns had whipped off gorgeous prose profligately in V-mails. *A Cry of Children* reads as if, having had the wind and spirit knocked out of him and being buffeted by advice from everyone around him, Burns had written in a straitjacket. Either that, or Italy was indeed a distraction. Or, just as plausibly, all that cognac was finally exacting a toll: alcohol was no longer revealing or intensifying Burns's vision, but clouding it. How, otherwise, could someone so talented have taken so long and labored so hard to have written something so poor?

Harpers was shocked by what Burns had sent. *Lucifer*, which had been excused as an off day for Burns, now looked stellar by comparison. "It was terrible," MacGregor later recalled. So terrible, in fact, that like Canfield before him, he consulted others just to make sure he hadn't lost his judgment. "I got as many of my colleagues as I could to read it, and I asked, 'Is this as bad as I think it is?' and they all said, 'Yes, it's just as bad as you think it is,'" he later remembered. "What do you do? I was hoping that, as time went on, he would get over some of his bitterness, and, second, that he would grow up a little and become the writer he gave promise of being. And this was just way below his previous work. It was just a lousy book."

Burns didn't see this—"It's closer to my heart than anything I've yet done," he wrote—and his blindness puzzled his friends.

"His own disturbance—what the war did to him, what his surroundings did to him, and I don't know—whether the fact of his
homosexuality had anything to do with it?—overwhelmed his talent in a way," Beulah Hagen later surmised. "There must be *some*
reason why he was convinced that he was writing better all the
time, and he was writing the best book he was capable of, when he
was instead doing the opposite." Even MacMackin—whose relationship with Burns had clearly waned: by now he had stopped
receiving, or at least saving, his letters—called the book "awfully
inept." Still, Harpers accepted it as it was, on the diminishing
chance that somewhere in him Burns still had another *Gallery*.
"I finally reasoned, 'Well, I will publish this'—and others agreed
with me—'because, if I don't, I'll lose him and we may regret it,'"
MacGregor remembered. "'It's not that bad. I don't like it and a
lot of people here don't like it, but it isn't disgraceful in publishing
terms.'" So he put on a brave face. "CONGRATULATIONS AND OF
COURSE WE WANT TO PUBLISH," he telegraphed Burns on March
10. Burns fell for the ruse. "I'm of course delighted at everybody's
reaction," he replied.

Warburg was far kinder than the Harpers folks, telling Burns
it was "a moving and powerful and at times, extremely funny
novel." "Superlatives are justified," he added. He scheduled publication for October, and asked about an option on Burns's next
two novels. Perhaps affection and loyalty had clouded his judgment. Or perhaps he was just being diplomatic.

Burns resolved to stay in Italy indefinitely; "I'm getting to look
more Tuscan and Medicean all the time," he told MacGregor. He
weighed voting in an Italian election simply to shed his American citizenship. He planned to set his fourth novel in Italy, one he
hoped to finish by Christmas. But for the first time, even with potent dollars at his disposal, he was going broke, another sign that
all that Hollywood money Burns had bragged about was a myth.
In late April 1952 he implored Strauss by cable for funds. "If I

don't get a check by the end of the week, I'm thinking of selling my 35-year-old body to rich American doxies who pass through here," he wrote Warburg. To Warburg he joked about someone finding his starved corpse sprawled along the Arno.

Perhaps because he was no longer writing against the backdrop of epochal events, perhaps because he simply stopped sending them, Catherine Burns also was no longer saving his letters. But in the summer of 1952, Mother Burns visited Florence. She went to Villa La Bicocca and met Sandro, photographing him and Jack on their front balcony, and accompanied them to Ischia. Catherine Burns hadn't approved of any of her children's spouses, but she appeared to like Sandro, in part because she never acknowledged who, or what, he was. He even won a place in her scrapbook. One evening, sporting a blue straw hat with cherries on top, she put in

Mother Burns, flanked by Jack (L) and Sandro at Villa La Bicocca, summer 1952

an appearance at the Excelsior. Burns actually approached Berny Wolff and his wife at their table that night and asked if he and his mother could join them. "I think he wanted to show off to his mother that he knew a straight couple," Wolff later recalled. The new book was due out in the United States on September 3, and Burns had his usual case of "pre-publication jim-jams." Warburg predicted a mixed reaction, "for not everybody can take your brand of frankness and the very racy language."

In fact, nothing about the reaction was mixed. In the *New Republic*, Whitney Balliett called *A Cry of Children* "a confused, stale, empty book." In the *Saturday Review*, which had usually treated Burns respectfully, James Gray found it "as strained, over-blown, and obvious as a soap opera," adding that "unfortunately, Mr. Burns has no assets of style, wit and poetry." The squeamish Victor Hass of the *Chicago Tribune*, who'd also panned *Lucifer*, complained that Burns "continues to write like an angel but (unfortunately, to my mind) he has not yet raised his sights above the slime of neuroticism, homosexuality, and assorted perversions." *A Cry of Children* "is certainly a powerful and finely written novel," he noted, but it was also "a singularly unattractive one, with a heavy taint of human degradation"; to reach its finer passages, "the reader is forced to consort, tho only imaginatively, with a wide range of sluts, lesbians, homosexuals, and incipient sadists. Add to these a lot of obscenely drunken people and a frightful sequence in an abortion den and you have a sort of novelistic nightmare. It made my flesh crawl."

The unkindest cut, though, came from the *New Yorker*, where the book had the extreme ill fortune to be reviewed jointly with *The Old Man and the Sea*. If Ernest Hemingway's latest was "sure to be considered one of the best-written books of the year, *A Cry of Children* should win a place for itself among the worst written," stated Brendan Gill. Burns's dialogue, he said, was "of sequoian woodenness," and his exposition even worse. "Mr.

Burns may yet learn his craft, but here he seems to have far to go," Gill concluded. "In publishing this book, Harper & Brothers show distressingly little respect for the author, for writing, or for themselves."

By this point those reviewers with longer memories—that is, who went back a mere five years—could only scratch their heads. "It all seems like a waste of time: Burns's writing it, Harper's publishing it, the reader's reading it," John A. Lynch wrote in *Commonweal*. "One wonders what has happened to John Horne Burns." The kindest thought critics like James Kelly of the *New York Times Book Review* could offer was that they were *still* waiting for the author of *The Gallery* to pull it all together again. "Lacking in real significance, flawed by excessive malice and nightmarish distortions, Mr. Burns's novel, nevertheless, reaffirms the artist's status as one of America's gifted young writers," Kelly declared. "Perhaps the next one will bring both talent and subject-matter into sharper focus."

Readers, too, once again reacted indignantly. Like Marta Cohn of Santa Monica, California, the more they had once admired Burns, the more betrayed they felt:

> *Surely you must realize Mr. Burns is a sick man. Only a person mentally ill could have written such a depraved, anti-social, anti-Semitic, anti-Catholic, anti-Negro tract. That Mr. Burns is a homosexual can be no secret to anyone who has read his previous books. But that is beside the point. The author of* The Gallery *was a great writer, regardless of his sexual inclinations. The author of* A Cry for [sic] Children *is a poor writer, a vicious writer, a sick man. It is indeed difficult—almost impossible—to believe the same man wrote both books.*
>
> *Naturally, those of us who read* The Gallery *will buy whatever is written by Burns, expecting if not as fine a*

*work at least another "try." We do not expect to be tricked
into contributing a cent toward this sort of malicious filth.*

*What, may I ask you, is worth reading in Mr. Burns's
book? What is he trying to say? What is he trying to prove?
That all women are hateful, scheming whores? That the
mother of every man by Freudian concepts turns her son
into a pervert? That Jews are money-hungry cheats and
Catholics warped maniacs and Negros [sic] Communist-
spouting lunatics and that all men are filthy, depraved
animals?*

*I paid three dollars for this book hoping to place it on
my shelves along with the thousands of other books I am
proud of owning. This, in all conscience I cannot do. I
cannot allow it to be read by my sons, I cannot lend it to
my friends. I cannot myself ever look at it or touch it again.
I feel cheated. You, as publishers have tricked me into
spending my money for the ravings of a sick man.*

She demanded, and received, a refund.

Critics are often wrong in unison, particularly with anything
adventurous or avant-garde. His old friend William Weaver later
wrote that his detractors had fundamentally misread Burns; they
took him for a war writer, steeped in realism, when he was anything but. Or, as he put it, "the critics wanted Norman Mailer,
and Burns gave them Céline."* But Burns himself seemed more
resigned than indignant. "The *New Yorker* review of *A Cry* depressed me with its uncalled-for superciliousness; but since I've
seen many others, particularly from the South and Midwest, I
feel a trifle better," Burns wrote Beulah Hagen in early October.
The reviews had crushed him, he told Weaver, but he consoled

---

* Louis-Ferdinand Céline (1894–1961), French author of *Journey to the End of the Night* and
other black, bitter novels.

himself by recalling how Keats had been devastated by slams in the *Edinburgh Review*. But had Keats read the British reviews of *A Cry*, he'd have felt himself fortunate. In the *Spectator*, for instance, the book warranted but a brief reference. "The only reason I now mention *A Cry of Children*, which has an American setting, is that so lamentably cheap and nasty a piece of work is likely to contribute in a small way to the anti-American prejudice in this country which at the moment is so dangerous," wrote the reviewer, R. D. Charques (who had also panned *Lucifer*). Coming from an Englishman, this must have especially stung; Burns couldn't write it off as classic American provincialism.

When a fan who believed Burns to be the greatest living writer complained he couldn't find his last two books, a discouraged-sounding Burns urged him to call off his search. "I'll bet that, if you liked *The Gallery*, these last books would not be to your taste," he wrote. Meantime, he did what he always did: he turned to his next novel, and returned to the Excelsior. But even in his sanctuary at the near end of the long wooden counter, he could not escape his predicament, as George Armstrong later wrote.

The writer from Massachusetts would become annoyed when someone would come up to him and praise to the skies his first book without even mentioning the other two. Burns had a glittering kind of charm when he chose to employ it but that was usually only early in the evening. He very rarely became noticeably drunk, but one could tell how much he had had by the amount of sarcasm he put into his conversation. It may have been defensive but the effect was certainly offensive. He could be very insulting to total strangers and was almost always, sooner or later, insulting to his acquaintances, including myself. One of his favorite tricks was to parrot what was said to him in an imbecilic voice, particularly picking up clichés and parroting them

back, even though you may have been using them as a
conscious attempt at humor.

Even more offensive to Burns than the idea he'd written but one good book would have been the notion, now abroad, that he'd written none. "One rumor, probably of local (and low) birth, and one that Burns surely did not start, was that 'he didn't write *The Gallery*, everyone knows that,'" Armstrong was to reminisce. "But no one ever seemed to know who did write it, if not Burns." One very quickly learned to bid him *buona sera*, and then move on.

The article on Florence Burns was doing for *Holiday* might have given him a chance to show his stuff or, if he were so inclined, to work out his frustrations. He told people that several of the Excelsior's regulars would appear in it, presumably unflatteringly. For more than a year it had been the subject of speculation around the place. It's "rumored that John Horne Burns is writing a saga for *Holiday* magazine that is supposed to be quite moving," *Il Mattino* reported. "[E]veryone is wondering in what direction." But whatever bile Burns included must have been leeched out in New York. The piece, which appeared in October 1952, was not as luxuriant as the one on Naples; while Burns appreciated Florence more, it didn't hold for him the same power or pathos. But it was another gem, filled with the passion, insight, and elegance MacGregor had hoped he could once more channel into his fiction.

Burns's Florence still reeled from the war, yet its allure endured. "It can't be *done* in four hours, or probably four years, for Florence is a celestial sort of flypaper," he wrote. "People have been known to come for a brief stay and end as Tuscan grandfathers." Burns's tour led through stores, churches, and museums to, inevitably, the local bars, including, less inevitably, his own; evidently he had concluded that buttering up the management (and, probably more importantly, the bartenders) was worth any additional noisome encounters with—and reproaches from—disappointed readers.

> *For Americans and British, the most gracious bar is*
> *at the Excelsior, a huge and excellent hotel on the Arno,*
> *run with grim Swiss discipline by the brothers Kraft and*
> *their heirs . . . The bar at the Excelsior is operated by two*
> *concessionaires who are brothers-in-law, Raffaello Sabatini*
> *(Ralph) and Enrico Mariotti (Henry). Raffaello is a trifle*
> *bald, introspective and serious until he gets to know his*
> *customers well—then he opens up with flashes of Florentine*
> *wit. Enrico is his fit counterpart, jesting and chortling.*

But this was the happy part of Burns's Florence. Overlaying the
rest was a certain melancholy.

> *The turmoil and the sense of proportion that brought*
> *Florence into being are gone. And they are gone forever,*
> *because there's nothing more to say in the Florentine*
> *pattern. It flowered and it died, leaving a trace far more*
> *permanent than a rocket. In spring and autumn no city*
> *possesses more witchery. It's the city of cities for falling in*
> *love. Yet at midnight during her dismal rainy winter one*
> *feels here a tremendous sadness, a weight of six centuries*
> *of human striving—gone, gone, gone, but frozen into*
> *massive beauty. At such times Florence reduces modern*
> *man to a pygmy, nervous, dehumanized, and concerned*
> *with murderous nonsense. One senses that long ago there*
> *were giants in the earth, and hopes there may be again.*
> *And one is proud still to be a member of the civilization*
> *that engendered this flower of stone, tile, low towers and*
> *honeyed sunlight.*

So the Excelsior crowd survived the *Holiday* article, but still
faced a more menacing prospect: Burns's novel about Florence.
There, he would enjoy far freer rein to settle scores, or so the

thinking went. *Il Mattino* had hinted at this apprehensiveness, too, back in November 1951. "At one corner of the bar stands in lonely splendor the literary set of Florence, Mr. John Horne Burns," it noted. "He is working night and day to finish his next novel by November 20th. It seems the new novel is all about Florence and believe us all those who have snubbed and have been unkind to Mr. Burns had better be looking for greener fields as he has really poured forth his opinion on these lowly ones. It's rumored the final chapter takes place at his favorite bar, where his icy stares turn all the characters to stone and the author lives happily ever after."

Around the time *A Cry of Children* appeared, a *Holiday* editor named Harry Sions came to Florence with his wife, Louise Lux, and visited Burns. The couple had already passed a pleasant day or two sightseeing and shopping with him when, after dinner one night, they decided to go to the Excelsior bar on their own. There they spotted Burns, with what Lux later described as the biggest bunch of weird-looking homosexuals she'd ever seen, all painted and dressed up, wearing wigs. When she and her husband waved at him, Burns first refused to acknowledge them and then, as they continued to seek his attention, got up and walked out. To Lux it was "excruciatingly sad": "Mr. Burns felt we had 'blown his cover,'" she wrote, when of course, with them and nearly everyone else who knew him well, he had had no cover to blow, nor any need for one. She later recalled Burns as "a lovely, sad, torn, handsome young man."

30

In early 1953 Burns, now thirty-six years old, wrote a short self-portrait for a reference book called *Twentieth Century Authors*. "In 1949 his second novel, *Lucifer with a Book*, met with raucous opposition," one portion of it read. "His third book, *A Cry of Children*, was admired by practically no one. He is at present living in a chilly villa outside Florence, Italy, finishing his fourth novel, which will deal with Saint Francis of Assisi in modern life. If that novel is a fiasco, he will take up gardening and write a book about that, too. He has written this account in the third person because, with all his faults, he is shy about his worth, even to the point of doubt, a sin against the Holy Ghost."

Burns had no problem naming novels long before they were complete, nor in saying reassuring things about them. His fourth was to be called *Maiden Voyages*, and in November 1952 he told Warburg that he'd never written anything "with such love and calm . . . It seems to have an equilibrium I never before possessed," he claimed. With any luck, he said, it "will silence the critics for a spell." He described his new, Italian writing regime: every afternoon he began writing at four, which meant that every afternoon he began getting anxious at three. Playing with his white kitten, Micio, or Lucky, his Alsatian shepherd dog, didn't help. "When I write I experience agonies that only the damned could conceive, even though I've thought it all out in advance, and strange changes happen when I sit down before this damnable Italian 'writing machine,'" he said. Silencing his critics was probably unrealistic, Warburg replied, "for they seem to bay like bloodhounds on your trail." But for all the greats he'd published, Warburg went on, "there are few if any writers on my list from whom I look forward to reading a new volume with more sense of excitement."

The new novel was, indeed, about the life of the Florentines, Burns told Armstrong; "everyone" was in it—even Bernard Berenson. Because the title had already been taken, it was now to be called *The Stranger's Guise*, and in late February 1953, Burns told Warburg he hoped to deliver it within a few days. Far from disdaining or ignoring his detractors, Burns was now trying to anticipate and placate them. He was writing the way Loomis students had once written for him, anticipating—and fearing—the barbed responses. "I've never worked so hard in my life," he wrote Warburg. "I've tried to iron out all the faults that the best critics speak of in my work. This time I've attempted to produce something that will please and move—not irritate, if that's possible, given my peculiar psychology. The chosen few—what a phrase!—who have read it say that it has something I never had before. But that's what comes of living in Italy, and writing about Her. The whole novel takes place here; but it's no re-write of *The Gallery*. When I start copying myself, I'll raise pigeons and train dogs." Warburg called his letter "unexpected and wholly enthralling." "All this seemed to me a new John Horne Burns," he gushed. To

MacGregor, too, Burns promised a new Burns. There had better be one: Harpers had contracted to publish only his first three books. On this one it had made no promises.

But in late March, Warburg lamented to Bessie that he had still not received the manuscript. Harpers, meantime, sought to coordinate things with the British publisher. "Don't you agree it would be a good idea this time if neither you nor we said anything directly to Burns until we had compared notes?" Bessie asked. Harpers had printed ten thousand copies of *A Cry of Children*, he noted, and had sold barely half that; it didn't want Warburg's enthusiasm restricting its maneuvering room, including the freedom, if need be, to turn Burns down. "Reading between the lines seems to indicate that you had rather a flop with *The* [sic] *Cry of Children* and lost perhaps a bit of money," Warburg replied. "We came out with our shirt but it was somewhat tattered."

The walls were closing in on Burns; his greatest ally was wavering, and his book simply wasn't coming together. But when Ruth Langdon of the *Boston Sunday Globe* caught up with him that April, Burns acted utterly carefree. Langdon, another American living and writing in Florence, very correctly diagnosed Burns as "a puzzling contradiction in terms": "Scornful of the epithet 'expatriate,' which he says is a sapping and deadening state for an author, he appears well-ensconced in his lovely Tuscan villa, La Bicocca," she reported. By now, she noted, Italian came more easily to Burns than English; when she'd seen him sipping brandy at the Excelsior bar, he had been reading Dante in the original. Burns boasted that the money was "rolling in" from *A Cry of Children;* he claimed to have just gotten a check for seven thousand dollars, prompting friends tired of seeing him catch the midnight bus back to Corbignano to press him to buy a car. But the Burns she saw around town didn't look any more prosperous than he really was. "In a battered tweed coat and tired green pull-over," she wrote, he looked "more like a small-town college professor than a successful Continental novelist." The topic turned to Sinclair Lewis, who had been living in Florence when Burns moved back. Lewis, who had died in January 1951, had once praised *The Gallery*, but when Langdon asked Burns about him, Burns wasn't so kind. "A pitiful and tired old has-been" he called him. Had he any sense for his own predicament, he might have shown more pity. But Lewis was another writer, after all, and Burns wasn't given to fraternal feelings.

In the spring of 1953, another famous American made her way to Italy: Clare Boothe Luce, the glamorous and flamboyant playwright, journalist, and congresswoman—and wife of Time-Life cofounder Henry Luce—was now America's ambassador to Rome. Soon, Burns was the answer to a riddle posed by George Armstrong in *Il Mattino*. "What modern living American writer, a Florentine resident, was offered the job of chief interpreter and aide to Madame Clare Boothe Luce but refused to leave Tuscany . . . ?" he asked in late April. It's hard to imagine a more improbable match: the ambassador surely didn't know of Burns's oft-voiced contempt for *Time*, let alone his left-wing politics or curmudgeonly ways. Burns wisely turned down the offer—if, indeed, such an offer was ever made.

By this time Armstrong had inherited the English-language "Around the Town" column in *Il Mattino*, a version of which also appeared in the *Rome Daily American*. Only then, he was to recall, did Burns deign to deal with him: "I was no longer the barbarian American he was fleeing from." The two men joked about what a fixture Burns was at the Excelsior. "We often told him that someday we would have put a commemorative plaque on the floor, saying: 'John Horne Burns stood here nightly, from seven to nine—sometimes longer,'" Armstrong later wrote. Burns's face, he recalled, "was always too flushed." MacGregor was more brutal. "He settled in Florence and became an irredeemable drunk," he said many years later. "He was at the Excelsior bar so drunk, so often, that they finally told him he couldn't come there any more."

In those heady moments of his in Florence just after V-J Day, Burns told his mother how contentment impaired his work. "I find writing a better catharsis than castor oil, and I only do it well when I'm not at ease," he observed. He'd told Herbert Kubly the same thing. By 1953, working in the languor of the Tuscan hills—where everything had coexisted beautifully for so long that there seemed no particular need, and certainly no rush, to add anything new—both the quality and speed of Burns's output continued to decline. Only in mid-March did he finish *The Stranger's Guise*. Another month passed before he sent it to Warburg, and then, only the first third. "I hope it's the best thing I've done—as indeed it had better be," Burns wrote him. It was remarkable, touching even, to see how tentative he had become.

But his timidity was once more warranted. *The Stranger's Guise* represented a further, shocking deterioration in his skills. The premise—the doomed relationship between an unmarried American woman in Italy on a Fulbright-like fellowship and an Italian man intent upon the priesthood, set largely in Tuscany—was reasonably promising but neither Helen Morton nor Mario Mezzasoma is interesting or appealing. Morton, a thirtyish "domestic science" teacher who chases Mezzasoma as assiduously as she evangelizes about the dubious virtues of American canned vegetables, is priggish and provincial. Mezzasoma is also priggish, along with conniving, cold, self-righteous, and humorless. Only Burns could love him, both for sharing his peculiar brand of religiosity—it features pounds of learning and grams of compassion—and his "appalling physical beauty," to which Burns repeatedly, even obsessively returns (he has a "small, perfect body," is "marvelously beautiful and agile," and, by the way, "made one catch one's breath at the glory and generosity of God"). Some of Burns's language (e.g., his "ruddy lips . . . that glowed like an azalea on his white face") sounded disconcertingly like the populist "drivel"—i.e., "her lips were a slash of carmine"—he'd ridiculed to that *Globe* reporter back in Connecticut only a few years before.

Once more, the subsidiary characters, particularly the other Americans, are built for easy and repetitious ridicule. What's puzzling is Burns's preference for such nonentities, given all the large, real-life figures who regularly walked into his life, creating limitless literary possibilities. As *Il Mattino* chronicled, the list was endless—Noël Coward, Andrés Segovia, Beniamino Gigli, Walter Lippmann, George Balanchine, Samuel Barber, Bill Mauldin, Tyrone Power, to name but a few. If he'd only done what he was rumored to be doing, he had countless targets upon whom to heap his scorn. But Burns was afraid to take on people his own size. Worse, he disdained them. In the spring of 1952, nearly a half-century after writing *A Room with a View*, which was set largely in the city, E. M. Forster returned to Florence, but Burns passed up the chance to see him, and was proud of it. "He was here the other day, but I didn't go and pay court," he told Warburg. "*Everyone's* in it," Armstrong told his Florentine readers about Burns's latest book. In fact, no one was.

Actually, *one* person was. That is the man Burns describes as "an old mandarin, not Chinese," whom Morton visits at his baronial hilltop villa. An ancient American émigré who'd come to Italy sixty years earlier, collects art, and writes on scholarly topics: there's no doubt it was Bernard Berenson. In Burns's rendering—clearly retribution for his unpleasant visit to I Tatti—Berenson is an old windbag who brooks no disagreements, never bothered learning Italian, and who curbed his lifelong lechery only when his sexual machinery conked out. "Incredibly wise and incredibly senile," Burns calls him.

It is nasty and maybe very unfair, but at least it crackles. And again, it makes one ponder the opportunities Burns wasted. What other expatriated wrecks washed up at the Excelsior? What Florentine grandees did he get to know? What was Sinclair Lewis like at his most dissolute? How about Madame Clare Boothe Luce? Burns ducked them all.

His timidity even extended to his choice of locales. The book isn't set in Florence, with its limitless thematic and descriptive possibilities, but Fiesole, the picturesque but far less interesting hilltop town overlooking it. In fact, nowhere in the book does Burns say anything of consequence about Italy or the Italians. There was more insight, and craftsmanship, in one of Burns's letters home than in the entire book. True, it was written in a lighter vein; but it's not funny enough to be satirical, yet is too satirical to say anything serious.

"She had lost her sense of timing and urgency—an Italian disease that sucks the life blood of foreigners, for the vital spark is gone in Italians, except their desire to survive by fair means or foul." It's Burns's take on the lovesick Morton, but it described him, too. Were he to retreat into the beauty of Tuscany, he had told his mother eight years earlier, "anything good I might do with my life would be smothered." But he'd upped and done just that. And whatever the Italian air had done to sap his strength, the alcohol had only intensified.

By early June, Burns had sent Warburg the entire book. When he heard nothing for two weeks, he grew worried. Had it been lost, or was Warburg too scared to say what he really thought? "You will understand my reaction, which is one of frustration, doubt, and downright terror," Burns wrote him. Warburg in fact liked portions of it, but even his barely lukewarm reaction was the minority view; his colleagues were far more critical, believing that the characters were labored and the writing stylized and irritating. (One also found Burns's obsession with food tiresome. "We all know—or most of us do—that Italian food is infinitely better than American," he observed.) There was, Warburg confessed to an associate, "a strong minority feeling in favor of throwing Horne Burns overboard."

With Burns, Warburg was more diplomatic. "Our reactions to the book are not by any means wholly favourable and we think the critics, especially in this country and perhaps also in the United States, may be waiting to jump on you and throttle you," he wrote. Burns, who by now was inclined to agree with any or all criticism, thanked Warburg for his frankness. In a long critique sent in mid-July, David Farrer—Warburg's colleague and the man who first vouched for George Orwell's 1984, told Burns that as it stood, the book was unpublishable, in part because—remarkably—it was too poorly written. He all but said that English had become Burns's second language.

> In parts the writing is very careless; at times it slips right over into the lurid and lush style of a woman's magazine: "The idea of being possessed by him seemed to her the most violet dream in this world." Frequently too you give to verbs a meaning quite alien to the meaning assigned to them in current speech. You don't, for example "execute" an opera, and surely the whole sentence "I am going to the opera. They are doing the first ever executed in Florence some centuries ago" is appalling English.

While *The Stranger's Guise* contained "the best things that you have ever written," Farrer wrote generously, it also contained the worst. "I get the impression that in parts of it neither your mind nor your emotions were really engaged," he said. But with the right fixing, he went on, it could be turned into something "immensely worthwhile." Burns quickly agreed that ninety-eight percent of Farrer's points were just, and, acknowledging that he couldn't afford "another scalping," he pledged to "take the blue pencil" and "set myself again at this blasted machine." He pledged to have it back in a month. No rush, Farrer replied: three months would be fine, particularly with a Florentine August looming. "Whether now he will turn in a worth while [*sic*] book, remains to be seen," Farrer wrote Bessie at Harpers.

In fact, Harpers, which now had the book as well, had already made up its mind: MacGregor, unlike Farrer, considered it unsalvageable. "He turned in a manuscript that was more than I could take, altogether," MacGregor later recalled. "It was a sad experience to read this, when I had hoped for so much more." MacGregor finally lowered the boom, apparently through Helen Strauss. Then, with considerable tenderness, he wrote Burns himself. "By now Helen must have told you of our most difficult decision," he wrote Burns on July 20, 1953. "Aside from the business aspect, you must know that it means much to me personally. For your sake I can only hope that we are wrong. Perhaps all of us have blind spots." Years later, MacGregor still recalled that letter. "I wrote back and said 'I'm sorry. I'm just sorry,'" he said. "I made no attempt to say, 'Why don't you do this or that?' My experience with John was that he wouldn't, or couldn't, revise; anyway, he didn't." Harpers then passed along the word to Warburg. "This was not an easy step to take since we considered *The Gallery* one of the best books we have published since the war, and we have carried on through two other [of] Burns's books about which we were not completely enthusiastic, but which we felt ought to be published to keep publishing him," Bessie wrote Farrer. The matter wasn't entirely settled; as long as Warburg remained interested, Harpers left its own door ajar—a crack.

"I m-i-g-h-t come back for a while when my fourth [novel] is published," Burns had written Beulah Hagen the previous September. But if his return home depended on that, Burns would never get back at all.

31

Like all of Italy, Florence clears out in August and heads for the beach, leaving its cities to the tourists. On the first of the month—a Saturday, and only a week or so after his book had been rejected—Burns set out with Sandro. It was a major operation: accompanying them were Burns's cook and his dog, Lucky, recently freed of the last of her fifteen puppies. Burns would not be returning to Villa La Bicocca, at least not for very long: soon, George Armstrong reported, he would be moving into another villa, in Settignano. For Burns it would represent a change in scenery and, perhaps, a fresh start. And perhaps a cheaper rent, even though it came with the person whom Burns called the best chef in all of Tuscany. Probably because money was tight, the men passed up Ischia this time and stayed closer to home—Sandro's boyhood home. Along with Sandro's mother, they had rented a relative's small beachfront bungalow in Marina di Cecina, a few miles from where Sandro had grown up. "John Horne Burns goes

The fish and lobster here practically jumped onto Burns's famous table.

in *villeggiatura** beginning today at his sea-side seat, just south of Leghorn," Armstrong noted. It's unclear whether the party went by car or train. One way or another, they'd have headed west toward Pisa, then south to Livorno and beyond along the Tyrrhenian Sea, which Burns had mentioned in *The Gallery*.

It wasn't Burns's only connection to the place: Shelley had been shipwrecked, and had washed ashore, nearby. So the place had its romantic associations for Burns. And his sojourn, too, promised to be romantic. By now, Burns had been with Sandro Nencini for three years, longer than any of his prior relationships. Just what bonded the highly literate American and the more rudimentary Italian isn't clear. According to Nencini's daughter, at least a few of Burns's letters to her father, which may provide some clues, survive. But she either can't, or doesn't choose to, find them.

---

* A country vacation.

Marina di Cecina was a simple fishing village that in summers grew into a simple resort, catering to visitors of modest means, along with a wealthy few craving something unpretentious and serene. There was little to do except swim, sail, read, or watch the sunsets, and very little to buy except basic groceries, wine at the local bars, and fresh fish from the local *pescatori*. Burns's cottage, at the foot of Via Baldissera, had a narrow balcony wrapping around it, overlooking a beach of dark volcanic sand and gravel leading to the turquoise sea which, because it dropped off quickly, was colder and more treacherous than it looked. Like the Villa La Bicocca, the Villino Brunella—named for one of Sandro's relatives—sounded more impressive than it was; it had actually been the housekeeper's quarters for a larger residence that had been claimed by the ever-eroding shoreline. From it on a clear day you could make out Elba, Corsica, and the small islands of Capraia and Gorgona, which, as Burns would have remembered from Harvard, Dante had joked about in *The Inferno*.

Five days into his stay there, Burns wrote his mother about the place. It appears to have been his first letter home in a considerable while, maybe six or seven months. And this letter Catherine Burns saved—or, perhaps, she just never had the chance to throw it away. It was dated Wednesday, August 5, 1953.

> *Darling mother,*
>
> *Above you'll see the address of my summer palace. It's a beautiful little house that Sandro and his mother have taken for the month of August, practically in the sea, on the Tuscan coast just across from the islands of Elba, Corsica, and Sardinia. Sandro often says you'd like it even better than Ischia. We have our own private beach, take our meals in the garden in a pergola that looks like a pagoda, and the surf is exactly ten seconds away from*

our door . . . It is much nicer than a pensione, *and much cheaper; we buy the food we want to eat—it costs less here than in Florence—and of course our table is famous. The fish and the lobster here would make you drool: they jump out of the waves onto our table.*

Burns thanked his mother for the package that had arrived just before he'd skipped town, filled with wonderful things for the beach, like the blue shirt and shorts he was wearing as he typed. Sandro, too, was delighted with his presents: a wallet with a penny in it, along with an alligator belt. Several of his friends had fallen ill during the recent brutal winter, Burns told his mother, but he had mercifully been spared. "All I produced was a book," he wrote. "And now I'm turning a lobster color, which (I hope) will become a tan. My hair is almost ash-blond from the sun . . . Tonight we're having curry of shrimp with rice and iced white wine." He closed with "All my love, and thanks for the gifties."

The next day, August 6, Burns went out sailing. Given his extreme sensitivity to the sun, such a venture was chancy, and suddenly he began to feel sick. He started to shiver, his arms and legs went into spasm, and his vision became cloudy. He was taken back to shore, and a doctor was summoned from the local navy base. Asked for his medical history, Burns mentioned a head injury sustained in the military—that he'd gotten hit in the forehead once by a rifle butt. He said nothing about brass knuckles or, for that matter, falling off a bus. The doctor diagnosed sunstroke. Burns's faith in that magical Tuscan sunlight which, he'd written a few years before, "vitalizes but does not burn," had been misplaced.

He spent the rest of that day in bed. On the next, he ventured out into the garden. For three days after that, August 7, 8, and 9, he did not leave home, and his symptoms gradually abated.

Around seven o'clock on the evening of August 10, he even went for a swim, then had dinner before going to bed at eleven-thirty. But by the following morning Burns had fallen into a coma, and shortly after nine o'clock he was admitted to the local hospital. He was breathing laboriously, and sweating copiously; his limbs were rigid and his right eyelid drooping. Now and then his legs trembled for a few seconds. The American consulate was informed of his condition. He did not seem to be in any imminent danger, but late that afternoon Sandro arranged to have another doctor, a brain specialist from nearby Volterra, come to check Burns out. But before he could get there, at around five, Burns had a particularly wild seizure, and for a minute or so was foaming—it was a grayish liquid—at the mouth. Then it stopped and, once more, his condition appeared to ease. But soon it all began again. And this time, Burns died. He was two months shy of thirty-seven years old.

As Armstrong later put it, the hospital summarized things with "awesome simplicity": "Burns, John Horne; entered 0930 hours, 11 August 1953; exited 1715 hours, 11 August 1953." At 1725 hours, ten minutes after Burns had expired, the doctor from Volterra arrived. Reviewing the medical history, he attributed Burns's death to seizures brought on either by an old brain injury—perhaps that "mere concussion to the brain," as Burns had characterized it to MacMackin in August 1942—aggravated by sunstroke, or a cerebral hemorrhage.

Burns had joked periodically in his letters about getting older—about throwing beds out of the hotel windows at American Legion conventions when he was forty-five or, as he put it, "beating all the life insurance raps and living to the age of 104." "I don't understand your vitality," a friend in Naples once told him. "You'll probably live to be 100." Notwithstanding his self-destructive habits, Burns clearly agreed. Any sense of urgency he had stemmed not from a feeling that his time was short, but from how much he felt he still

The death certificate

had to write, or how many things were still to be enjoyed, or, at least briefly, how much good he still had to do. But he'd also told his students that he didn't expect to live beyond forty—not necessarily anticipating anything tragic, but as if to say, since old age was such a drag, what was the point? Anyway, the various indignities of old age he'd identified in his Harvard sonnet—all those songs dissolving "in cadences of tears"—he would now be spared himself.

Almost daily, Burns's parents went on walks around their neighborhood in Back Bay: down Gainsborough Street to Huntington Avenue, then up to the opera house and back. They were slow going, for by now Joseph Burns had had five or six strokes and wore a brace on his leg. On the afternoon of August 11 they went for their walk as usual, but when they returned they found under their door a cable from the American consulate in Florence. Their son had died, they read to their horror, and incidentally, the hospital had to be paid, for Burns hadn't left enough behind to

From the Italian papers

settle up. Neither went into histrionics—Joseph Burns because he was not well, Catherine Burns because she was, by nature, stoic. But for Burns's mother in particular, it was an absolutely crushing blow. The two never took one of their walks again.

Burns himself seemed no more inclined to return to America in death than he had in life. He no doubt would have been satisfied with something less prestigious than a plot in the English cemetery alongside Elizabeth Barrett Browning, as long as it was local. But the family quickly decided—that is, Catherine Burns decreed—that Jack was to be brought back. The repatriation of Americans abroad was the province of the State Department and, thanks to the family's political clout—Tom Burns knew Elliot Richardson,* then a key aide to Senator Leverett Saltonstall of Massachusetts—the matter reached all the way up to Secretary of State John Foster Dulles. So it was that an agency of government that had spurned him in life, and an American establishment that he had in turn rejected, quickly mobilized to return John Horne Burns to a place he'd forsaken and from which he'd have happily continued to stay away.

"FAMILY DESIRES AIRSHIPMENT BURNS EMBALMED REMAINS AUTHORIZATION INSTRUCTIONS FOLLOW," the State Department cabled the American consulate in Florence two days after his death. The undertaker in Cecina yielded to his counterpart in Florence; it was he who presumably preserved the body. In *The Gallery*, Burns had speculated about the faces of the GIs buried in Fedhala who, having been denied "the finished peace of the ordinary dead, embalmed in funeral homes," must look "as though a cop had surprised them in the orgasm of life." Burns himself would now be spared that indignity. Not that his next of kin would know it: the State Department warned them that the process would probably drag on long enough that he would best not be viewed by the time his body got back to Boston.

The family sent a check for $950, payable to the secretary of state, to cover expenses. But things proceeded glacially; after all, it was still *Ferragosto*, and the Italians, including bureaucrats in Cecina responsible for the death certificate required for Burns's departure, remained on vacation. It was one of those quintessential Italian traditions that foreigners living in Italy, Burns included, both cherish and disparage; as a consular official explained to Burns's impatient family, the summer holidays "completely denude practically all Italian Government and business offices." Despite repeated prodding, it took until August 28 for

---

* Later attorney general of the United States.

the death certificate to reach the consulate. Burns then made his final trip—first to Rome, and then Pan American flight 115 to Boston. The matter was handled by American Express, at a cost of $583.97. The family still had to settle with the two undertakers, the hospital, Burns's landlord, the local wine dealer, and a dry cleaner, due $1.92.

For nearly three weeks, the family had little to do but wait, excruciatingly, for Burns's body. Finally, on the morning of September 2, an undertaker from Roxbury, Massachusetts, named William Gormley picked up the handsome hand-carved casket at Logan Airport in Boston. It was strangely shaped—contoured to its contents, like something for a stringed instrument—with a small, engraved plaque on top. The names were scrambled: BURNS HORNE JOHN or something similar. No one ever did open it up. It was taken directly to St. Ann's Church on St. Stephen Street—what Tom Burns called "this dinky little church in Back Bay, off Mass Ave. that Jack never saw, never went to"—where the funeral was presided over by a plump priest whom Burns had never met. None of Burns's friends, such as they were, attended. "There were about four people in the church," Tom Burns later remembered. At the very least, he thought, it should have been held back at St. Augustine's in Andover. The body was then taken to Holyhood Cemetery in Brookline, where Rose Kennedy's father, the former mayor of Boston, John "Honey Fitz" Fitzgerald, and other Boston Irish luminaries were buried (and where Rose and Joe Kennedy themselves would one day come to rest). Burns was interred in the family plot, alongside his maternal grandparents and two of his brothers—William, who'd died in infancy, and Bobby, who had strangled in his crib. Probably at his mother's insistence, when Burns's name was carved onto the back of the obelisk, he got top billing. Afterward, the family gathered back at 89 Gainsborough Street. Phillip Isenberg (the model for the Jewish student in *Lucifer*, who'd gone on to

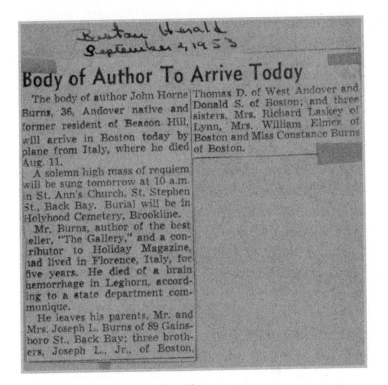

A clip from the Boston Herald

Harvard Medical School), was casually going with his roommate to their apartment upstairs when one of Burns's sisters poked her head outside requesting quiet: there was mourning going on, she explained.

Tom Burns always thought his brother should have been left in Italy. "That's where he loved it," he said. To Armstrong, too, there was something unjust about his fate, but darkly humorous as well. "His love for this part of the peninsula was probably more complete than that of the 19th century English poets whose bones now rest beneath Tuscan cypresses," he wrote a few days after Burns died. "But his family has the right to want his body in Andover [*sic*] if it gives them comfort. I imagine Burns, wherever he is, as sneering at all the bother."

32

A tan leather Gladstone bag, valued at $4.00. New shirts: $6.00. Worn ones: $3.00. Three pairs of pants—gray flannel, gray denim, and blue denim: $6.50. A gray suit: $6.00. A gray tweed overcoat: $10.00. An Unda radio: $10.00. Eleven framed pictures: $5.00. Packages of typing and carbon paper: fifty cents apiece. Part of the job of the American consulate in Florence was to collect, evaluate, and disperse Burns's personal effects. So some functionary traveled to Villa La Bicocca to itemize what Burns had left behind. The inventory was paltry. Burns had never been acquisitive, but it was startling to see just how little he had accumulated. His estate, if you could call it that, included very nearly as many packages of Lucky Strikes (eighteen, worth $1.50) as books (twenty-four, valued at $12.00).

Burns had had no cash on him when he died and, contrary to what the family had heard, by donating $160 to help cover his funeral expenses, Burns's Italian publisher, Livio Garzanti, had

```
                    INVENTORY OF EFFECTS
                         Estate of
                     JOHN HORNE BURNS
                      Florence, Italy
```

Quantity	Description of Effects	Value in Dollars	Total
	LUGGAGE		
1	Tan leather gladstone bag	$4.00	$4.00
	WEARING APPAREL		
1	Pair leather sandals	nil	
1	Pair brown shoes	nil	
1	Pair walking shoes	nil	
3	Shirts, new	$6.00	
3	Shirts, worn	3.00	
5	Pairs socks	1.50	
1	Pair gray flannel trousers	4.00	
1	Pair gray denim trousers	1.50	
1	Pair blue denim trousers	1.00	
1	Gray tweed overcoat	10.00	
1	Gray tweed suit	5.00	
1	Aligator belt	3.50	
1	Pair leather gloves	nil	
1	Pair swimming trunks	nil	
1	Gray suit	8.00	
2	T-shirts, cotton	nil	
2	Pairs shorts	nil	$43.50
	MISCELLANEOUS EFFECTS		
1	Radio, "Unda"	$10.00	
1	Typewriter	15.00	
24	Books	12.00	
11	Framed pictures (prints)	5.00	
6	Pottery soupbowls with covers . . .	3.00	
18	Packages Lucky Strike cigarettes . . .	1.50	
1	Package typing paper	.50	
1	Package carbon paper	.50	
1	Manuscript	nil	
2	Folders containing correspondence, statements, clippings, etc. . .	nil	$47.50
	JEWELRY		
1	Wristwatch, "Recta"	$5.00	
1	Pair gold cufflinks, monogrammed . .	3.00	
1	Gold medal on chain	1.00	
1	18 karat gold ring, blue chipped stone .	5.00	14.00
		TOTAL	$109.00

Burns's estate

more than discharged any debt he had had. With a Recta wrist-watch, a pair of monogrammed gold cuff links, a gold medal on a chain, and an eighteen-karat gold ring with a chipped blue stone, the value of his worldly goods totaled $109.00. The most valuable item was his "blasted" *macchina da scrivere*: his typewriter, worth $15. But the last thing to have emerged from it—the manuscript of *The Stranger's Guise*—was assigned the same value as his sandals, shoes, and swim trunks: "nil."

The *New York Times* and *Herald Tribune* ran obituaries of Burns that were generous, respectful, and evasive. (The *Times* finally mentioned Momma, for instance, but identified her only as "a woman tavern proprietor.") But the tributes were few. In the *Saturday Review*, Bennett Cerf noted his passing, including him among several "good people going far before their time," reminders "of what constant stress and tension were doing to thinking souls these days." In the Italian press, the obituaries were almost nonexistent, which was why, the *Rome Daily American* explained, it had commissioned George Armstrong "to supply additional details on the life and death of the brilliant American author," which he provided in a couple of installments. Eventually, Burns collected more tributes in Italy than in the United States, and for one simple reason: there, he was considered a friend.

Once the news got out and the shock wore off—actually, that's not quite right, for as young as Burns was, to those aware of his self-destructive ways, like Holger Hagen, Vidal, and Warburg, his death, though premature, was not exactly unexpected. "I felt no shock," Vidal later wrote. "It seemed right. One only wondered how he had achieved extinction." "An extraordinary and somehow appropriate end for an extraordinary life, wasn't it?" Bessie wrote Warburg. "It is true that Johnnie lived, let us say, with unduly exuberant zest in Florence, and perhaps it is this that has caused him to pay a price than which nothing is higher—I don't know," Warburg wrote Helen Strauss. "When all is said one of America's most talented (and undisciplined) younger writers is dead and no country is sufficiently rich in creative talent to do other than mourn."

In Florence and Rome and London and New York and Windsor and Boston and Cambridge and Andover, the topic quickly turned from the official version of Burns's demise to what had *really* happened. That the reports were so sketchy only fanned the speculation. Some, like Warburg and Weaver, believed Burns had effectively drunk himself to death. "In Italy John had even found a group of critics that were smarter than those in the United States," Weaver was to write. "But he had also found a place where he could live the way he wanted to live. Unfortunately, he wanted to drink, and maybe he even wanted to die." Some speculated that the drinking that killed him wasn't habitual but targeted—that is, despondent over the state of his career, he drank himself into a stupor, lay out too long in the sun, and willed himself to die. Or that he was inconsolable over a love affair gone bad with a Florentine boy. Others assumed suicide by different means, followed by some nefarious cover-up. When Burns's former student John Stuart Cox told Burns's Florentine "fiancée"—the woman whose picture Burns kept on the bookshelf of his apartment at Loomis—that officially at least, Burns had died of a cerebral hemorrhage, she burst into wicked laughter. "Yes, a cerebral hemorrhage caused by a bullet to the brain," she declared, conveying not the slightest hint of sadness or distress as she did.

Even Ernest Hemingway, who knew something about suicide—his father had shot himself—weighed in. "There was a fellow who wrote a fine book and then a stinking book about a prep school, and then he just blew himself up," he mused a few years later to Robert Manning of the *Atlantic*. (And the rumors persisted: long afterward, the authors of a book called *Final Drafts: Suicides of World-Famous Authors* devoted a segment to Burns.)

Another school of thought had Burns murdered. Richard Johnson, the Loomis student who'd studied Hart Crane under him—and whom Burns sought out when Johnson worked at the American consulate in Florence—had heard that a drunken Burns had been killed in a bar brawl. Or Burns hadn't really been on a boat off the coast of Livorno with his veterinarian lover, but off the coast of Naples with a doctor and his wife in a ménage à trois; the doctor had killed Burns, then signed his death certificate. Or Burns had jumped from a window. Or that he had been pushed. Or been killed by a soldier he'd propositioned. Helen Strauss had heard—maybe from someone who'd been reading about Shelley—that Burns's body had washed ashore on a beach in Leghorn.

Frank MacGregor went to Florence to try to learn something for himself. "It was soon enough thereafter for people to remember whether he was just drunk and fell down, whether he was in a fight as he could easily have been, whether he was murdered deliberately, but I couldn't find out," he was to recall. "It was a sad, mysterious end, very tragic. At one time I thought it might be a suicide, although he wasn't a suicidal person. He was a violent person when he got drunk, I know that, or could be fought with, let's say. He would irritate people, provoke a fight." But Mac-Gregor left Florence knowing little more than when he arrived.

Among those who lived there, few would have mourned. "Everyone who had read Burns's three books knew that he was not a peaceful man and that his evident bitterness might lead him to depression and suicide," wrote Armstrong. "But what made the story more readily acceptable in Our Town was that Burns was pretty generally disliked, in varying degrees, by most of the people who knew him—or thought they knew him. That was the sad truth, though one always wondered if *he* found it sad. I suspected that he felt solitude became him—as an artist and observer of life. But beneath his façade of sarcasm, there may have been a frightened and shy man who was afraid of being 'taken in' by friendship." (To Armstrong, all the talk of suicide would have been just the sort of rumor Burns himself might have started.) "Had he lived longer than those 37 years, John Horne Burns might never have given us a book as true and good as *The Gallery*, but we were all hoping that he would," Armstrong later observed. He likened Burns to the filmmaker Roberto Rossellini, who would never match the greatness of early classics like *Open City* and *Paisan*. "Both men seemed to reach the heights of greatness only when great things were going on outside of them," he wrote. "What glimpses we have been given, subsequently, of their *insides* have been puny, confused, and tasteless in comparison."

A British woman named Searles, who, with her husband, ran a small hotel outside Florence that Burns frequented (and to which he sometimes sent patrons), grew so outraged by what she considered Armstrong's impudence that, in an angry letter to him, she supplied another possible cause of death, one Burns himself would have savored: he had fallen victim to his own brilliance, along with everyone else's idiocy. True, "he was certainly rude to those people who, because he was a celebrity, tried to gate-crash his acquaintance at the Excelsior bar," she conceded. But that only proved his sound judgment. "It is no wonder," she wrote, "that a brain so finely balanced should not tolerate fools gladly, [nor] that one with such power of observation should find so many people ridiculous." Burdened by the foolishness of those around him, she speculated, his "nervous system finally gave up the struggle." Later, Burns's hometown paper offered another, equally flattering postmortem. "The war killed John Horne Burns," the *Boston Globe* opined. "A young man generous and compassionate, the misery and horror which he saw inflicted on his 'enemies,' the Italian people whom he had come to love, burnt him out and broke his heart."

Themselves dubious about the official explanation, Burns's family hired a well-connected American lawyer in Rome named

Peter Borre to investigate his death. He found nothing suspicious. Some years later, when a magazine reported that Burns had killed himself, Tom Burns demanded, and got, a retraction. But nearly sixty years later, his own suspicions of suicide persisted. "Don't forget," he said, "his last book was a total flop. And I don't know what his finances were at that time. He was an extremely proud man, and I think he may have looked upon himself as a failure, as an author and as a man . . . I wondered whether he was happy with his sexual orientation . . . I think he probably wasn't."

Shortly after Burns died, so, too, did the Excelsior bar; "Ralph" and "Henry" opened up Harry's Bar nearby. One very hot summer day many years later, Tom Burns stopped by there and asked the manager whether he'd ever met his brother. "The Professor!" the man exclaimed. "He was my best customer!" Tucked into the mirror behind the counter was a picture of John Horne Burns.

Since Burns's death occurred when it was in summer recess, Loomis had an excuse to ignore it—not that it really needed one. The alumni bulletin took no note of Burns's death, as it would normally have done for someone who'd taught there six years. But the *Hartford Courant* marked the occasion with an editorial. "*Lucifer with a Book*, known as 'the book' among Loomis students, will long be read by boys at this school as they look around to see what masters are pictured there," it predicted. "An enthusiastic teacher, he held his English classes spellbound with his erudition and delivery," it went on, before noting his music, his dramaturgy, and his supervision of the literary magazine. "Admired and a little envied by some of the members of the faculty," Burns, it said, had "died too young."

Perhaps the most emotional tribute came from James Michener, who recalled in his 1991 memoir how devastated he had been to hear about Burns's death. (He, too, suspected suicide.)

I began to appreciate the great loss I had suffered,
for men often thrive when they have competitors against
whom to test themselves, and had Burns lived I am sure
he and I would have competed, honorably and vigorously,
throughout our lives, each checking what the other was
doing, meeting now and then as adversaries and in time
as friends, each going his unique way, each presenting
a mirror-image of the other. He would have been one
of the notable esthetes, I a stolid representative of the
stable middle class; he a writer of traceries and shadowy
intimations, I of conflicts in blazing sunlight; he the head
of a coterie and immensely popular in universities, where
his acerbic wit would be appreciated and encouraged, I off
by myself plugging away at my own goals. Side by side we
would have marched through the decades, and tears fill
my eyes when I think of the enormous loss I and the world
suffered with his death. My alter ego had vanished in the
mists of sunset. I think of John Horne Burns every week of
my life.

It's a pretty thought, but Michener was flattering himself: unless he'd been assigned to review another one of them—and then agreed, without compunction, to do it—it's doubtful Burns would have read any more of Michener's later books, let alone have compared Michener's work to his own. And rather than being moved by Michener's affectionate, even touching tribute, Burns would probably have ridiculed his purplish prose.

33

Harpers settled up with the Burns estate. From January 1 through June 30, 1953, Burns had earned $271.66 in royalties. Subtracting the $200 he'd been paid left $71.66. With the $2.36 due the estate from the sale of nine copies of *The Gallery*, minus the $12.38 due Harpers from the return of thirty-three copies of *A Cry of Children*, the estate was owed $61.64. But even that could still be offset by additional returns. There was also a stray letter from a fan, who enclosed a note he'd received from Burns "for possible use someday when his fame begins to grow." When the man asked where he might find a copy of *Lucifer*, the publisher suggested he look in a secondhand store.

In November Tom Burns attempted to interest Harpers in publishing the partially revised *Stranger's Guise*, which had been returned to the family. But shortly before Christmas its editors rejected the book once and for all. Burns's lawyer brother toyed with taking it somewhere else, but never did; as he later put it, it wasn't exactly *The Last Tycoon*. The final item in the "Burns, John Horne" file in the Harpers papers, dated March 12, 1954, granted the Library of Congress permission to transcribe *The Gallery* into Braille.

The book continued to sell, though. By September 1953 the Bantam paperback edition had sold almost half a million copies, and the company was printing a quarter million more. Shortly after the hardcover had been published, CBS filmed the chapter on Giulia. From time to time after that, there was talk of a film version of the book. Sidney Poitier was to have starred in one; another stillborn incarnation involved Burt Lancaster, and the film producer David Susskind spoke of it, too. Inspired by *South Pacific*—it, too, had been a disparate collection of stories—in January 1951 Tom Lehrer began turning it into a musical; he wrote a couple of songs, one of them a takeoff of "O sole mio" in which a young boy pimps for his sister. The narrator was named "Moe," and there were also scenes in Momma's bar. But it never came off; once again, Michener had bested Burns.

Lucifer lived on only around Loomis. Faculty members rarely lent out their copies, for fear either of revealing that they owned them, or, worse, of never getting them back. Or they hid them: William Speer, who succeeded Batchelder as headmaster, inverted the jacket cover on his copy, so that it could sit anonymously on his shelf. For several years after Burns's disappearance and death, it was a tradition for rebellious students to track down and pore over scarce copies. When John Nichols reached Loomis in 1954, reading *Lucifer* was—along with buying early issues of *Playboy*, wearing dungaree jackets and motorcycle boots, keeping a shotgun in his room, and selling switchblades to classmates—a way to rebel against a conformist place and era. But to Nichols, the mockery was only part of the book's appeal. Another was its raw sensuality—not the bogus lovemaking of its purportedly heroic couple, but its infinitely more persuasive accounts of teenage boys, their libidos coming into bloom, playing with themselves and one another, accompanied by the "rhythmic creaking of Academy cots." It was an appeal grown-up critics would of course have missed: *Lucifer* was really a book of, for, and by adolescent boys. And while Nichols quickly forgot the particulars, the spirit of the novel stayed with him as he began writing well-regarded novels of his own.*

But interest inevitably tailed off. When David Gates attended Loomis in the early sixties, he later recalled, Burns had become "a black hole: nobody talked about him . . . one got the impression that The Love That Dare Not Speak Its Name found a paradigm in Burns's Loomis career. The scarlet letters JHB were expunged from the general consciousness." When it finally appeared in a cheap paperback edition in 1977, few people, even at Loomis, would have ever heard of it. David Haller, who began teaching at Loomis three years after Burns left, kept a copy, and compiled his own list of who was who. So did George Hickok, who arrived in 1954. So did David Sherman, who ran the school bookstore. He never stocked it, of course, and no copies ever seemed to turn up in used bookstores near Hartford or Springfield, Massachusetts. But twice—in Hollywood and Boston—he actually found the book. The Hollywood edition was annotated.

Burns rated only one unilluminating paragraph in Loomis's official history, *The Harvest of Our Lives*, written in 1964, even though (or perhaps because) its author, a crusty old history teacher named Lloyd Wright Fowles, would have remembered Burns well. He said nothing of Burns's teaching, nor of *The Gallery*; only *Lucifer* mattered, and just barely. "Reactions to the book were varied,"

---

* *The Sterile Cuckoo; The Milagro Beanfield War; The Wizard of Loneliness.*

wrote Fowles. "It merely strengthened the opinions of those who disliked the school and headmaster; it irritated others who knew the real worth of Mr. Batchelder; it interested the faculty more than incensed them; and as for Mr. Batchelder—to all outward appearances—he read it and dismissed it from his thoughts."

Occasionally, some new Burns lore would surface, like the Sunday morning when a group of prostitutes in a red convertible supposedly showed up behind his dormitory looking for him, or some ghostlike remnant of his presence would emerge. When a newly hired French teacher named David Simpson moved into what had been Burns's apartment in 1959, the walls had been stripped, and beneath the wallpaper was a solid coat of bright red paint which, he was told, Burns had applied one night while drunk. Once it was covered up again, the last physical trace of Burns's presence at the place was gone. Then, even his ghost was too undernourished to stick around. The most amazing thing about my having been clued into *Lucifer* forty-seven years ago is that it ever happened at all. Why would anyone have cared enough to tell me, and why would I, a fourteen-year-old boy, have cared enough to remember? But only because of that exchange did I write this book; so it was that the winner of the 1970 Norris Ely Orchard Prize in English became Burns's Boswell. One wonders how Burns would have felt about that. While Loomis Chaffee (the two schools officially merged in 1973) has never commemorated Burns, Andover did: in October 1961, his parents established a prize in his name, providing thirty-five dollars to the author of the best original short story. It seems an odd choice, since Burns never published a short story. Then again, his most enduring work was really a collection of them.

For a time, *The Gallery* cast a long shadow over others trying to write their own books about World War II, like Joseph Heller. But with some exceptions, like the contrarian British critic Brigid Brophy—who in 1964 called Burns "by far the most talented, and the most *attractively* talented, American novelist to emerge since the war"—Burns increasingly became the province of gay writers, critics, and scholars.

Probably the first was Daniel Edgerton, in the pioneering gay magazine *ONE* in October 1958. A friend of Burns's described him to Brophy as "the most committed homosexual I have ever met," but Edgerton wasn't buying: echoing Aldridge, he charged that Burns toyed with but did not write wholeheartedly gay material. "The sexual theme dies of malnutrition, not to say poisoning," he wrote. "After providing abundant evidence that his heroes are inverted, he seems to feel obliged to leave the reader with the notion that they are heterosexual." Surprisingly, Burns's greatest champion was Gore Vidal. He *had* outlasted him, and could now afford to be more kind. And Burns's family had been kind to him: learning a year after Jack's death that Vidal planned to write something about him, Catherine Burns invited Vidal to dinner when he was next in Boston, enclosing her telephone number to make sure he called the right Burns.

Twelve years passed before Vidal actually produced that piece, but his respect for the man hadn't waned in the interim. "Of the well-known books of the war, I have always thought that only Burns's was authentic," he wrote in a long essay in the *New York Times Book Review* in May 1965. "To me the others were redolent of ambition and literature, and their talented authors have since gone on to better things. But for Burns the war was genuine revelation. In Naples he fell in love with the idea of life." Vidal made his mistakes in that piece: he placed Burns's birth, and death, five years later than they happened. But more deeply than anyone, Vidal plumbed the two great riddles of Burns's story: why he fell so far so fast, and why he died so soon.

Burns was a gifted man who wrote a book far in excess of his gift, making a kind of masterpiece which will endure in a way that he could not. Extreme circumstances made him write a book which was better than his talent, an unbearable fate for an ambitious artist who wants to go on, but cannot; all later work shadowed by the splendid accident of a moment's genius. I suspect that once Burns realized his situation, he in fact chose not to go on, and between Italian brandy and Italian sun contrived to stop.

(By "outing" Burns—he repeated Burns's claim that to be a great writer, one had to be a homosexual—Vidal incurred the wrath of Burns's sister Cathleen. "She wrote me an intemperate letter . . . denying that he was ever homosexual—in fact, he was going, she said, to marry "a contessa," Vidal later wrote Mark Bassett. "The social climbing of the lace-curtain—or even bog—Irish is genetic.")

But Vidal's attitude toward the man and his work evolved, and varied. "The book was badly written in many places," he said of *The Gallery* to the journalist Israel Shenker in 1968, but "despite a quite clumsy style he was able to make one feel deeply." "He was an awful man. Monster. Envious, bitchy, drunk, bitter," he told the writers John Mitzel and Steven Abbott of *Fag Rag* in 1974. "Which was why *The Gallery* was so marvelous. It was his explosion into humanity at a fairly late date. I think he was in his early thirties, after a half-assed career as an English teacher and writing unprintable novels." But Vidal told the playwright and gay activist Larry Kramer in 1992 that the critics had "obliterated" Burns, not so much because his work was bad but simply for being gay, just as they had with him. *Lucifer* he called "the most savagely and unjustly attacked book of its day." Homophobia had practically destroyed him as a novelist, Vidal said, and *had* destroyed John Horne Burns, whom he now described as "my friend."

(It was a point on which Vidal and his erstwhile antagonist, Norman Mailer, agreed. Mailer, too, had criticized Burns; in a letter from 1954, he called him "minor" and added, "I've gotten halfway through *The Gallery* and have no desire to finish it." But five years later he'd mellowed, even recommending that the book be translated into Japanese. "John Horne Burns is dead, a nice talent, sexual, not too dishonest, oversweet but tender—the poisonous stupidities of the reviewers toward his last two novels hurried his going, and who knows what could have happened to his talent, for it had the promise of size," he wrote.) Long after Burns had ceased to matter to just about everyone, Vidal continued talking about him, regaling guests in late-evening discussions at his home above the Mediterranean with gossip about his life and death.

Burns's death was clearly not, as Vidal famously said of Capote and assorted others, a "good career move." Vidal was among the few to help keep Burns's reputation alive, but by framing him principally as a gay writer, he also helped typecast, and marginalize, him. Because Burns's homosexuality was something his family would not acknowledge, and because so much of Burns's life could be reconstructed only from letters whose content, under copyright law, the family controlled, Burns's survivors could, and effectively did, shut down Burns scholarship. The gatekeeper—"the keeper of the flame," as Tom Burns called her—was Cathleen. She, too, had literary credentials (including a degree in English from Smith) and aspirations, which was why, before her death in 1976, Catherine Burns had named her Jack's literary executor, entrusting her with the variety of materials—college papers, early novels, wartime letters—she had saved. For a long time, Cathleen planned to do her own book about her brother, whom she once described as "one of the most accomplished and beguiling, complex and contradictory persons it was ever a close observer's delight and dismay to know." So in addition to whatever other baggage they brought to the project, anyone proposing to write about Burns was also a competitor.

The first person to study him at any length was John Mitzel, a gay activist, writer, and operator of a theater in Boston showing gay pornography who, having learned of Burns from Vidal, set out in 1973 to write a short biography of him. He interviewed, among others, Burns's mentor at Andover, Emory Basford, along with Tom and Donald Burns. But the family's cooperation stopped there. Burns's story, Mitzel quickly concluded, touched the three taboos in Irish Catholic culture: alcoholism, suicide, and homosexuality. As eager as family members were to see Jack celebrated, they were more eager to maintain his, and their, secret. "Their whole goal in life was not to have him presented as an important figure in an emerging gay literary culture, but only as someone in the standard American literary pantheon," he recalled. "I can understand their point. They were old-fashioned Irish Catholics who'd done very well."

Tom Burns's equivocations with Mitzel over the threshold question of Jack's homosexuality suggested just how difficult the subject remained for him twenty years after his brother's death:

> *Well, I don't know that he was. I've heard it suggested that he was. This was something he wouldn't want to talk about with his brother. I never thought about it. I think he probably was. What did I know about it? Nothing . . . This business of homosexuality was nothing that was talked about in the family. I suppose subconsciously I've always known he was . . . I really never before sat down to think about this, about him in that context. It doesn't surprise me. I suppose I always considered that he was one. My wife always said he was. But there was never anything that was overt about him.*

Cathleen found various excuses to block Mitzel: her own proposed book; fears that Mitzel's scholarly credentials were too meager to restore her brother to his rightful place; worries that Mitzel would reduce Burns into a gay cult figure like Judy Garland. Her brother, she said, "deserves a happier fate than this."

JOHN HORNE BURNS
a forgotten faggot

. . John Horne Burns was by far the most talented, and the most attractively talented, American novelist to emerge since the end of the war.
—*Brigid Brophy*

is July marks the 21st anniversary of death of John Horne Burns. Few le today recognize the name of this , even fewer are familiar with his s. In the popular mind Norman Mailer entified as the man who wrote *the* rican War Novel of WW II. But in fact is a book by John Horne Burns: *The* ry, published in 1947. This book was tseller, and Burns was proclaimed by *aturday Review* as the best writer of

John Horne Burns was a faggot, and as certainly no claquer for America. wo following books, *Lucifer with a* and *A Cry of Children* were fiercely cruelly attacked; some reviewers to the level of personal abuse. hy wrote: The subsequent career of eputation illustrates not so much the usness as the whirligig irresponsi- of literary circles." They certainly job on John Horne Burns, and it was ry deliberate; if not personally co- ated, then at least a shared reaction

unpleasant to the prevail But this was the path Brophy: "Horne Burns ha and sufficiently overcome to commit himself to his im where he was artistically more can be asked of the gift to make as explicable world. It is the commitmen nation, and the *quality* of t in detailing his world by w must be judged, not merely vealed thereby, though o orient him on the political in the area of brilliantly world, Burns excelled. Br prototype is Dickens. We n pare him, making small with Tennessee Williams. and an active *imagination* novels of John Horne Bur tion are perhaps what Bool are least equipped to handl

Orville Prescott in the *Ne* ". . . a novel . . . so drench venom that it is hard to tak *Lucifer with a Book* is a v novel, tedious and someti . . . Mr. Burns seems to hav

The family's nightmare

"Cathleen figured out long before the rest of them that the faggots were going to take over her brother, and she wanted him," was how Mitzel later put it. He proceeded on his own, publishing an article—"John Horne Burns: a forgotten faggot," in the summer 1974 issue of *Fag Rag/Gay Sunshine*—that he then expanded into a "sympathetic biography." His thesis, like Vidal's, was that Burns had been done in by the homophobic American literary establishment. "That Burns was known to the Literary Mobsters as an aggressive faggot guaranteed that his books would never be well received," Mitzel wrote. They'd trapped him, demanding that he submerge his own sexuality, only to fault him for being "unconvincing." "America had done its work well, wiped out the most interesting writer of his time and turned John Horne Burns into a forgotten commodity," he concluded.

In 1980 Mark Bassett, a gay graduate student in English at the University of Missouri intrigued by "Momma," decided to write his doctoral dissertation on Burns, even though he was convinced that studying a gay literary figure would be, as he put it, a "career-killer." His research was much broader than Mitzel's, including an "author's query" in the *New York Times Book Review* that led him, through Tom Lehrer, to the mother lode: David Mac-Mackin. Alcohol had stunted MacMackin's life and work, and turned him into a paranoid recluse. Having long ago abandoned writing Burns's biography, he appeared to have forsaken Burns, too. His sister recalled the time in the late 1950s when, perusing his Loomis yearbook together, he'd suddenly slammed the book shut, then denounced prep schools for letting older men hang around young boys without proper supervision. (Whether it was Burns he was talking about wasn't clear; she'd never asked him to elaborate.) At one point MacMackin had inexplicably dumped his copy of *What Wondrous Life*—the novel (or fragment thereof: it ended in mid-sentence) Burns had dedicated to him—on Tom Lehrer. Still, he'd kept most of what Burns had given him; as much as Cathleen, he was his archivist.

MacMackin now gave it all to Bassett: manuscripts of Burns's other early novels; his Harvard honors essay; his translation of *The Inferno*; various photographs, including the portrait from Camp Croft with the aureole around his head; an inventory of Burns's record library; some recordings Burns had made. Then one day Bassett received a shoebox, battered and uninsured, in the mail. Inside were all of Burns's wartime letters to MacMackin. When, having transcribed them, Bassett attempted to give them back, MacMackin reacted violently: clearly, he wanted to be rid of them. It seemed like a form of exorcism.

"Burns wore many hats," MacMackin wrote Douglas McKee, who had spotted Bassett's ad and called him to MacMackin's attention. "That is to say, he changed persona to fit the given circumstance. (He wore no headgear.) Therefore, the Biographer's problem appears to be the reconcilement of various reports from different periods of his life. (I have a recurring nightmare in which Gore Vidal and Merle Miller conspire to kill the man on the Johnny Carson Show.)" Whatever that may have meant, MacMackin wanted to help Bassett. That a new and unauthorized biography of Thomas Mann had just appeared, he told him, proved that he could "do his number without access to family-held material (read: homosexuality) and garner plaudits."

But Bassett's sole meeting with MacMackin—in the same overstuffed apartment in the Musicians Building on West Sixty-seventh Street in New York where MacMackin had lived since the war—was a disaster. Most of it was spent having MacMackin decipher obscure references in various letters, while Bassett's more serious questions—like the origins of "dreadful"—were met with either blank stares or cryptic smiles; MacMackin seemed more interested in Bassett's boyfriend. Bassett never did learn whether "dreadful" had lofty literary roots—Oscar Wilde, perhaps, or Balzac—or was simply a pet term of Aunt Olive's.

About Burns himself the two barely talked. Ideally, that would happen in subsequent meetings. But MacMackin preferred communicating by cassette tape, and he became so incoherent and abusive in those recordings that Bassett stopped soliciting them, and the two lost contact. MacMackin lived out his days in utter isolation, a spooky and occasionally violent presence in his building, which he left only to fetch food and vodka a couple of blocks away. Nights he'd spend staring through his keyhole as music students arrived for their lessons next door; he'd sing to, or at, them from behind his door as they passed. He died of lung cancer at the age of sixty-eight; Burns's letters to him landed in the trash.

When Glenway Wescott suggested to Beulah Hagen that she sell her manuscript of *The Gallery* and Burns's letters, she wondered who would even want them. But the gay diarist Donald Vining, to whom Bassett read portions of Burns's letters to Mac-Mackin shortly after acquiring them, quickly recognized their historic significance, as his entry for July 8, 1981, indicates:

*Mark has rounded up a marvelously frank and campy
set of letters John Horne Burns wrote to a man Mark
thought might be his lover. After I'd heard a few I said they
didn't sound like letters written to a lover to me but more
like what one would write to a gay "sister," as we used to
say in the old days.*

Bassett retraced some of Burns's steps, including to Loomis,
where he interviewed a few of Burns's surviving Loomis colleagues. Francis Grubbs, who had gone on to become the school's
headmaster, insisted he'd never known he'd been the model for
Lucifer's "pockmarked and platitudinous" Dell Holly. But Burns
himself, Grubbs most certainly recalled. "The word 'snide'
comes to mind," he said. "He sneered at an awful lot of stuff."
Burns could teach, Grubbs admitted, but he'd not have wanted
his kids to have studied under him. Grubbs wrote of his encounter with Bassett to Tom Brush, then chairman of Loomis's board
of trustees.

*I find that I have not said anything about Burns except
to call him a bastard. Maybe that's enough. He was a
repulsive person and all I can say is that Mr. B sometimes
made a mistake in his selection of teachers—but Jack made
a good impression in a superficial interview. There is no
question that he was a brilliant mind, but that was his
trouble perhaps.*

Brush could splutter when the topic of Burns arose. But coun-
seling Bassett on how to obtain the cooperation of Burns's family, he was more measured: "John Horne Burns had a tragic life,
and I think if you can bring that out in your book and make
him sympathetic—even though he was, at least when I knew
him, an unpitiable swine—you may be able to break through

the stone wall so far maintained against you by Burns's brother and sister."

Bassett promised Burns's siblings that his work would be more serious and less polemical than Mitzel's. "Let me admit to you now that I am gay, too," he wrote Tom Burns. "That is certainly part of my interest in John Horne Burns. But I am certainly not a Boston 'faggot.'" But Cathleen Burns, in particular, remained unconvinced. She had now reconsidered the matter, she claimed, and had come to doubt whether her brother merited a biography at all. "Respectful though I am of his genius and his memory, I also believe that as a writer he was a one-book man, a cultural phenomenon of World War II, though that one book, without doubt, was a modern miracle," she wrote Bassett. But the books that followed had been "one-dimensional and overwrought, written in haste and under extreme pressure to sustain the exalted reputation he had earned with *The Gallery.*" Better even to denigrate her beloved brother privately, it seemed, than to acknowledge his homosexuality publicly.

Some of her brother's papers, Cathleen told Bassett, had been "irretrievably lost"; this he took to mean that anything pertaining to his gayness had been destroyed. And she set severe limits on the material that remained: references to Burns's sexual orientation must be kept "to a decent minimum," for instance; she could review, or delete, anything "prejudicial to Jack's memory and reputation and/or his family's privacy." Backing up her demands was a series of threatening letters from Tom Burns, written on the imposing letterhead of his law firm, which had become one of the largest in Boston. Even from the grave, a gay brother could cause problems for someone of such prominence and respectability: a leader of the bar, a club member, someone with children in the finest schools. Having his brother come back to life, and as a gay man, Tom Burns later reflected, "wasn't going to help me at all." Bassett completed his dissertation. But he shelved plans to turn it into a book and, fearful of opening himself up to a lawsuit, kept it very much under wraps. It was never even microfilmed, as doctoral dissertations invariably are. He then put aside his Burns materials for the next twenty-five years—until, that is, retrieving them for me. Other gay scholars were similarly thwarted. In the early 1990s David Bergman asked the family for a look at *The Stranger's Guise.* "Neither you nor anyone else is going to see that novel," he was told. It may have been no accident that when the *New York Review of Books* reissued *The Gallery* in 2004—with jingoism running high at the outset of the war in Iraq, the editors felt the time ripe for a more skeptical look at the American military—it chose Paul Fussell, a historian of war rather than a gay scholar, to write the introduction. The family must have been pleased; Burns had been rescued from his gay admirers.

But time softened the family's resistance. Having grown infirm and uncommunicative, Cathleen yielded her role as literary executor to Tom Burns. And when I approached him, then nearing ninety, a few years ago, he could not have been friendlier or more cooperative. He had come to terms with his brother's homosexuality, and to realize his brother's historical significance. He, too, wanted to know more about him, conceding that he'd never really known him at all.

Getting reacquainted wasn't easy, however. Jack had been no kinder to him than he had to many others. As Tom read his wartime letters for the first time, old resentments resurfaced, particularly about Jack's apparent indifference to him and his brothers, all of whom had been in far greater peril than he. Especially rankling was Burns's description of their encounter in Naples sixty-six years earlier. "He spent more time describing the glassware in which he served me some cognac than how I looked or what I had been through or what I said or how I'd survived the southern invasion of France," Tom Burns observed. To him, Jack's letters, like Jack himself, were a bit of an act, written for posterity and, before that, to flatter their mother. "They're the biggest bunch of garbage," he said at one point. "Who the hell is this guy kidding? He was a total narcissist." Only over time did the full tragedy of his brother's life—so many secrets, such extraordinary talent so squandered—become apparent. But it still didn't make him any easier to love.

As Gore Vidal said, Burns's death, even coming when it did, "made sense." It is hard now to imagine it *not* happening then, or shortly thereafter. But what if it hadn't happened? He did not need much to live on; could he have put aside his novels for a while, curbed or stopped his drinking, taken refuge in teaching, travel writing, and translating until he had regrouped? Could he, as the more tolerant world he had called for in "Momma" slowly and painfully materialized, once more have written penetratingly of what he knew and loved? Or would it have taken another cataclysm for him to recover his gift?

34

Situated in the now-fashionable hills outside Florence, Villa La Bicocca has considerably more cachet than it had in Burns's day. But tourists have discovered, and vulgarized, Marina di Cecina; a coffee bar now sits right below Villa Brunella. Sometimes, though, Sandro Nencini, who got married sometime in the late 1950s, went there with his three children. (Nencini, who became an antiques dealer, died in 2005.)

It's a pity they never installed that plaque in the floor of the Excelsior bar, because the place has been remodeled beyond recognition, and there's no one still around Florence who remembers Burns at all, let alone where he once stood every night drinking, and drinking in the scene. But in Naples, the San Carlo Opera House is perfectly intact. The Banco di Napoli, the Fascist-era building turned Allied officers' club where Burns played Brahms and watched a black officer humiliated, is once again a bank. "Mussolini's fairgrounds," the Mostra d'Oltremare, where Burns was treated for syphilis, is once more a site for exhibitions, looking both too new and too immaculate ever to have served such a purpose.

What's changed the most dramatically is the Galleria Umberto. Architecturally, it is as imposing as ever. But more than the GIs and the *scugnazzi* and the souvenir sellers and the bartenders have moved on; so, too, have the citizens of Naples. They have found other places to shop, and linger. The pulsating and wicked place Burns described, and the more respectable place to which he returned, have vanished. The angels with their trumpets still look down, but they see very little going on. The place feels cavernous and empty. Its old din has been replaced by a hollow sound, punctuated by the occasional stray shouts of young boys kicking around a soccer ball. Only a few forlorn chairs line the marble floor. The stores are marginal; there's not even a bookstore selling *The Gallery*, nor has anyone ever heard of it in the hotel upstairs—located, perhaps, where Momma and Poppa once lived. The Galleria is now more shortcut than destination. The place, at long last, is largely free of vice; prostitutes, dependent as they are on foot traffic, find it a bad bet. Even something timeless can become anachronistic. The Galleria's demise makes John Horne Burns seem even more dead.

Loomis has spread and opened itself up, losing—for both better and worse—the intimate, hermetic quality of Burns's day and mine. He would neither feel so suffocated nor be such a personality at the school today. But the core of the campus still looks the same, and though the graceful elms of his day have died and a couple of new dormitories have been built, you can stand in the original Quadrangle and imagine him, in his jacket and tie, walking briskly to class or, cigarette in hand, pacing nonchalantly on the porch outside his suite. Or, for that matter, suitcase in hand one frosty December evening, marching off to the Boston bus as Christmas carols resounded through the chapel.

Founders Hall looks and smells the same, though the library where *Lucifer* was banned has been replaced by a new building a short walk away, where copies of the book are readily available but seldom sought. Just around the corner from the old library is another gallery. In it, hanging on both sides of a narrow corridor, are framed portraits of the school's most venerable and durable teachers, many of whom saw John Horne Burns come and go, then come and go again, then drop his bomb on the place. No image of him appears in this gallery, nor is one ever likely to: he didn't—he *couldn't*—stay long enough to qualify. But maybe, somewhere at the school, one should. And perhaps one day, no matter how thoroughly dreadful Burns may have been, one will.

John Horne Burns, undated

Permissions

All letters from John Horne Burns—from the Howard Gotlieb Archival Research Center at Boston University, Princeton University, and various private collections—reprinted with permission from the Estate of John Horne Burns.

Excerpts from John Horne Burns, *The Cynic Faun* (1937) X812 B937, Rare Book & Manuscript Library, Columbia University in the City of New York, reprinted with permission from the Estate of John Horne Burns.

Selections from the journals of William Weaver courtesy, The Lilly Library, Bloomington, Indiana, reprinted with permission of Mr. Weaver.

Materials from Selected Records of Harper Brothers courtesy, Manuscripts Division, Department of Rare Books and Special Collections, Princeton University Library.

Frontispiece, pages 13, 16, 23, 26, 166, 329, and 350: From the John Horne Burns Collection, Howard Gotlieb Archival Research Center, Boston University

Page 12: Courtesy of Thomas D. Burns, Esq.

Pages 36, 37, 41, 51, 179, and 229: From the collection of the Loomis Chaffee School Archives, Loomis Chaffee School, Windsor, Connecticut

Pages 52, 59, 128, and 380: Courtesy of Mark Bassett

Page 75: Courtesy of Eugenia Klein

Page 86: Courtesy of Reinhold Pauly

Page 159: Henry Holiday, *Dante and Beatrice* (1884), reprinted with permission of the Walker Art Gallery, Liverpool, England.

Page 198: Loring Studio, *New York Times*

Pages 210 and 276: Dust jackets for *The Gallery* and *Lucifer With a Book*, HarperCollins.

Page 218: From *Harper's Bazaar*, November 1947 © Ronny Jaques / Trunk Archive.

Page 227: From *The Boston Globe*, December 11, 1947 © Boston Globe. All rights reserved. Used by permission and protected by the Copyright Laws of the United States. The printing, copying, redistribution, or retransmission of this Content without express written permission is prohibited.

Page 235: *Saturday Review of Literature*, February 14, 1948

Page 249: *Life*, January 1, 1949 © Nina Leen / Time & Life Pictures / Getty Images

Page 285: Courtesy of Lucretia Hickok

Page 299: From *The Andover Townsman*, November 10, 1949, reprinted with permission from *The Andover Townsman*

Page 306: *The Gallery* paperback covers, Bantam Books

Page 309: Courtesy of the Excelsior Hotel

Page 353: From the *Boston Herald*, September 2, 1953 © Boston Herald.